LIBRARY MAKERSPACES

LIBRARY MAKERSPACES

The Complete Guide

Theresa Willingham

with contributions by

Chuck Stephens
Steve Willingham
Jeroen de Boer

ROWMAN & LITTLEFIELD
Lanham • Boulder • New York • London

Published by Rowman & Littlefield
A wholly owned subsidiary of The Rowman & Littlefield Publishing Group, Inc.
4501 Forbes Boulevard, Suite 200, Lanham, Maryland 20706
www.rowman.com

Unit A, Whitacre Mews, 26-34 Stannary Street, London SE11 4AB

British Library Cataloguing in Publication Information Available

Library of Congress Cataloging-in-Publication Data Available

ISBN 9781442277397 (hardback : alk. paper) | ISBN 9781442277403 (pbk. : alk. paper) | ISBN 9781442277410 (electronic)

∞™ The paper used in this publication meets the minimum requirements of American National Standard for Information Sciences—Permanence of Paper for Printed Library Materials, ANSI/NISO Z39.48-1992.

Printed in the United States of America

To two of my favorite Makers: Steve Willingham, my husband, business partner, and best friend of almost 40 years, and my great visionary and accomplished friend, Chuck Stephens. This book wouldn't have been possible without their combined expertise, patience, support, and encouragement. Thanks for Making it awesome!

CONTENTS

PREFACE

> *Makerspaces in libraries allow everyone to develop critical thinking and problem-solving skills; they facilitate opportunities for collaboration and community engagement that will aid in entrepreneurial thinking, as well as the next generation of STEM jobs. They provide access to tools (from books to 3D printers) and, most importantly, "access to each other." Library makerspaces are powerful informal learning spaces that give local community members the ability to create, hack, and make their future.*
>
> —American Library Association[1]

Library Makerspaces: The Complete Guide comes to press at the height of the growth of creative public spaces in public and academic libraries worldwide. Intended for librarians interested in developing intentional, community-driven makerspaces and related programming in their libraries, this book will take the reader from the most preliminary steps in identifying both library and community capacity to support a space to developing inventory and hosting related programming and events. It draws from the best practices of spaces that have been in existence for two or more years, as well as my own extensive experience as a consultant for libraries interested in developing public makerspaces.

There are plenty of good reasons to embark on the makerspace journey for your library, if you haven't done so yet, or enhance the space you have now.

"Makerspaces are enabling libraries to transform their relationship with communities and to empower community members of all ages to be creators of information, not just consumers," said American Library Association (ALA) president Barbara Stripling, in a 2014 ALA statement of support for makerspace development in the nation's libraries.[2]

It's a telling statement. When I wrote *Makerspaces in Libraries* with Jeroen De Boer just two years ago, and not long after the issuance of the ALA statement of support, we referenced "dozens" of library makerspaces then in development. As of this writing, we have personally facilitated staff development for hundreds of librarians in the United States and Europe, and helped with the development of several new library makerspaces in our respective communities. There are now hundreds of public and school library makerspaces throughout the United States, Canada, and Europe, and hundreds more "pop-up" and soft making spaces, which provide access to such items as 3D printers and sewing machines. Today, "library makerspace" is even a thing on Wikipedia (https://en.wikipedia.org/wiki/Library_makerspace). There is also an abundant and growing body of research on the topic of makerspaces in libraries and elsewhere, examining everything from equity to community impact.

WHY LIBRARY MAKERSPACES MATTER

In a March 2016 article for the *Atlantic*, Miguel Figueroa, director of the Center for the Future of Libraries at the American Library Association, identifies makerspaces as part of libraries' "expanded mission to be places where people can not only consume knowledge, but [also] create new knowledge."[3] In a related *Atlantic* article, titled "The Library Card," author Deborah Fallows identifies three areas of service that fix libraries as vibrant centers of U.S. cities and towns: technology, education, and community.[4] Makerspaces in libraries clearly address these three areas of service and impact, and function as a natural extension of the library's institutional legacy.

Says John Palfrey in *BiblioTECH: Why Libraries Matter More Than Ever in the Age of Google*,

> The library as an institution has been fundamental to the success of our democracy. Libraries provide access to the skills and knowledge necessary

> to fulfill our roles as active citizens. Libraries also function as essential equalizing institutions in our society. For as long as a library exists in most communities, staffed with trained librarians, it remains true that individuals' access to our shared culture is not dictated by however much money they have.[5]

Makerspaces in libraries amp up that equitability by providing, in addition to books and Internet access, access to tools and other creative resources. However, while there's a lot of interest in creating these new spaces, inspired by success stories of existing spaces like we share in *Makerspaces in Libraries*, there's also some confusion by newcomers on just how to go about doing that and sometimes why to do it at all. School and public library librarians are finding themselves with new collections among the stacks, namely 3D printers, MaKey MaKey and littleBits kits, and these things called Arduinos, along with sometimes-vague, new directives from above and from without, about creative content delivery.

TAKING NEXT STEPS WITH *LIBRARY MAKERSPACES: THE COMPLETE GUIDE*

The following question is naturally arising in some libraries and communities: Are we creating new spaces and programs because they're needed or just because everyone else is doing it? That's a good question and an important one to ask for libraries and any institution or organization considering a journey into the makerspace/hackerspace/FabLab field of dreams.

In the 1991 book *Crossing the Chasm*, author Geoffrey Moore proposes that a gap exists between the early adopters of technology and the mass market that uses that technology.[6] The book mostly focuses on product technology but also has applications in the adoption of almost any new concept or idea. In "Rethinking Crossing the Chasm," written 15 years later, ReadWrite blogger Alex Iskold makes some sage observations that have even more relevance to library makerspace development. He writes,

> Often, what works for early adopters does not work for the mainstream, and the other way around. Early adopters are typically techies; they want power tools; they eat, sleep, and drink tech; they are spoiled. Mainstream users are technophobic; they need one button at most; they freak out when things

change . . . the lucky ones that do get to the chasm today are going to face a big problem that did not exist just a few years ago.[7]

"Freak out" and "technophobic" are extremes that probably don't apply to most librarians, but the basic tenet holds true: It's easier for early adopters of anything to jump right on board with a new idea they're already interested in and totally get. It's something else entirely, with a potentially steep learning curve, for those learning about a new idea or concept for the first time. Expectations should not and cannot be the same. Later adopters will need a little more help crossing the chasm, clearer purpose, more resources, better illustrations, and a stronger helping hand.

What is the same, however, is the approach to developing sustainable spaces. In each case we reference in our previous book, and in this one, the unifying theme is the need for a community-defined and community-led space. From the veteran Fayetteville Free Library's Fabulous Laboratory in New York to the young but thriving Land O'Lakes Library Foundry makerspace in Florida, librarians with successful creative programs and spaces counsel the same things: Start small; understand your community and its needs; and collaborate and cooperate with one another, stakeholders, and potential community partners.

Another issue entering the discussion about makerspaces in libraries and elsewhere is that of diversity and inclusion, a challenge identified by Maker Media's own surveys, which found that the "movement is overwhelmingly male, well-educated, and affluent."

With economic impact from the Maker movement expected to top $8 billion by 2020, it is worth asking, says writer Will Holman in the *Places Journal* article "Makerspace: Towards a New Civic Infrastructure," "whether we are witnessing the birth of a durable movement or another trendy notion about civic innovation."[8]

These are important considerations that require an intentional and thoughtful approach, which includes ways to measure access and impact to create spaces and programming that help libraries serve their inherent missions and users have truly positive and meaningful experiences. Understanding community needs, as well as the inherent passions and interests of library personnel, can help make the difference between idle 3D printers no one is interested in using and sewing machines that never stop thrumming, or active mechanical and woodworking programs in a community that prefers these things to electronics and Web design.

Library Makerspaces breaks new ground for the next level of library makerspace development, presenting the best foundational start for new spaces, as well as new resources for veteran makerspace librarians to help them explore ways to beef up their existing spaces with more inclusive and diverse programming.

WHAT'S NEW

With more than 9,000 public libraries in the United States and almost 100,000 public-school libraries,[9] the opportunity to develop accessible infrastructures for creative endeavors and skills development is immense and important. And with a number of those libraries well into their second, third, or more years of makerspace development, there's a growing well of best practices and resources from which to draw so newcomers can get off to a better and more sustainable start to their own makerspace development and programming.

Library Makerspaces draws on those best practices through the results of a comprehensive survey for veteran library makerspaces, developed just for this book, as well as some of the latest research on inclusive makerspace development for all ages and abilities. This book addresses three areas of program and space development, which roughly equate to knowledge, design, and management:

- Makerspace culture and climate, and best practices from libraries throughout the United States (chapters 1–3)
- Methods for designing physical space and creative programming, and evaluating the effectiveness of both (chapters 4–6)
- Resources and information for stocking, staffing, and managing space and programs (chapters 7–9)
- Summary wrap-up with quick reference checklists (chapter 10)
- Comprehensive reading and resource recommendations

Throughout *Library Makerspaces*, we'll be using an adaptation of the uTEC Maker Model,[10] created by Bill Derry, David Loertscher, and Leslie

Preddy, to assess measures of library makerspace success, both potential and actual. The uTEC Maker Model describes "developmental stages of creativity" that can be generalized from individuals to groups, "as they develop from passively using a system or process to the ultimate phase of creativity and invention." The four stages are using, tinkering, experimenting, and creating. Today, most library makerspaces are largely serving the "using" category of Maker, with classes, workshops, and tool orientations, with just a few spaces serving Makers at the "tinkering" stage.

We'll further discuss the uTEC Model in greater detail in subsequent chapters, but we believe that for library makerspaces to become the center of what John Seely Brown, of the Deloitte Center for the Edge and the University of Southern California, calls an "ecosystem for innovation,"[11] libraries have to become more agile, innovative, and less risk averse. Only then can library makerspaces become a place of true creation, where users can come—freely, often, and with limited supervision—to experiment and create independently and in small groups, helping the library makerspace make the leap from trendy tool room to a vital community resource and valuable economic commodity.

Designing 21st-century programs and spaces from the ground up, intentionally and with purpose, helps everyone, from librarians to the communities they serve, cross the chasm together and make new tools, resources, and opportunities available to everyone. Creating an enduring and sustainable program with measurable impact is the real challenge, and *Library Makerspaces* aims to provide librarians with a comprehensive tool kit for achieving long-term success that serves patrons, staff and volunteers, and our communities well into the future.

NOTES

1. "American Library Association Supports Makerspaces in Libraries." *News and Press Center*. 2014. Accessed July 11, 2017. www.ala.org/news/press-releases/2014/06/american-library-association-supports-makerspaces-libraries.
2. "American Library Association Supports Makerspaces in Libraries."
3. Fallows, Deborah. "How Libraries Are Becoming Modern Makerspaces." *Atlantic*. March 11, 2016. Accessed July 11, 2017. www.theatlantic.com/technology/archive/2016/03/everyone-is-a-maker/473286.

4. Fallows, Deborah. "The Library Card." *Atlantic*. March 11, 2016. Accessed July 11, 2017. www.theatlantic.com/magazine/archive/2016/03/the-library-card/426885.

5. Palfrey, John G. *BiblioTECH: Why Libraries Matter More Than Ever in the Age of Google*. New York: Basic Books, 2015.

6. Moore, Geoffrey. *Crossing the Chasm: Marketing and Selling High-Tech Products to Mainstream Customers*. New York: HarperBusiness, 2006.

7. Iskold, Alex. "Rethinking 'Crossing the Chasm.'" *ReadWrite*. August 6, 2007. Accessed July 11, 2017. http://readwrite.com/2007/08/06/rethinking_crossing_the_chasm/.

8. Holman, Will, Keller Easterling, Jim Robbins, and Jeremy Till. "Makerspace: Towards a New Civic Infrastructure." *Places Journal*. 2015. Accessed July 11, 2017. https://placesjournal.org/article/makerspace-towards-a-new-civic-infrastructure/.

9. "Number of Libraries in the United States: ALA Library Fact Sheet 1." *American Library Association*. September 2015. Accessed July 11, 2017. www.ala.org/tools/libfactsheets/alalibraryfactsheet01.

10. Derry, Bill, David V. Loertscher, and Leslie Preddy. "Makerspaces in the School Library Learning Commons and the uTEC Maker Model." *Teacher Librarian*, December 1, 2013, 48–51.

11. Garmer, Amy K. "Libraries in the Exponential Age: The Aspen Institute Dialogue on Public Libraries." *Aspen Institute Dialogue on Public Libraries*. January 8, 2016. Accessed September 4, 2016. www.libraryvision.org/libraries_in_the_exponential_age.

LIBRARY MAKERSPACES 101

We can empower ourselves to hack our way to better tools, a better library, and a better world.

—Nicholas Schiller, "Hacker Values ≈ Library Values"[1]

For those new to the makerspace discussion, the words and concepts discussed here may seem fresh and new. To those researching for any length of time, the thought of yet another "History of Makerspaces" and "Makerspaces 101" may be cause for eye rolling. Anyone dabbling in library makerspaces in recent memory may know that the development of the first public library makerspace is credited to Lauren Britton Smedley, who launched the Fayetteville Free Library Fabulous Laboratory (FabLab) in New York in 2011. Commensurately, various general histories of makerspaces may have been encountered along the way, and Googling "History of Makerspaces" will provide ample reading for anyone interested in the topic. Moreover, most librarians by now are familiar with, if not fairly well versed in, such new technologies as 3D printers, and many probably have at least one among the stacks by now, if they don't have a makerspace, per se.

Thus, for our purposes here, we'll present a high-level overview of the history of makerspaces, before examining the different forms makerspaces can take, the types of programming that might be found within them, and who can benefit from using them In subsequent chapters, we'll explore these concepts and ideas in greater detail.

CHAPTER 1

DEFINING TERMS

There are some basic terms that occur in any discussion about makerspaces. They are as follows:

- *Makers and making:* "Maker" became a proper noun in about 2005, becoming commonplace shortly thereafter. No less than President Obama has embraced the "Maker" culture, celebrating it annually during his presidency beginning in 2014, at the White House Maker Faire. But just what is a "Maker" and what do we mean when we say "Making"? Chris Anderson, in his book *Makers: The New Industrial Revolution* (2012), perhaps puts it best:

  > We are all Makers. We are born Makers (just watch a child's fascination with drawing, blocks, LEGOs, or crafts), and many of us retain that love in our hobbies and passions. It's not just about workshops, garages, and man caves. If you love to cook, you're a kitchen Maker and your stove is your workbench (homemade food is best, right?). If you love to plant, you're a garden Maker. Knitting and sewing, scrapbooking, beading, and cross-stitching—all Making.

  The term *Maker* is inclusive of artists and crafters, electrical or mechanical hobbyists and woodworkers, citizen scientists, and tinkerers, and characterized by a zeal for the creative task at hand and a passion for sharing it. "Making," with a capital M, is no less than a "social revolution: in how we learn, how we share, how we collaborate, how we consume and produce—making changes everything," says Lauren Britton Smedley.[2]
- *Makerspaces:* Places where Makers congregate and, ideally, have access to the tools, spaces, and resources that help them create the things they Make.
- *Hacking:* A more hardware- and software-oriented form of Making. Despite lingering and sometimes justifiably negative connotations, the term largely refers to the original intent of the word *hacking*, as in taking something apart. Hardware hackers like to modify, rebuild, upcycle, repurpose, and redesign. Software hackers like to do the same with programming and app development.

WHY MAKE?

In a 2016 article by that title, in *Public Libraries Online*, author Elizabeth Hartnett observes the following:[3]

> A satisfactory definition for makerspaces might be as follows: A makerspace is a physical space that provides access to equipment and guidance in a flexible format that responds to the interests and skill levels of users collaborating on self-directed projects.
>
> The connection between makerspaces and public libraries or other cultural institutions may be puzzling to some initially, but their inclusion supports the overall goals of these institutions: equity of access, community development, creating relationships among patrons, and encouraging lifelong learning. These are all potential benefits of public access to makerspaces as well.
>
> Evidence of the beneficial effects of makerspaces is beginning to be documented. In a 2013 report, high-school-age users of YOUmedia at the Chicago Public Library listed these effects:
>
> - Feeling of safety, community, and belonging.
> - Greater involvement with chosen interests.
> - Improvement in at least one digital media skill.
> - Improved academic, communication, and writing skills.
> - Better understanding of opportunities after high school.

Additionally, a growing body of evidence supports the benefits of the Maker movement to economic development,[4] community development,[5] and civic activism.[6] Libraries have been at the forefront of makerspace development from the very beginning.[7]

HISTORY

One of the more interesting histories of library makerspaces on the Internet takes a broader look at "making" in libraries than the standard histories often allow. The blogger of Bound, in "A Brief History of Makerspaces in Libraries,"[8] goes back to 1873, in New York, to the Gowanda Ladies Social Society, the members of which came together to drink tea, quilt, knit, sew, socialize, and swap books. From their social club grew the Gowanda Free Library, which is still active today.

Mita Williams, in the blog New Jack Librarian, sources makerspaces back a little further, to what he calls the "proto-species of the makerspace," the Mechanics' Institute. Begun in Edinburgh, Scotland, in October 1821, to "provide libraries and forms of adult education, particularly in technical subjects, to working men,"[9] the Mechanics' Institute was financed by local industrialists looking to create a more skilled workforce. At one time, there were more than 700 Mechanics' Institutes worldwide.

Bound also includes the Carnegie Library of Pittsburg in his history, which, in 1905, regularly organized sewing and basketry workshops for local children, and the Manitoba Crafts Museum and Library in Canada, which was dedicated in 1933, to preserving the area's cultural heritage by teaching legacy skills to youth. One of the earliest tool libraries was the Rebuilding Together Central Ohio Tool Library, made possible by a federal community development block grant. The Central Ohio Tool Library (www.rtcentralohio.org/tool-library/) is still in operation today and offers more than 200 different types of tools, with more than 5,000 individual hand and power tools.

However, what we now know of makerspaces and hackerspaces in the United States, outside of libraries, hearkens back to the European hacker movement of the late 1990s.[10] Hackerspaces, which are typically more hardware oriented and focused on electronic and computer technologies, were the forerunners of today's more broad-based creative spaces we usually call makerspaces, which embrace everything from arts and textile work to all-purpose tinkering. The first hackerspaces to open in the United States were NYC Resistor and HacDC, in Washington, D.C., both of which opened in 2007, followed by Noisebridge in San Francisco in 2008.

Makerspaces began to appear in 2005, in spaces as small as private garages and as large as the 30,000-square-foot TechShop chain. At about the same time, *Make:* magazine hosted its first Maker Faire, in San Francisco, launching the growth of even more makerspaces. By 2014, the two flagship Maker Faires in San Francisco and New York had drawn 215,000 people to the Maker celebration, and by 2015, dozens of independent Maker festivals had cropped up throughout the world, including many library Maker festivals. Makerspaces and "making" are now officially—in the vernacular of the time—a "thing."

In Europe, makerspace growth has perhaps been even more robust. In 2008, there was one makerspace in the United Kingdom. By 2015, there were nearly 100, appearing in almost every region, with most major cities in the United Kingdom being home to at least one makerspace.[11] In Europe and many other parts of the world, the FabLab typically dominates.

The Makery, Europe's go-to resource for all things hacking and making, has the most comprehensive directory of spaces overseas, identifying more than 500 FabLabs, hackerspaces, art, media and other creative spaces.[12] Africa boasts more than 200 spaces, supported by the Fab Foundation and BongoHive, and the American Society of Mechanical Engineers supports more than 150 and 75 spaces in India and Southeast Asia, respectively.[13]

The typical community hackerspace or makerspace, then and now, is membership based, operating like a hobbyist's health club. There are usually different membership levels, offering varying degrees of access to a variety of tools and resources. In 2013, almost 34 percent of makerspaces required membership, and a smaller percentage required membership or a daily usage fee, with membership costs ranging from $30 to $200 per month,[14] usually to help cover operational and maintenance expenses.

MAKERSPACES IN LIBRARIES

The idea of creating makerspaces in public libraries was a natural outgrowth of the mission and goals of the library as a community resource. Dr. David Weinberger, senior researcher at Harvard's Berkman Center for Internet and Society, and codirector of the Harvard Library Lab, makes one of the best cases for makerspaces in libraries when he talks about the library as platform.[15] Rather than a "portal we go through on occasion," he says, we should think of the library as "infrastructure that is as ubiquitous and persistent as the streets and sidewalks of a town, or the classrooms and yards of a university."

The library as platform, says Dr. Weinberger, "would give rise to messy, rich networks of people and ideas, continuously sparked and maintained by the library's resources. A library as platform is more how than where, more hyperlinks than container, more hubbub than hub."

Nicholas Schiller further disrupts traditional notions of the library with his ideas in "Hacker Values ≈ Library Values," drawing parallels between the core values of both—sharing, openness, collaboration, and hands-on activity. "With an injection of hacker values into library services," he writes, "we no longer have to remain at the mercy of the default setting. We can empower ourselves to hack our way to better tools, a better library, and a better world."[16]

That notion of collaborative community is what drove Lauren Britton Smedley to develop the Fayetteville Free Library FabLab. In a Library as Incubator Project article, in 2012, Britton writes, "Makerspaces are places where people come together to create, collaborate, and share resources and knowledge—an idea and concept that fits perfectly with the mission and vision of public libraries."[17] Adding 3D printers to the library resource collection was, ultimately, no different from having 2D printers like copiers and scanners. And, in fact, the Fayetteville Free Library FabLab was originally focused on 3D printing, a new technology in 2010.

Britton saw libraries and makerspaces as a natural fit, noting, "Libraries create an opening for people to experience the Maker movement for free."

In 2012, Dutch librarian Jeroen De Boer launched the FryskLab project, which became Europe's first mobile FabLab, a "place where physical and

FryskLab. ***Jeroen De Boer***

digital use and knowledge-sharing converge."[18] The FryskLab project is a mobile platform, with the goal of building creative, technical, and entrepreneurial skills in youth, and, ultimately, they hope, inspire an increase in the innovative capacities of the province as a whole.

By 2013, when author and librarian John Burke launched his "Makerspaces in Libraries Survey," he found that 41 percent of his 109 respondents were already providing makerspaces or maker-style activities and programs in their libraries, with another 36 percent working on developing such programs in their institutions.[19] More than half of the makerspaces identified at the time were in public libraries, with most of the rest in academic libraries and a small percentage in public-school libraries.

With more than 50,000 public libraries in Europe, the Europeana Association Network Task Force on Public Libraries took a serious look at where they were and where they wanted to be. In their 2015 final recommendations report, the makerspace movement was front and center:

> Europe's public libraries are currently engaged in a process of transformation for the digital era. The erosion of demand for their traditional services (such as book lending and printed information sources), as a result of the pervasiveness of the Internet and changes in patterns of public consumption, has led to a need to transform their portfolio of services to match demand, whilst capitalizing on the trust which people have in public libraries as neutral and ethical civic institutions.[20]

The task force set specific goals and guidelines for the establishment of a permanent European library makerspace network with tools and resources for member libraries, creating the basis for a strong library makerspace infrastructure.

Libraries are natural partners for innovation, contends Aspen Institute president Walter Isaac. "Forming communities and collaboration is the core of what libraries do," he writes in the Aspen Institute report on public libraries. Innovative programming and use of space are simply a "return to the institution's origins." "Public libraries didn't start out as only repositories for books. They were places for dialogue and conversation. They were 'knowledge tanks,'" says Mary Lee Kennedy, chief library officer at New York Public Library, in the same report.[21] Makerspaces make them knowledge tanks with toolboxes.

But perhaps the most compelling reason libraries are embracing innovative use of space and programming might simply be, as Britton found with the Fayetteville Free Library FabLab, that "people who had never visited the library began streaming in."

So just what, you might ask, are they streaming into? What's the difference between a FabLab, a hackerspace and a makerspace, or an Innovation Center, or any of the other name variants by which these spaces are called?

TYPES OF SPACES

There are many different terms for creative-use spaces, and many of these terms, like hackerspace and makerspace, are often used interchangeably, sometimes to the chagrin of those who feel there are sufficient distinguishing features between the two to warrant more selective use of terms. Others, like co-working spaces or technology hubs, are more commercial in nature, and while they may have elements of makerspaces or hackerspaces, they are not terms often connected with libraries. Thus, for our purposes, we're chiefly going to use the generic term *makerspace* in discussions of tool- and resource-stocked creative library spaces. But it's worth noting some of the differences, both for the sake of cultural and historical awareness and the potential value of integrating some of the more traditional elements of these different spaces in library designs.

Makerspaces

We touched on these briefly at the beginning of this chapter. Generally, makerspaces tend to be focused on independent craft, repair, and construction. They can vary considerably in scope and size, from a classroom to several thousand square feet, and be stocked with anything from basic art supplies and small hand tools to ventilated paint booths and CNC machines. Most library spaces can rightly be considered makerspaces in that they can be adapted to a wide variety of existing spaces to accommodate interests ranging from arts and sewing to small or large electronic and mechanical projects.

FabLabs

Fabrication Labs, or "FabLabs," are usually affiliated with academic institutions or sponsored by a foundation or organization and focused on manufacturing and business incubation spurred through rapid prototyping and patent development. The Fayetteville Free Library FabLab is a friendly wordplay on the concept, standing for "Fabulous Lab." Most FabLabs, however, tend to stay pretty true to the spirit and intent of the Fab Charter, which outlines several elements, from tools to purpose, that all FabLabs should have in common. These broadly include that a FabLab should:

- Serve as a "community resource" and be open to the public for at least part of the week
- Respect open-source ideas
- Support commercial activities incubated in the lab
- Have a common set of tools, capabilities, and processes to facilitate sharing within the lab and project development
- Participate in the larger international community of FabLabs

FabLabs are most common in Europe, where they got their start, although there are several well-regarded FabLabs throughout North America.

Hackerspaces

Hackerspaces, also known as hacklabs or hackspaces, grew out of the computer science and programming community, and have a heavy technical focus. While FabLabs are also highly technical in nature, hackerspaces are more freewheeling, with no formal common theme or charter uniting them. These spaces are typically stocked with a robust assortment of tools and equipment, ranging from sophisticated electronics to specialized power tools.

Mobile Makerspaces (or Mobile FabLabs)

A mobile makerspace is just that: a book mobile of making, stocked with tools instead of books. FryskLab, Europe's first Mobile FabLab, developed by coauthor Jeroen De Boer, has desktop versions of a laser cutter, a CNC, a vinyl cutter, 3D printers, a 3D scanner, and computers and laptops fitted into a former "librarymobile" to take the making experience to rural and remote communities.

Pop-Up Makerspaces

Like a mobile makerspace or FabLab, a pop-up makerspace is a way to maximize access in limited spaces. For libraries that are unable to build or repurpose sufficiently large spaces or whose communities lack enough interest to justify capital outlay for space development, tools, or equipment, the pop-up makerspace provides an affordable and accessible option. This type of makerspace can consist of mobile Maker stations in the form of specially configured carts that can be easily stored when not in use. Depending on community interest, pop-up makerspaces can use art carts, mobile sewing stations, carts equipped for culinary creativity, and even zine workshops that connect writing with crafting.[22]

Youth Makerspaces

Libraries, especially school libraries, can turn their youth areas into youth makerspaces that focus on arts, crafts, game making, cosplay prop making and costume creation, anime, music making, and more. It can be easier to start with a youth makerspace and build from there to support growing interest resulting from increased awareness.

Innovation Centers

In many parts of the world, particularly in South America, India, Africa, and parts of Asia, Innovation Centers focused on design and fabrication training for local communities are creating spaces where people can gather, learn, and create. Affiliated with the International Development Innovation Network, these spaces make available shared tools and equipment for prototype and product fabrication in a variety of materials. These spaces intentionally distinguish themselves from makerspaces, FabLabs, and hackerspaces by virtue of a "mission toward creating social good."[23]

TYPES OF PROGRAMMING

Programming can be a sticky wicket. One of the greatest assets of the library in developing public makerspaces is also one of the biggest challenges library makerspaces encounter: the public library administrative model. Where member-based makerspaces are either collaboratively managed by those members or run by an established charter, library makerspaces are being retrofit into a civic governance system with varying layers of bureaucratic processes completely unrelated to making. What Makers might do with ease and autonomy in a member-based facility—like simply walk in and start using tools—might require preregistration and time limits in a library makerspace.

Additionally, the structured model of library programming—children's story time, lectures, workshops, and classes—can inadvertently force library makerspaces into a classroom-model situation where they're providing an extensive suite of "Maker"-style programming, for example, 3D printing classes, Arduino workshops, computer-aided design, video editing, and other tech-related classes and workshops but little independent making capability. While some facilitated learning is desirable, the most effective makerspaces, in public libraries or elsewhere, are those that function as open-access facilities where people who have become fluent in equipment

Library MakerFest program, Tampa Bay Library Consortium. ***Theresa Willingham***

use can freely come and go to work independently on projects. That said, good programming helps them get there, and good administrative models help keep them coming back to create and explore.

When we speak of "programming" here, we're referring to everything from curricular-style classes and workshops to the creation of intentional opportunities for unstructured, collaborative, and independent making. Programming can consist of the following:

- Workshops and classes on everything from 3D printing software to cosplay costume making
- "Open make" sessions, where people have open access to makerspace resources
- Contests
- Repair Cafés
- Maker festivals
- Heritage craft and other "traditional" making and learning opportunities
- Robotics
- Ham radio
- Project-based programming (e.g., zine workshops, do-it-yourself [DIY] media, digital storytelling)
- Citizen science projects and opportunities

The best programming for your library is the programming your user community most values and enjoys, and sometimes there will be no packaged programming at all. In the "Making in the Library Toolkit,"[24] the condition of HOMAGO, an acronym created by Mimi Ito, a professor of anthropology at the University of California, Irvine, is suggested as the ultimate goal for good Maker programming.

HOMAGO stands for "hanging out, messing around, and geeking out." The tool kit suggests that this is the ideal experience for patrons, in this case, teens, who can socialize and set their own pace for creativity and new skills acquisition. "If teens leave your program with a new skill and a smile on their face," the tool kit advises, "that's a great indicator of success and another way to evaluate your programming." That same benchmark of success holds for adults using makerspaces, too.

Ultimately, the goal of the library makerspace is to provide opportunities for library users to create something that didn't exist before, says Vicki Rakowski, assistant director of Youth Services at Lisle Library District and cocreator of Make It at Your Library, an idea that "strengthens the importance of the old 'third space' concept."[25] The third space, or place, concept, discussed in some detail in *Makerspaces in Libraries*, essentially identifies the library as one of those places that is neither home nor work/school, but a place where we go to socialize, converse, think, and explore together.

LEVELS OF PROGRAMMING

The uTEC Maker Model, exploring types of Makers, was created by Bill Derry, David Loertscher, and Leslie Preddy, and first appeared in the December 2013 issue of *Teacher Librarian*.[26] It describes the evolutionary journey of the empowered Maker from the most rudimentary User (U) to the

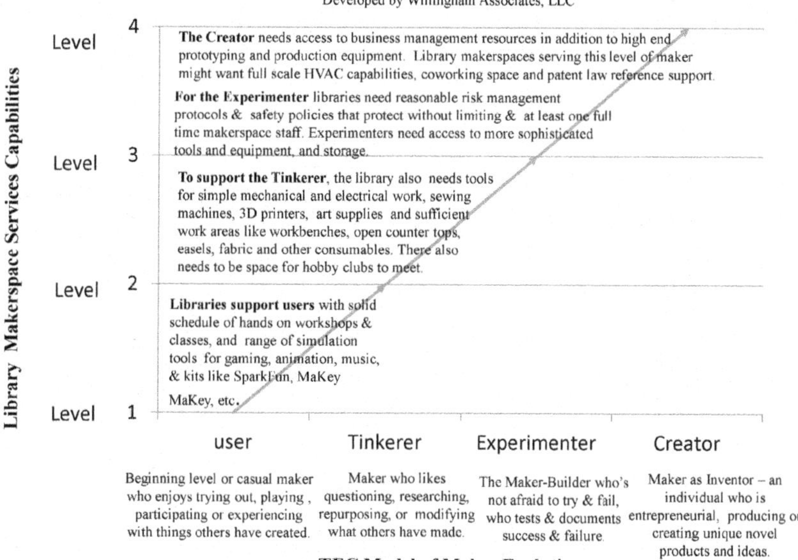

Library makerspace growth goals guide. ***Theresa Willingham***

top-level Creator (C), a concept that can be helpful in developing and evaluating library makerspace programming. Depending on the scope and intent of a library makerspace, if capabilities can only support targeted workshops and classes, makerspace users will likely stay at the User level, sampling new things like tools or devices at the most basic level, recreating what others have already done, for instance, 3D printing keychains.

Programming that supports the Tinkering level of this concept allows Users to explore a bit more independently, modifying others' creations and using tools or resources in unexpected or unintended ways to create something new. "Modifying" is the operative word here, and makerspaces with programming that allows users to wander off the beaten path of instructions are expanding users' abilities from basic interest to skills development.

The third level of the Maker journey in the uTEC model is Experimenting. This is the point at which the Maker embarks on a new way of doing things, creating new knowledge and content of her own. This is where expertise develops and modification might become complete repurposing. Failure is a powerful and necessary component of the Experimenting level and can often result in a new direction of creation. Libraries that can allow users to reach this level of making have to be willing to overcome varying degrees of risk aversion and give more autonomy to space users.

At the highest level of the uTEC Maker experience is Creating. This stage is characterized by independent thinking, invention, innovation, and intentional action. At this level, the Creator has made something new, had an impact, and made a difference through active exploration and engagement.

The levels or categories of making can be viewed as progressive or standalone levels of interest. Some people may simply want to tinker, with no desire to advance beyond that level. Others may be inspired to create at a more sophisticated level as they learn what's possible; however, none of this creative expression, at any level, is possible simply by providing the space and resources, and waiting. "Access is not enough—just because you put a makerspace in a library, doesn't mean that that is enough. Outreach needs to be done. If you just offer access and nothing else, the people that use it (are) very self-selected."[27]

To that end, staff development is vital for the successful implementation, management, and promotion of makerspace resources and programming to reach the most people and have the most far-reaching community impact.

STAFF DEVELOPMENT

"How do you train a librarian to teach a patron how to make?" asks Melody Clark in "Libraries and Makerspaces: A Revolution?" "The first part is helping librarians understand why this is part of their job," writes Clark. She continues,

> Another part is helping them to understand they don't have to be experts with this, that they are coming at this at a more equal playing field. Think of the librarian as a facilitator, rather than librarian as an expert. This doesn't just apply to makerspaces, but also to helping librarians deliver a lot of new services. Let librarians know it's ok to just learn by trying and doing—you don't have to know what you're doing.

From our experience as library makerspace designers and staff development providers, as well as tinkerers, experimenters, and creators in our own right, we would modify that a bit: We don't think librarians have to "teach a patron how to make" any more than they generally need to teach a patron how to read. Certainly, literacy tutoring is part of the library experience, but the majority of people using a library already read and simply come in to indulge their love of reading and explore the shelves for new reading experiences. In the same way, librarians working with makerspaces among the

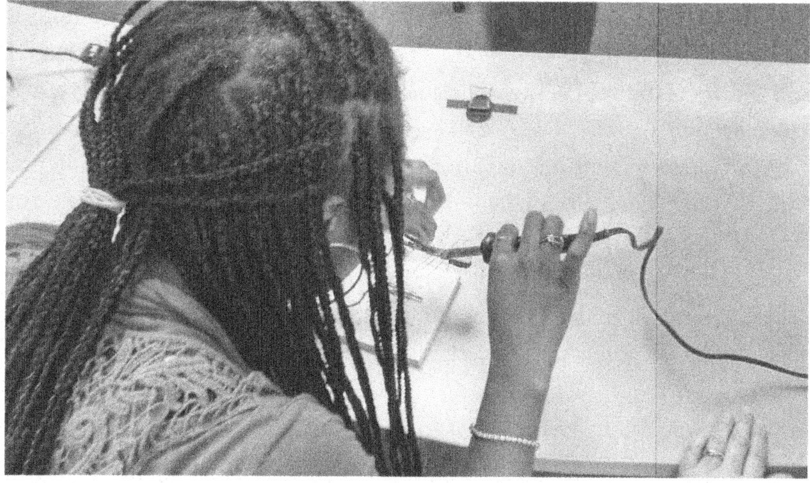

Staff development training, Tampa Hillsborough County Library. ***Theresa Willingham***

stacks simply facilitate patrons' discovery of their inherent ability to make or their desire to create something new.

Understanding why Maker programming is part of the 21st-century librarian's job is vital, of course, and we agree that it's not only okay, but also essential, to learn by trying and doing. But to the notion that you don't need know what you're doing, we would suggest that, yes, it's pretty important to know what you're doing, too. It's uncomfortable and difficult to facilitate any experience if you're totally out of your wheelhouse.

While we're not suggesting that librarians have to understand or even appreciate the inner workings of a 3D printer or 3D modeling, any more than a circulation librarian needs to understand or appreciate James Joyce's *Ulysses* or Kafka, we do believe that librarians working with makerspaces need a love and understanding of making to be the most effective makerspace librarians. People entering a library understandably expect librarians to enjoy and have some level of expertise about books. Similarly, people using library makerspaces should be able to have a reasonable expectation that facilitating librarians are themselves practiced purveyors of making.

The best staff development will help library administrators identify the innate talents and inherent creative interests of staff and volunteers, and leverage those talents and interests to help those librarians bring their native passion and enthusiasm to the Maker table, because ultimately the Maker experience and the makerspace is about the people in the space, not the physical space itself. The Maker movement and the Maker community is about sharing what's made, modifying creations, building on them, and reimagining creations in new ways. Effective and enduring library makerspaces are staffed by people who equally love making, experimenting, and creating.

Staff development that taps into everyone's inner Maker not only produces well-trained librarians who can effectively facilitate library makerspaces and programming, but also happier staff whose passion for their work is infectious—the essential elements of a good makerspace. Good staff development for makerspaces should take place during several days or in a period of a few weeks and include the following:

- Orientation to Maker history and culture
- Exposure to a wide variety of creative experiences, from arts to textiles to electronics and more

- Hands-on tinkering opportunities
- Facilitated discussion on creativity, design, invention, and innovation
- Open make sessions
- Tool orientation
- Training in asset mapping to identify potential collaborative community partners

Staff development is successful when librarians come away from the experience not with a dread of more work in roles they don't understand, but with new ideas about themselves as empowered creators excited to share in the experience of making with their patrons. Enthusiastic and passionate staff who understand the core tenets of the Maker movement and consider themselves makers are key to creating vibrant, thriving library makerspaces about which patrons are equally excited and passionate to be part of, in the same way that librarians who love books make the best circulation and reference staff.

DEMOGRAPHICS SERVED

Library makerspaces should serve the same demographics libraries serve with current programming and also tap into an underserved segment of the community, for whom current programming is inadequate or not of interest. The population served by library makerspaces tends to be a little different from that served by member-based spaces, where high-end hobbyists, inventors, or entrepreneurs are looking for more sophisticated tools and resources, and are willing and able to pay for them. Library makerspace users tend to be teens and young adults, families, and women—a positive trend in the evolution of the Maker movement, where there has been growing awareness that, for the most part, the movement has been largely white, male, and well educated.

Of the more than 160,000 Maker Faire attendees in 2012, almost 70 percent were male, and almost all of whom had graduated from college and had an average income of $117,000.[28] At the third annual FabLearn conference at Stanford University in 2013, Dr. Leah Buechley, a former associate professor at the Massachusetts Institute of Technology, pointed out that between 2005 and 2013, *Make:* magazine themes leaned overwhelmingly toward electronics, which were cover features more than half the time, followed by features on vehicles (31 percent), robots (22 percent), rockets (8 percent), and music (5 percent). She also pointed out that of the 40 people featured on the cover of *Make:*, 85 percent were white men and boys, and she called for broadening considerations of making to include ceramics, costuming, weaving, and other nontechnical craft skills and interests.[29]

"If technical tinkering, STEM, and digital fabrication are the economic forces that will empower Makers, and women and people of color are not participating in these activities in a visible way," writes Britton, "that power will remain unequally distributed."[30]

Fortunately, because Makers are, for the most part, also good, kind, and socially aware people who want to grow their communities, there has been an active movement toward becoming more inclusive of and accessible to the able and differently abled, people of all ethnicities and backgrounds, any gender orientation, and all types of communities. Libraries are the Maker movement's best hope for true accessibility and inclusion, providing access for the price of a library card and being situated in the hearts of our most diverse neighborhoods. As libraries build creative spaces, they're in a prime position to create them using principles of universal design,[31] which will be explored in greater depth in chapter 4, to ensure that spaces, tools, and resources are accessible to everyone and more representative of the interests, culture, and needs of the communities they serve.

COMMUNITY IMPACT: THE MAKERSPACE SUCCESS QUOTIENT

Community impact has to be examined by different measures of success than might be typically employed since, in makerspaces, failure is always, necessarily and vitally, an option. Measures of impact can also vary widely by community served. In short, it's not an exact science, but it's a necessary one if libraries are to continue being able to fund creative programming and space expansion.

Britton cites research that shows that the "creativity and divergent thinking that (making) requires is central to the health of society, is good for individual happiness, and when done collaboratively, can transform the quality of life in communities."[32] Quantifying that transformation can be a little challenging, but Auckland Libraries have given it a shot, identifying four rather creatively named qualities by which to measure the success of library makerspaces.

1. *Grow-like-weed-itude* measures the resilience and sustainability of the idea of a makerspace from library staff and systems perspectives. The measure of *grow-like-weed-itude* can be determined by the number of libraries with permanent or semipermanent Maker activities and the annual growth rate of Maker events in the libraries.
2. *Social-interesting-ness* measures how well makerspace ideas and activities engage the library community's imagination online, as well as in person. Auckland Libraries use the social media formula of "likes + shares (X2) + comments (X4) = number of fans." If stories are appearing in the local paper about a library makerspace, that's a solid measure of "*social-interesting-ness.*"
3. *Filling-in-form-ability* measures the rigor and quality of the library's makerspace business model, based on the degree to which the information on the Social Lean Canvas form can be filled in. The Social Lean Canvas is a tool designed to help social entrepreneurs understand and build business models. Being able to fill in all of the Social Lean Canvas information helps ensure a replicable library makerspace model.
4. *What-would-Andre-say* is a measure of success derived from an outreach event for illiterate children in Auckland and is determined by storytelling impact. What kind of enduring story can the library makerspace tell? How many projects or activities are demonstrably linked to positive community impact? The highest level of achievement here would be a communication from someone who believes the library makerspace made a powerful and positive impact on his or her life.[33]

The community impact of library makerspaces is clearly viewed through a different lens, one that looks at the deeper values of empowerment, increased skills, and knowledge. Where circulation was previously a measure of community impact, now those measures are more esoteric. Auckland

Libraries have found one method for evaluating their "Makerspace Success Quotient." There are other measures of success libraries can look at for their own communities.

Library makerspaces may contribute to economic development by encouraging entrepreneurship, supporting small-business growth, providing workforce training and professional development, and increasing workforce retention. They can also contribute to their communities more generally through education, resiliency, and community development.

In 2014, the University of Washington Information School (iSchool) launched its third and most refined release of the Impact Survey, created to get more useful and useable feedback from libraries.[34] Previously, the survey focused largely on technological services, but the 2014 release looked at other library services, including children's programs. Even without specifically examining the impact of library makerspaces, which is probably only another release or two away, the current data shows that libraries contribute to the economic health of the community by supporting the small-business community, with 8 percent of the public access technology users at U.S. libraries reporting they had used these resources for entrepreneurship purposes in the last year.

As libraries move forward in the development of creative spaces and programming, identifying what measures of success are most relevant will help put intentionality behind the design and implementation of these spaces to help ensure the creation of sustainable and enduring spaces.

NOTES

1. Schiller, Nicholas. "Hacker Values ≈ Library Values." *ACRL TechConnect Blog, Association of College and Research Libraries*. November 13, 2012. Accessed July 5, 2017. http://acrl.ala.org/techconnect/post/hacker-values-%E2%89%88-library-values.

2. Smedley, Lauren Britton. "'Making' the Future: Conclusion of Making and the Maker Movement Blog Post Series." *Technology Social Change Group*. December 14, 2015. Accessed July 5, 2017. http://tascha.uw.edu/2015/12/making-the-future-conclusion-of-making-the-maker-movement-blog-post-series.

3. Hartnett, Elizabeth J. "Why Make? An Exploration of User-Perceived Benefits of Makerspaces." *Public Libraries Online*. November 28, 2016. Accessed July

25, 2017. http://publiclibrariesonline.org/2016/11/why-make-an-exploration-of-user-perceived-benefits-of-makerspaces/.

4. Tierney, John. "How Makerspaces Help Local Economies." *Atlantic*. April 17, 2015. Accessed July 25, 2017. www.theatlantic.com/technology/archive/2015/04/makerspaces-are-remaking-local-economies/390807/.

5. Paonessa, Laura, and Arianna Orozco. "What Is a Makerspace? How Does It Promote Community Development?" *Beeck Center*. October 5, 2016. Accessed July 25, 2017. http://beeckcenter.georgetown.edu/makerspace-community-development/.

6. Smith, Adrian. "Tooling Up: Civic Visions, FabLabs, and Grassroots Activism." *Guardian*. April 4, 2015. Accessed July 25, 2017. www.theguardian.com/science/political-science/2015/apr/04/tooling-up-civic-visions-fablabs-and-grassroots-activism.

7. Hartnett, "Why Make?"

8. "A Brief History of Makerspaces in Libraries." *Bound*. March 30, 2014. Accessed July 5, 2017. http://boundbooksandlibraryblog.blogspot.com/2014/03/a-brief-history-of-makerspaces-in.html.

9. Williams, Mita. "Hackerspaces, Makerspaces, FabLabs, TechShops, Incubators, Accelerators. . . . Where Do Libraries Fit In?" *New Jack Librarian*. February 2, 2015. Accessed July 5, 2017. http://librarian.newjackalmanac.ca/2015/02/hackerspaces-makerspaces-fab-labs.html.

10. Benton, Cristina, Lori Mullins, Kristin Shelley, and Tim Dempsey. *Makerspaces: Supporting an Entrepreneurial System*. Working paper, Michigan State University, 2013.

11. "Open Dataset of U.K. Makerspaces: A User's Guide." *Nesta*. Accessed July 5, 2017. www.nesta.org.uk/publications/open-dataset-uk-makerspaces-users-guide.

12. "Map of Labs." *Makery*. Accessed July 5, 2017. www.makery.info/en/map-labs/.

13. Brown, Anna Waldman. "Definitive Maker Map Mapping." *District: Stories of Digital Design*. April 21, 2015. Accessed July 5, 2017. http://district.life/2015/04/21/definitive-maker-map-mapping/.

14. Smedley, Lauren Britton. "Democratized Tools of Production: New Technologies Spurring the Maker Movement." *Technology Social Change Group*. August 18, 2014. Accessed July 5, 2017. http://tascha.uw.edu/2014/08/democratized-tools-of-production-new-technologies-spurring-the-maker-movement/.

15. Weinberger, David. "Library as Platform." *Library Journal*. September 4, 2012. Accessed July 5, 2017. http://lj.libraryjournal.com/2012/09/future-of-libraries/by-david-weinberger/#.

16. Schiller, "Hacker Values ≈ Library Values."

17. "The Oh-So Fabulous Lab at the Fayetteville Free Library." *Library as Incubator Project*. March 21, 2012. Accessed July 5, 2017. www.libraryasincubator project.org/?p=3335.

18. De Boer, Jeroen. "The Business Case of FryskLab, Europe's First Mobile Library FabLab." *Rafelranden*. February 2016. Accessed July 5, 2017. http://jeroendeboer.net/2016/02/12/publication-the-business-case-of-frysklab-europes-first-mobile-library-fablab/.

19. Price, Gary. "Results from 'Makerspaces in Libraries' Study Released." *LJ INFOdocket*. December 16, 2013. Accessed July 5, 2017. www.infodocket .com/2013/12/16/results-of-makerspaces-in-libraries-study-released.

20. "Final Recommendations Europeana Association Network Task Force on Public Libraries." *Europeana Pro*. December 2015. Accessed July 5, 2017. http://pro.europeana.eu/files/Europeana_Professional/Europeana_Network/europeana-task-force-on-public-libraries-final-report-dec2015.pdf.

21. Garmer, Amy K. "The Aspen Institute—CHAPTER II—Leveraging the Exponential Edge." *Aspen Institute*. 2015. Accessed July 5, 2017. http://csreports.aspeninstitute.org/Dialogue-on-Public-Libraries/2015/report/details/0143/Libraries-2015.

22. Rogers, Melissa. "Compositional Craft: Zine Workshops as Pop-Up Makerspaces." *Digital Rhetoric Collaborative*. April 7, 2016. Accessed July 5, 2017. www.digitalrhetoriccollaborative.org/2016/04/07/compositional-craft-zine-workshops-as-pop-up-makerspaces/.

23. "International Development Innovation Network." *Innovation Centers*. Accessed July 5, 2017. www.idin.org/innovationcenters.

24. "Making in the Library Toolkit." *Young Adult Library Services Association*. 2014. Accessed July 5, 2017. www.ala.org/yalsa/sites/ala.org.yalsa/files/content/MakingintheLibraryToolkit2014.pdf.

25. "Making in the Library Toolkit."

26. Derry, Bill, David V. Loertscher, and Leslie Preddy. "uTEC Maker Model." *UTEC Maker Model*. 2014. Accessed July 5, 2017. https://sites.google.com/site/utecmakermodel/.

27. Clark, Melody. "Libraries and Makerspaces: A Revolution?" *Technology Social Change Group*. June 13, 2014. Accessed July 5, 2017. http://tascha .uw.edu/2014/06/libraries-makerspaces-a-revolution/.

28. Britton, "'Making' the Future."

29. Quattrocchi, Christina. "MAKE'ing More Diverse Makers." *EdSurge*. October 29, 2013. Accessed July 5, 2017. www.edsurge.com/news/2013-10-29-make-ing-more-diverse-makers.

30. Britton, "'Making' the Future."

31. "Making a Makerspace? Guidelines for Accessibility and Universal Design." *DO-IT*. 2015. Accessed July 5, 2017. www.washington.edu/doit/making-makerspace-guidelines-accessibility-and-universal-design.

32. Britton, "'Making' the Future."

33. "Measuring Makerspaces." *Feddabonn*. October 1, 2014. Accessed July 5, 2017. http://feddabonn.com/2014/10/measuring-makerspaces/.

34. Becker, Samantha. "Impact Survey: Measuring Your Library's Impact." *Public Libraries Online*. July 22, 2015. Accessed July 5, 2017. http://publiclibrariesonline.org/2015/07/impact-survey-measuring-your-librarys-impact/.

2

FIRST THINGS FIRST

Getting Organized

Makerspaces are collaborative learning environments where people come together to share materials and learn new skills . . . makerspaces are not necessarily born out of a specific set of materials or spaces, but rather a mindset of community partnership, collaboration, and creation.

—Library as Incubator Project[1]

The most successful library makerspaces, whether in public libraries or school libraries, are those that are sustainable, adaptive, and dynamic. Library administration has an enormous amount to do with those three key characteristics. Thus, it needs to be a significant partner in the development of these creative public spaces. It's not enough for a library system to throw its librarianship hat into the makerspace arena just because everyone else is doing it. Any library system embarking on the development of public makerspaces needs to be self-aware, well organized, and committed to the idea of "making" as complementary to and, in many cases, integral with the library's mission to empower and inform.

This is a crucial aspect of library makerspace development that has to be addressed at the earliest stage of makerspace development. The decision to be "cutting edge" necessitates a healthy amount of risk-taking and an acceptance of possibly being cut on that sharp edge of innovation. "There are no rules here," Thomas Edison famously said. "We're trying to accomplish something."

Obviously there have to be some rules, but Edison's point should be well taken. Achievement and success blossom with as few restrictions as possible. Risk-averse administrations that expect to micromanage every aspect of library makerspace operation can and usually do negatively impact the effectiveness of the effort. It's almost impossible and, at the very least, counterproductive to expect a library makerspace to function the same way as other library operations and programs. By nature and design, the best and most successful makerspaces are busy, messy, community-driven, heavily volunteer staffed, often spontaneous in programming and activity, and noisy. Branches instituting makerspaces and the administrations that run them need to enter into the experience with eyes and minds wide open, and the flexibility to best serve them, even and especially if that means doing the business of the library in new ways.

Anything less than full institutional and community support is a waste of time and public dollars. Full-spectrum support of library makerspace initiatives, however, can reinvigorate libraries like few other programs and effectively establish libraries as epicenters of their communities economically, as well as socially and academically.

This chapter begins with the premise that an engaged, flexible, and supportive administration supporting a library makerspace has already been established. With that crucial support base in mind, we'll look at methods, tools, and resources for creating the most effective and enduring makerspace program for your library in a way that truly meets the needs of your library community, efficiently leveraging the capabilities and financial and human capital with which you have to work.

The single best first step in this journey is to understand your library community's needs and interests. If you're lucky and smart enough to get administrative support first, understanding your community will help you develop the most useful and well-used space possible. If you don't already have administrative support or have only limited "we'll see" support, being able to quantify community needs and interests, and identify how the library can better serve them through updated programming and space use, can be pivotal in launching your space or save you the trouble of doing so if it turns out there is no real support in your community for this type of programming.

ASSESSING COMMUNITY NEEDS AND INTERESTS

The Community Tool Box (http://ctb.ku.edu/en) is a fantastic online resource developed by the University of Kansas to assist groups and organizations "working to build healthier communities and bring about social change." Library makerspaces fit the bill in both categories, and many of the organizing resources provided by the Community Tool Box are directly applicable to the development of public creative spaces and programming in libraries.

One of the most useful tools in the Community Tool Box, especially for a public library makerspace effort and directly applicable to the first step here, is "Chapter 3: Assessing Community Needs and Resources."[2] Before you embark on the makerspace journey, it's vital to understand what needs you're trying to serve and how—and if—serving them serves the bottom line of your library's principle mission and goals.

The Community Tool Box defines needs as the "gap between what is and what should be." Moreover,

> A need can be felt by an individual, a group, or an entire community. It can be as concrete as the need for food and water or as abstract as improved community cohesiveness. . . . Examining situations closely helps uncover what is truly needed and leads toward future improvement.
>
> Resources, or assets, can include individuals, organizations and institutions, buildings, landscapes, equipment—anything that can be used to improve the quality of life.[3]

If the development of creative space doesn't serve any particular community need or attempts to provide solutions to problems that don't exist or resources for interests that aren't there—like stocking 3D printers where people would really like sewing machines—the effort to create such space can be a waste of time, money, and human capital, with limited to no return on the investment. But taking the time to understand the surrounding community and patron needs and interests can position your library for long-term success and viability.

Whether libraries use professional needs assessment tools, for example, the Impact Survey;[4] hire an outside consultant like Eureka! Factory (co-owned by author Theresa Willingham and her husband Steve) to provide third-party focus groups and evaluate results; or conduct their own studies, the seven basic steps outlined by the Office of Community Services apply equally well to assessing library community needs and interests. This holds true whether the community is a neighborhood, town, or school community.

1. *Define the scope.* Figure out just what it is you want to figure out. Are you exploring makerspace creation because of waning patronage, administrative directive, or community requests? Has it been a while since you've assessed program effectiveness and you simply want to take the pulse of the community in general?
2. *Determine how to conduct your assessment.* Do you just want to do some patron surveys and run your own focus groups, or do you have the budget to hire third-party support? Might it be better to collaborate with current and potential community partners to assess community needs? Running a collaborative assessment with community partners helps engage the community at a fundamental level, which can help increase engagement and raise awareness of the library as a community asset in the process of reevaluating services and support. It can also help leverage more assessment resources, tools, and funding. More importantly, collaborating with other community agencies and partners can help strengthen relationships that can be helpful in moving forward to address the findings of the assessments.
3. *Collect data.* There are two basic types of data you'll be collecting: primary and secondary. Secondary data will be things like census data about your immediate community—demographic data about work, income, ethnicity, and so forth—as well as historical library data about patron habits, circulation, and current program engagement. Primary data is what you'll collect from surveys and in-house focus groups with different types of stakeholders, which will include patrons, community agencies, and youth. For the primary data, it's important to ask the right questions to get the most useful information. You may want to know what kinds of things patrons and stakeholders would like to see or experience at the library, but don't forget to ask what skills and resources they may be able to share as well. We'll look at the details of data collection a little later.

4. *Determine key findings.* You can use both qualitative assessment measures, for instance, a basic SWOT Analysis,[5] to identify strengths, weaknesses, opportunities, and threats, along with quantitative data-driven information that looks at everything from circulation figures to through-the-door patronage. Numbers are necessary to establish baselines for comparisons and measure progress, but it's also vital to understand the opinions and feelings of everyone from staff to community stakeholders to get the full picture for strategic planning and decision-making.
5. *Assess your qualitative and quantitative information* in terms of strengths, gaps, challenges, and opportunities.
6. *Set priorities and create an action plan.* The action plan should be as specific as possible, addressing challenges and the actions that can be taken to address them, taking into consideration opportunities and strengths identified in the key findings and key people to take the lead. Some of those people may arise through focus group discussions.
7. *Share your findings.* Sharing your findings with those with whom you engaged in your discovery sessions, as well as library stakeholders both within and outside the library system, helps make everyone a part of the journey and imparts ownership and engagement at the most fundamental and effective levels. If everyone feels included and informed, everyone has a sense of ownership, and your library has the best chance at leveraging available human and fiscal capital.[6]

Focus Groups

Focus groups are a great tool for gaining a deeper understanding of any community or issue. With respect to library makerspaces, using focus groups in concert with surveys can help organizers get a handle on everything from staff and volunteer capabilities to patron preferences and help gauge the interest and support of the general public and potential community partners for any new program development.

The difference between the information gained from surveys and that gained from focus groups is that surveys are typically more narrowly focused to generate quantitative data, while focus groups provide opportunities for more open-ended qualitative discussion that speaks to the heart and soul of issues and needs. These two types of data sets provide the most comprehensive picture of the library as it currently is and as it could be.

To make the best use of focus groups, it's important to be able to identify the categories of stakeholders whose views will be helpful to the task at hand, in this case to gain a better understanding of the development of makerspaces and new "Maker"-style creative programming. Generally, for Discovery Sessions organized by Eureka! Factory, we break out four primary groups of stakeholders in most libraries:

1. Staff and volunteers
2. Community leaders
3. Patrons and friends
4. Youth and young adults

Each library is different, however, and there may be more appropriate ways to break out groups at your library. Nonetheless, the idea is to identify general categories of users and service providers, and bring them together within their own groups with a discussion facilitator to explore a specific set of questions.

Recruiting focus group members isn't an exact science, but there are some basic best practices that can be employed in selecting Discovery Session participants. A few things to take into consideration include the following:

- Participants' existing levels of interest and engagement with the library
- Stakeholder categories—are they patrons, volunteers, friends, or passersby?
- Potential for future partnership, whether fiscal, skills-based, or programmatic

Participants can be invited in person, individually, or through a RSVP request letter (see the sample focus group invitation in the appendix.) The invitation should be clear on focus and intent, length of the focus group session, the general range of topics, and how feedback will be used and disseminated. Groups shouldn't be any larger than 10 or 12 participants to ensure that everyone has an opportunity to speak and that information can be comfortably gathered by a notetaker.

Asking the right questions is important and sometimes takes a little trial and error. Generally, we've found it helpful to have slightly different sets of questions for different groups. We might ask some more outward-focused questions of community business leaders than we would of patrons and staff, for instance. In each case, we use a PowerPoint slide deck to project the question being discussed to stay on topic. We give a short introduction about the purpose of the focus group and have found it helpful to define some of the words we use, for example, "Maker" and "makerspace," so we're all speaking with the same vocabulary. Questions we typically ask of patrons are as follows:

- How often and for what purposes do you use the library?
- What are some of your favorite things about the library?
- What are some things you think could be improved?
- How do you feel about the idea of "Maker" programming or "makerspace" development at the library?
- What do you enjoy doing for recreational fun, hobbies, arts, or crafts?
- What kind of classes, workspaces, or resources do you access outside the library?
- What kinds of things might you like to have access to in support of interests or hobbies at the library?
- What are your thoughts on space usage and allocation, hours of operation, and risk management?

While you don't want to ask "leading" questions that inadvertently suggest answers other than what participants might offer independently, we've also discovered in the process of hosting countless Discovery Sessions that without some sort of prompting, it can be hard to elicit useful responses. This is especially true in communities where there may be no existing frame of reference for makerspaces or the Maker movement in general. Thus, when we ask about tools and equipment, for example, we might include a number of generic tool images that pop up on the slide deck that are used for the focus groups. If we ask people what they enjoy making or doing when they're not at work or for relaxation and enjoyment, images of gardening, knitting, playing a musical instrument, or making art or jewelry might be employed.

For business-community discussions, additional questions can include discussions about programming or resources that might be helpful in terms of certifications, training or workforce development, or entrepreneurial support. For these groups we may use images related to invention, start-ups, mentoring, and so forth, to help participants get a better sense of the scope of programming that can be employed.

Conversation will naturally range, sometimes widely, as a result of some of the questions, especially those on hobbies or special interests with patrons or library-related topics for staff, volunteers, and friends. Let it range as long as you're getting useful information, and try to capture anything that is even remotely relevant. We've often found that in the course of discussing one topic, participants will hit on something else of value—the name of a potential community partner, some nugget of insight on resource usage, or some underlying challenge that hasn't previously been brought to the forefront. Come back to those points as needed. But once the discussion on a topic starts to ramble, move on to the next question. Be prepared, however, to add notes to previous topics of discussion that may come up in an unrelated question. The more information you can capture, the better.

Surveys

Online and hard-copy surveys can have questions similar to those discussed in focus groups, but to provide more quantifiable results, surveys typically force choices on responses. For instance, instead of asking respondents to provide open-ended replies to questions about what they might like to see in a library makerspace, the survey will offer a number of possible options, for example, game design, 3D printing, app development, traditional craft, and so on, with the ability to make multiple selections. Surveys shouldn't be longer than about 10 questions, with a couple of open-ended response opportunities, in addition to the multiple-choice options. The survey is also an excellent opportunity to gather contact information from those who might have skills to share with the makerspace or creative programming initiative, so be sure to include a question about shareable skills.

The Harvard University Program on Survey Research provides some great tools and information about developing useful surveys. The ideal question, according to Harvard University, accomplishes three goals:

1. It measures the underlying concept it is intended to tap.
2. It doesn't measure other concepts.
3. It means the same thing to all respondents.

Some good rules of thumb for developing good surveys are as follows:

- *Decide on mode.* Will it be online, in person, hard copy (self-administered or given by someone), or any combination of these?
- *Keep it short.* Try to keep surveys at less than five minutes, in any mode.
- *Mind the order of your questions.* Some questions can affect those that come after them, so plan accordingly. Start with general questions and move on to more specific inquiries.
- *Ask sensitive questions*, including those about demographics or socioeconomic status, near the end of the survey.
- *Ratings scales between one and seven are most useful.* Use radio buttons rather than drop-down menus for online surveys.
- *The best questions are clear and concise.* Avoid technical jargon, vague terms, complex sentences, and "double-barreled" questions that measure two or more things. Each question should reference only one topic or issue. Also avoid leading, evocative, or emotional language or tone.[7]

The more responses you can get the better, so run the survey long enough to reach as many people from as wide a demographic as possible; a month or longer is best, but no less than three weeks. Your chances for wide dissemination are best if you promote your survey heavily both within your library and your library's community, and make the survey easily accessible. Provide the survey in both online and hard-copy formats. The online version should be made available at a kiosk or reference or checkout stations in the library, where people will have easy access. The link should also be easily accessible via your branch website, as well as related social media, and promoted regularly during the time it's available.

If possible, go into the field and try talking to people who currently aren't using the library. A short form of the survey, consisting of no more than three or four questions that specifically look at whether a makerspace might more effectively engage nonusers, that can either be asked quickly or administered via a tablet, can aid this effort. Again, the more people you can get feedback from, the more useful the data you collect.

Evaluation

Data collection, via in-person and paper or online surveys, is one thing; evaluating the results of that data is something else entirely and can be challenging. That's one reason it's good to use an experienced third-party consultant who can properly evaluate results. But if you've asked the right questions, you can also do a reasonably good job of interpreting the results yourself.

Most online survey platforms can generate customized visual results reports with charts and graphs, as can Excel, which allows for even more precisely controlled examination of results among a variety of selected categories and fields. Look for patterns of responses that can provide insights into the general interests, needs, and expectations of a given library community, and trends in existing skills and trades.

Is the community generally more arts-oriented or tech-focused? What is the average age demographic? Are there cultural communities with heritage craft skills or trades interests? Especially useful is learning how many people are interested in sharing skills they may have, potentially adding a wealth of human resources and capital to your new makerspace. Understanding your library community through the interpersonal dialog of focus groups and patron and community survey responses will help ensure that your library develops the most useful programming and space allocation for those who will use it.

While focus groups and surveys help you understand your immediate user community, asset mapping provides another way to gain a deeper understanding of the resources outside your doors and in the surrounding city or town your library serves, and that may ultimately serve you back.

COMMUNITY ASSET MAPPING

One of the best descriptions of the value of community asset mapping comes from the work of John McKnight and Jody Kretzman, founders of the ABCD

Institute (Asset-Based Community Development). The basic principles of this place-based framework of community development, which applies equally well to the development of community-based public makerspaces in libraries, are:

1. Everyone has gifts.
2. Everyone has something to contribute.
3. Everyone cares about something, and that passion is his or her motivation to act.[8]

"Strong, safe, and healthy neighborhoods and communities are built on the strengths and capacities of their residents and associations that call the community home," writes Dan Duncan in the introduction to the Asset Mapping Toolkit developed by the ABCD Institute. "We cannot build strong, caring neighborhoods without unlocking the potential of residents. The most powerful question we can ask is, 'What can we do with what we already have to get what we need?'"

Diane Dorfman, of the Northwest Regional Educational Laboratory, in her *Mapping Community Assets Workbook*, another great planning tool to walk you through the rudiments of identifying the most helpful resources in your area, explains that asset mapping is an "exercise in community development. . . . If you don't know the place where you live, how will you know how to take advantage of all there is to offer? How will you know how to build a strong, active community without the foundation of assets that are already right there?"[9]

More importantly, she says, asset mapping can show the interconnections among assets, which, in turn, can reveal ways to access the assets. "How you get to the assets and use them, and the people involved in the getting and using, all these are also assets. Assets—the relations among them and access to use them—these are the grounds on which communities are built." And a library makerspace is simply a type of community—a creative community where identifying the assets around your library can help build that community and make it viable and enduring.

Participatory Asset Mapping is a complementary process of creating a "tangible display of the people, places, and experiences that make up a community, while asset mapping is the process of identifying those assets."[10]

The Community Research Lab, a project of Healthy City, an effort that seeks to address social inequity, uses Participatory Asset Mapping as a way to support strategic planning by building on existing community strengths—essentially the same process used to support the strategic planning for library makerspace development. Participatory Asset Mapping, according to the Community Research Lab, "recognizes human capital and the capacity of individuals to use their own hearts, heads, and hands to build and create positive structures in their communities."

"Human capital" is exactly what makes a makerspace work, in a library or anywhere, and community asset mapping can help chart the way forward. There are lots of ways to map community assets, but one of the easiest and most immediate ways we've found is to use Google maps and search on a variety of categories ranging from arts to manufacturing within a desired radius of the library location.

Your map of assets can include anything and anyone you think might be helpful in your makerspace development and programming. Depending on the results of focus group and survey analyses, assets can range from machine shops to garden supply centers, from tailors to woodworkers, from mechanical engineers to artists. Don't dismiss any potential asset, no matter how obscure or possibly irrelevant it might seem. A nearby frame shop, for instance, can become a source of makerspace materials, from mat board that's typically cast off or recycled to glass and wood, potentially becoming a valuable source of free materials and possibly even a partner in programming.

Once you've identified the many and varied assets within your chosen radius, you need to exercise an "ask." It's not enough to just know where your assets are, you need to talk to them. You can reach out to them individually, explaining what you're doing at your library, or host a special open house event where you invite your potential new assets to a meet and greet, where you explain what future plans are underway and how you'd like to connect in your community to make it happen, with these great assets as new program partners.

Be sure to close the connection loop either by having specific things your potential new assets can immediately become involved in or continuing to follow up regarding makerspace plans going forward. Be open to things like naming rights for rooms, classes, and programming, and a variety of nontraditional partnerships.

Once you've got a solid sense of what your community wants in a creative library space and the partners that you have to work with, you can start fleshing out your makerspace plan and budget.

DEVELOPING A PLAN AND BUDGET

There are as many ways to develop a library makerspace plan and budget as there are libraries. At Eureka! Factory, when we work with public libraries, we use a custom-made budgeting tool populated with a variety of makerspace tools and resources from which we can sort to create a budget to meet the needs of any library client. Budgets will vary based on size of the space being developed, sources of materials and supplies (in-kind donations versus off-the-shelf purchases), and intent and focus of the space (will it require tools or mostly meeting space?).

The Eureka! Factory Library Makerspace Budget Estimation Tool organizes makerspace elements into type (equipment, supplies, and software), location (within the makerspace), and category (akin to community interests). For each individual item, it collects the item name, brand and model example, example unit cost, quantity needed, total item budget, price source, and a URL link or notes to present the details. Items can be added in any order and filtered, grouped, or sorted as needed.

"The tool," says Steve Willingham, who developed it,

> helps the library consider the results of their makerspace survey against the fiscal reality of the actual equipment, supplies, and software that would help meet the requests, desires, and needs of the Makers in their community. Is the library spending an inordinate amount on electrical tools and equipment when their community is more interested in textiles and arts? Are metalworking equipment and supplies draining the budget when the community is more oriented toward audio/video production? Ultimately the tool helps expose and compare the financial realities of a proposed makerspace budget against the goals and objectives of the library makerspace, and helps move toward a mutually acceptable solution that fits within the fiscal constraints of the makerspace program.

A huge collaborative creative space may end up costing less than a small, tool-heavy space. And a small space with great community buy-in that's well

	Item Total
ALL Rows Total:	$ 54,385.50
Hidden Rows FILTERED:	$ 54,385.50

Type	Space Name	Category	Item	Example	Unit Cost	Quantity	Total Budget	Price source	Link or Notes
Equipment	Flex Space	Art	Easel – tabletop	American Easel 24 Inch	$ 13.00	8	$ 104.00	Amazon	https://amzn.com/B000MM49QC
Equipment	Flex Space	Art	Easel - floor	US Art Supply Al Studio Easel	$ 50.00	2	$ 100.00	Amazon	https://amzn.com/B00PR8XMJQ
Equipment	Flex Space	Textile	Sewing machine	Janome Magnolia 7325	$ 330.00	4	$ 1,320.00	Amazon	https://amzn.com/B00J8VEM8S
Equipment	Flex Space	Textile	Serger	Janome MOD-Serger	$ 260.00	2	$ 520.00	Amazon	https://amzn.com/B01BKTQ3CS
Equipment	Flex Space	Textile	Thread spool rack	Mini Mega Rak	$ 19.00	2	$ 38.00	Michaels	http://michaels.com/10453541.html
Equipment	Flex Space	Textile	Adjustable Dress Form	Singer DF251, Medium/Large	$ 230.00	1	$ 230.00	Amazon	https://amzn.com/B00OLNDFOK
Equipment	Flex Space	Textile	Assorted Quilting Rulers	Omnigrid Ruler Pack	$ 24.00	4	$ 96.00	Amazon	https://amzn.com/B001CE38JS
Supplies	Flex Space	Textile	General sewing supplies	Generic	$ 300.00	1	$ 300.00	Wal-Mart	
Supplies	Flex Space	Textile	General Art supplies	Generic	$ 400.00	1	$ 400.00	Michaels	
Supplies	Flex Space	Textile	Ironing board	Generic	$ 60.00	1	$ 60.00	Amazon	https://amzn.com/B0048F5GXO
Supplies	Flex Space	Textile	Steam Iron	Any	$ 35.00	1	$ 35.00	Amazon	https://amzn.com/B01D1P9V00
Equipment	Flex Space	Power Tools	Glue gun, high temp	Surebonder PRO2-100	$ 31.00	4	$ 124.00	Amazon	https://amzn.com/B006IY359K
Supplies	Flex Space	Material	Glue sticks – 50pc/bag		$ 5.00	4	$ 20.00	Harbor Freight	http://goo.gl/f3BGZs
Equipment	Flex Space	Automated Tools	Silhouette Portrait Vinyl Cutter	Silhouette Portrait	$ 150.00	1	$ 150.00	Amazon	https://amzn.com/B009GZUPFA
Software	Flex Space	Art	Gimp (free version of photoshop)		Free	2	$ -	Online	https://www.gimp.org/
Equipment	Culinary Space	Culinary Tools	Induction Compatable Cookware	Various, as needed (total budget)	$ 1,000.00	1	$ 1,000.00	Amazon	https://amzn.com/B00QQ7TYFI
Equipment	Culinary Space	Culinary Tools	Cooking Utensil Set	Amco Stainless Steel 5-Piece	$ 21.00	4	$ 84.00	Amazon	https://amzn.com/B002YKVM92
Equipment	Culinary Space	Surface & Storage	Mobile Kitchen Cart	Boraam 98520 Sonoma Kitchen Car	$ 230.00	4	$ 920.00	Amazon	https://amzn.com/B00RE1LM7S
Equipment	Collaborative	Furniture	Collaboration Station Seating	POWWOW modular	$ 8,100.00	1	$ 8,100.00	EKO	http://www.ekocontract.com
Equipment	Youth Space	Surface & Storage	Lego League Compitition Table	Custom built	$ 150.00	1	$ 150.00	Locally made	http://goo.gl/cPFxTb
Equipment	Florida Room	Textile	Quilting Frame	Edmunds American Legacy	$ 106.00	2	$ 212.00	Amazon	https://amzn.com/B0046HJ7DO
Equipment	Florida Room	Textile	Embroidery/Stiching Scroll Frame	Edmunds Stitchers Floor Stand	$ 53.00	2	$ 106.00	Amazon	https://amzn.com/B002WE1IUS
							0		
							0		
Total							$ 54,385.50		

Eureka! Factory Library Makerspace Budget Estimation Tool. *Eureka! Factory*

Type	Budget
Equipment	$ 49,210.50
Software	$ 3,608.00
Supplies	$ 1,567.00
(blank)	$ -
Grand Total	$ 54,385.50

Space Name		Budget
Collaborative	$	23,600.00
Culinary Space	$	2,614.00
Flex Space	$	16,207.00
Florida Room	$	318.00
Studio Space	$	11,096.50
Youth Space	$	550.00
(blank)	$	-
Grand Total	$	54,385.50

Category		Category Costs
Art	$	914.00
Audio	$	1,803.50
Automated Tools	$	3,350.00
Computer Hardware	$	22,119.00
Culinary Tools	$	1,694.00
Design	$	1,900.00
Electrical Tools	$	390.00
Furniture	$	10,500.00
Hand Tools	$	480.00
Material	$	220.00
Measuring Tools	$	60.00
Music	$	1,128.00
Power Tools	$	244.00
Surface & Storage	$	1,820.00
Textile	$	3,317.00
Video	$	4,446.00
(blank)	$	-
Grand Total	$	54,385.50

Eureka! Factory Library Makerspace Budget Estimation Tool. ***Eureka! Factory***

stocked with equipment stakeholders want may be infinitely more productive and better used than a large, generally stocked space with no particular focus and a disinterested user base. So, before you start, make sure you've got a handle on what your specific library community wants and what your administration will support.

PURCHASING CONSIDERATIONS

Materials can be sourced from a variety of places, few of which are exclusive providers of any needed supplies. While it may be easy for libraries to order from existing suppliers, it's usually not as cost effective. As agile as makerspaces need to be, so, too, must the systems that serve them. Multilayered, bureaucratic, or archaic purchasing or equipment request systems that make it time consuming for library staff to order and reorder supplies and resources should be revisited prior to embarking on any makerspace plan and work-arounds put in place if the current system is insurmountable. If it takes six months to get resupplies of 3D printer filament, or a library system has to share a half-dozen laptops for unrelated programs, or a dozen forms and three departments are necessary to request a resource, that significantly hobbles a library makerspace.

Similarly, if there is no separate library budget for a makerspace, but rather the space costs are integrated into the regular branch library budget, that can be a blessing or a curse, depending on the library system. Without line-item support, makerspace needs can be supplanted by other library expenses. Ideally, a library makerspace should be able to draw from its own budgetary pool with agility and ease. Working with the library's Friends group is often one of the most efficient ways to streamline purchasing and makerspace budget needs.

With an efficient budgetary allocation process in mind, libraries should make final decisions with an eye to patron and library needs, preferences, and budgetary limitations. Some key considerations include the following:

- *Staff:* Ideally, space should have dedicated staff. Will existing staff be reassigned to the library makerspace, or will the library be hiring professional program staff? Or will the space rely more heavily on community volunteers?
- *Consultants:* Will the library be using outside consultants for preliminary or development work on the space?
- *Equipment:* In 2015, when we wrote *Makerspaces in Libraries*, a basic 3D printer cost about $1,500. Today, you can purchase a pretty decent one for $300 to $500—the price we then gave for building your own. Other equipment, from hand tools to power tools, to sewing machines and A/V equipment, can be sourced from a variety of suppliers or acquired in-kind through local partnerships. There's also no need to buy everything at once. Equipping a new space with items most likely to be well used in the short term will inspire greater community engagement and can help justify relevant new acquisitions as increased needs arise in the long run. The *High School Makerspace Tools and Materials* guide, developed by Makerspace.com, provides some helpful equipment lists that are adaptable to library makerspace needs.[11]
- *Insurance:* Insurance coverage may need to be adjusted depending on new activities and increased risk management.
- *Building or remodeling:* If new space use can be incorporated into existing library spaces, costs are obviously lower than building from scratch. Things like portable walls, additional electrical drops, repurposing wall space with whiteboard paint or Chroma key paint for A/V

use, and adding HVAC ventilation systems if bigger tools will be used are costs that may need to be taken into consideration. In some cases, the addition of a portable or adding on to existing space may be more desirable.

- *Consumables:* Consumables are things like 3D printer filament, solder, art, craft and office supplies, vinyl sheeting, and so on. Some spaces charge a materials or consumables fee to help cover those costs, or you add consumables to your overall budget.
- *Maintenance:* Maintenance costs need to be considered, but they don't need to be high. Core library and volunteer staff can provide regular maintenance checks and repairs as needed for smaller items, but large machinery, for instance, drill presses, saws, and sometimes even sewing machines, may require regular professional inspection and servicing.
- *Software license renewal:* Software license seats will need to be renewed annually or every few years, depending on software packages, and may have associated costs.

With respect to space usage plans, third-party consultants are helpful, but basic library space design best practices[12] can be adapted as well. As with other library spaces, you're looking at four basic space uses: learning, experiencing, meeting, and creating.[13] The two major differences with makerspace design planning are the addition, in the "creating" spaces, of noise and dust or waste from projects that are probably larger or more complex than those that have previously been created in the library. These are not insurmountable challenges, but they need to be taken into consideration when laying out space usage. There are also a range of other space usage possibilities, including pop-up makerspaces, mobile Maker stations, and portable facilities.

DEVELOPING ORGANIZATIONAL DOCUMENTS

Codifying an organizational framework in the early stages of makerspace planning can not only help your makerspace get off to a strong start and stay there, but also make processes reproducible in other libraries. A makerspace handbook for your library should be a living document that is referred to often and reevaluated and updated regularly. This can be especially useful in a school environment, helping students see their makerspace as a unique and special place with a defined set of community rules they can help develop.

The documentation you create will vary according to the design, focus, and intent of your library makerspace. If your space is populated with hand or power tools, your handbook should include documentation about tool use protocols, orientation, shop management, safety, and required releases. If yours is principally an arts and crafts space, your documentation will be less robust but should still be in place to identify mission and goals of makerspace programming, and be ready for additional material as needed, if your space grows to include more sophisticated equipment.

The Basics

Your table of contents should include, as relevant to your space:

- Welcome from library administration, with a description of your space and its mission and goals
- Makerspace policy and rules
- Member/patron agreements

Makerspace Policy and Rules

Google "library makerspace policy" and you will get a couple hundred thousand results. The best policy, of course, is the one that best meets the needs and goals of your individual library. Starting with a basic mission or statement of purpose can help provide the framework to develop useful policies, so start there. Is the space intended to serve mostly children? Is it focused on the arts? Does it support skills training? Is it mostly for prototyping?

Focus group sessions with patrons and staff can help answer these questions and others about space use and focus. Once you've agreed on the purpose of your space, you can start fleshing out the details. The makerspace policy and rules section can include information on the following:

- *Hours of operation*
- *Membership:* Who can use the space and according to what conditions and terms of service? What ages? Are guardians required for children of a certain age? Is usage limited to members with library cards?
- *Library policy and rules:* Makerspace policies may be aligned with existing library policies or have their own unique set of rules, but those policies and rules should be clearly spelled out and easy to understand.
- *Code of conduct:* A clear code of conduct can help you stock your makerspace with nice things that will be respected by everyone who uses them. Be clear on the consequences of not adhering to the code of conduct.
- *Scheduling policy:* How will space use be scheduled, and how long can spaces be used?
- *Safety rules:* Ideally, orientation should be required before anyone can use tools or equipment. The safety section should clarify the requirements related to space use, from orientation classes to whether users will need to supply their own safety gear (e.g., safety glasses), and what types of creative activities are permitted and which are prohibited.
- *Housekeeping and maintenance:* Regular "town halls" can be useful to institute in makerspaces, providing an opportunity for active makerspace users to take some ownership of the facility and lessening the work of staff through agreed upon housekeeping and maintenance practices. This section can also identify how space is used and maintained on an individual user basis and the expectations of users within the space with respect to tool and equipment use.

Member/Patron Agreements

Each library makes its own makerspace policies and decides how to enforce them, so member agreements may or may not be in order depending on library organizational structure and space use intentions. But it can be useful to have some agreements in place for future, if not immediate, use, and if only to articulate expectations of patrons and staff regarding space use. Standard member agreements that are good to include in a handbook are:

- Makerspace use agreement, outlining expectations about meetings, guests, access, and cleanup

- User consent and release form, covering publicity and marketing, use of participant photos in brochures, use of websites and social media, use of personal equipment, and safety agreements attesting that the user has read and is informed about safety policies
- Hold harmless agreement, a basic boilerplate customized as needed, waiving (at least in theory) any library liability in case of personal injury or the loss or destruction of items made in the makerspace.

These agreements, or whatever variations of them you may wish to employ, can be completed annually and kept on file or "badged" on a patron's library card to show they've completed any prerequisite items, like the agreements or orientation, prior to using the library makerspace.

Your library makerspace handbook should be easily available and accessible in hard copy on-site, as well as online, and every space user should be provided with a digital copy of the handbook. As your space grows, adapts, and changes, your makerspace handbook should reflect those changes. Expectations and responsibilities are the heart of a makerspace handbook, leaving as little to chance as possible with respect to space, tools, equipment usage, and conduct. Additionally, having a makerspace handbook shows intentionality and a long-term commitment to safety, transparency, and quality management, setting a tone of maturity, professionalism, and respect.

FUNDING OPTIONS

The biggest challenge for any makerspace is achieving a sustainable business model, and even a library makerspace is in the business of staying viable. It's typically easy to get a starting budget, but failing to plan for long-term sustainability can shutter a library makerspace as easily as any other makerspace.

In *Makerspaces in Libraries*, we review the work of John Boeck and Peter Troxler, who conducted a FabLab Business Study in 2011, resulting in eight identifiable business models for FabLabs,[14] of which three, by extension, are applicable to library makerspaces:

- Grant-based model, with a main income stream from public or private funding
- Institutionally embedded model, with no main income stream but where expenses are covered and services are provided by the parent institution
- Educational activities model, with the main income stream generated from course and workshop fees, and services typically approved or accredited and led by makerspace instructors

We'll take a closer look at each of these.

Grant-Based Model

Grant-based programs require a steady application of dedicated staff or volunteer support to continuously write funding proposals. Fortunately, for the time being, at least, there are a lot of grant opportunities for funding makerspaces. Unfortunately, many grant-funding options may not provide structural operational support. As with any grant-based programming, this model requires understanding grant requirements, having the skills to write strong grant proposals, and having a strong lineup of grants to keep in the pipeline.

Institutionally Embedded Model

Library makerspaces are, by definition, institutionally embedded, and in many cases, existing library budgets may cover the costs of makerspace development and maintenance. In contrast to independent or private member-based makerspaces, institutionally embedded systems also have the benefit of on-site staffing, since the library has dedicated staff, or these systems can invest in focused training to give existing staff the necessary skills and resources to run a library-based makerspace. In conjunction with applying for project grants, this is typically the most reliable funding model for libraries; however, to provide consistent and long-term budgetary support, this model requires strong administrative, local, and sometimes state buy-in. It also requires significant back-end development, for instance, the aforementioned focus groups, surveys, and reports, to establish evidence of community need and value, and, ideally, an evaluative process to provide measurable outcomes to stay on the budget.

Educational Activities Model

This model can be more challenging for libraries, depending on their mission and goals within their community. There is, however, precedence for fee-based structures that generate at least modest revenue to help sustain the makerspace, ranging from materials use fees to user fees for everything from 3D printers to recording studios. It's easy to dismiss a revenue stream model for a public library makerspace, but it can be something worth considering as a supplemental funding option.

Other supplemental funding options can include more familiar things like naming rights, endowments, Friends groups, and private donors. Your Friends group can actually be one of your best allies in your makerspace development and operation. Including them at the earliest stages of planning and enlisting their interest and support can be key to everything from grassroots public engagement to streamlined funding and efficient ordering for your space. Friends are often an untapped resource for programming as well, since many Friends members are retired professionals, craftspeople, and artisans.

ORGANIZATIONAL RECAP AND RESOURCES

If you look at the preliminary steps to library makerspace development outlined earlier as a series of milestones, you might outline it like this:

- *Milestone 1:* Ensure administrative support.
  - Organize administration and library staff meetings prior to embarking on makerspace development to gain full understanding of the pros, cons, preferences, and requirements, and ensure everyone is on the same page with mission and goals of the space, and expectations of outcomes.
  - For most effective makerspace operation, administrative oversight needs to be reasonable, and the library has to have creative freedom

and operational agility with respect to programming, budgeting, and management.

- *Milestone 2:* Assess community needs and interests.
  - Organize focus groups.
  - Launch surveys.
  - Evaluate the results of the focus groups and surveys to determine stakeholder preferences at all levels.
- *Milestone 3:* Develop community asset maps to identify potential community partners and resources to support identified needs and interests.
- *Milestone 4:* Develop a makerspace budget and plan based on results of surveys and community assets and support.
- *Milestone 5:* Create organizational documents to codify your library makerspace mission, goals, safety, and code of conduct.

There are lots of organizational resources for libraries developing creative spaces and programs to achieve those milestones. Among the most useful, in no particular order, are the following:

- Section 8 of the University of Kansas' Community Tool Box, "Identifying Community Assets and Resources"[15]
- "MakerEd Program Planning and Management"[16]
- *Makerspace: STEM/STEAM Skills for the Creative Economy*,[17] a California-focused resource guide but highly adaptable to any library makerspace project
- John Burke's "Makerspace Resources,"[18] especially the section on makerspace funding and donation resources
- "Renovated Learning,"[19] a premier resource for school makerspaces, by school librarian Diana Rendina

There are more listed in the appendix.

If you put sufficient back-end work into the creation of your library makerspace, you'll have the strong institutional and community framework for an enjoyable, well-used, beloved, and enduring creative space that will serve your community well into the future.

NOTES

1. "A WAPL Recap." *Library as Incubator Project*. May 13, 2012. Accessed July 17, 2017. www.libraryasincubatorproject.org/?p=4594.

2. "Chapter 3: Assessing Community Needs and Resources." *Community Tool Box*. Accessed July 17, 2017. http://ctb.ku.edu/en/table-of-contents/assessment/assessing-community-needs-and-resources.

3. "Chapter 3: Assessing Community Needs and Resources."

4. Becker, Samantha, and Maggie Buckholz. "Impact Survey: Understand Your Community's Technology Needs." *WebJunction*. September 5, 2013. Accessed July 17, 2017. www.webjunction.org/events/webjunction/Impact_Survey.html.

5. Renault, Val. "Section 14: SWOT Analysis: Strengths, Weaknesses, Opportunities, and Threats." In "Chapter 3: Assessing Community Needs and Resources." *Community Tool Box*. Accessed July 17, 2017. http://ctb.ku.edu/en/table-of-contents/assessment/assessing-community-needs-and-resources/swot-analysis/main.

6. "CCF/SCF Tools Conducting a Community Assessment." *Office of Community Services, Administration for Children and Families*. September 18, 2012. Accessed July 17, 2017. www.acf.hhs.gov/ocs/resource/conducting-a-community-assessment-1.

7. "Tip Sheet on Question Wording." *Harvard University Program on Survey Research*. November 17, 2007. Accessed July 17, 2017. https://psr.iq.harvard.edu/files/psr/files/PSRQuestionnaireTipSheet_0.pdf.

8. Duncan, Dan. *Asset-Based Community Development: Asset Mapping. Asset-Based Community Development Institute*. Accessed July 17, 2017. http://hdaniels-duncanconsulting.org/pdfs/Asset Mapping Toolkit.pdf.

9. Dorfman, Diane. *ABCD Toolkit: Mapping Community Assets Workbook. Northwest Regional Educational Laboratory*. September 1998. Accessed July 17, 2017. www.abcdinstitute.org/docs/Diane Dorfman-Mapping-Community-Assets-WorkBook(1)-1.pdf.

10. Burns, Janice C., Dagmar Pudrzynska Paul, and Silvia R. Paz. *Participatory Asset Mapping. Community Science*. April 2012. Accessed July 17, 2017. www.communityscience.com/knowledge4equity/AssetMappingToolkit.pdf.

11. *High School Makerspace Tools and Materials. Makerspace.com*. http://spaces.makerspace.com/wp-content/uploads/2012/04/hsmakerspacetoolsmaterials-201204.pdf.

12. Lesneski, Traci. "10 Steps to a Better Library Interior: Tips That Don't Have to Cost a Lot." *Library Journal*. August 16, 2011. Accessed July 17,

2017. http://lj.libraryjournal.com/2011/08/buildings/10-steps-to-a-better-library-interior-tips-that-dont-have-to-cost-a-lot-library-by-design/#_.

13. "Zones and Spaces: Model Programme for Public Libraries." *Agency for Culture and Palaces*. December 6, 2016. Accessed July 17, 2017. http://modelprogrammer.slks.dk/en/challenges/zones-and-spaces/.

14. Boeck, John, and Peter Troxler. "Sustainable FabLabs." *FabWiki*. August 17, 2011. Accessed July 17, 2017. http://wiki.fablab.is/images/e/ef/Factsheet_Lab-Sustainability_Fab7.pdf.

15. Berkowitz, Bill, and Eric Wadud. "Section 8: Assessing Community Assets and Resources." *Community Tool Box*. Accessed July 17, 2017. http://ctb.ku.edu/en/table-of-contents/assessment/assessing-community-needs-and-resources/identify-community-assets/main.

16. "MakerEd Program Planning and Management." *Maker Education Initiative*. Accessed July 17, 2017. http://makered.org/resources/program-planning/.

17. Feinstein, L., M. Daniel DeCillis, and Laurie Harris. *Makerspace: STEM/STEAM Skills for the Creative Economy. California Council on Science and Technology*. April 2016. Accessed December 7, 2016. http://ccst.us/publications/2016/2016makerspace.pdf.

18. Burke, John. "Makerspace Resources." *Miami University*. March 28, 2013. Accessed July 17, 2017. www.users.miamioh.edu/burkejj/makerspaces.html#funding.

19. Rendina, Diana. "Renovated Learning." *Renovated Learning*. December 5, 2016. Accessed July 17, 2017. http://renovatedlearning.com/.

3

THE LAY OF THE LAND

A Look at the Current Makerspace Landscape

Overheard between two fifth graders: "Did you know Ms. MacLean has a SAW?"
"Yes, and she's not afraid to use it, either."
"That's what scares me!"

—Irene MacLean, elementary teacher-librarian and digital learning coach, the Inquiry Zone, Discovery Canyon Elementary School, Colorado

Since we wrote *Makerspaces in Libraries* in 2015, the number of public and school library makerspaces has grown significantly. We originally sourced a list of 70 library makerspaces from the Make It at Your Library directory.[1] Today, that list shows almost 80 library makerspaces, and a more robust directory created by Sharona Ginsberg, Learning Technologies Librarian at SUNY Oswego, which includes libraries in academic, K-12, and museum settings, shows 115 public makerspaces.[2] Accounting for duplicates between the two lists, the number of public, academic, K-12, and museum makerspaces is probably closer to 150, easily double the number from 2015.

As with the first book, we launched a library makerspace survey in advance of this work, but this time with a focus primarily on library makerspaces two years or older, to obtain best practices from established and successful spaces. We included a couple of makerspaces not quite two years old because there were some unique aspects to their operational models; however, most who responded have been in operation for two and a half to three years.

This time we looked at things like makerspace models, funding and budgeting structure, administrative and community support, staffing, user demographics, and best practice recommendations, as well as some things these established makerspaces might have done differently knowing what they know now. We also revisited some of the library makerspaces we reviewed in our first book.

We'll start with a look at some of the different types of library makerspaces generally and then examine some of the new case studies, as well as some of the old ones.

TYPES OF LIBRARY MAKERSPACES

In *Makerspaces in Libraries*, we introduce the idea of libraries as a "third place,"[3] a concept developed by Ray Oldenburg, Ph.D., author of *The Great Good Place*, which talks about the third place as the place that isn't home and isn't work or school. The third place is that other space where we gather with friends and family to eat, talk, and otherwise socialize. These "great good places," Oldenburg says, are the neutral safe spaces we voluntarily seek out and look forward to being part of. It's where we go freely, without obligations, responsibilities, or concerns.

The third place is that vital "place on the corner"—typically the café, bookstore, local pub, tea shop, or diner—that helps unify neighborhoods, serves as a port of entry for newcomers to an area, and provides intergenerational interaction and a place for discussion, entertainment, and friendship. This is also an excellent definition of the local public library, especially with the addition of a makerspace, which enhances the opportunity for active gathering. The library as a "third place" becomes a space where people can not only read, but also talk, create, have fun, learn things, and generally have a good time together in a safe, inclusive environment.

Library Spaces for Makers

The three most common manifestations of creative space in libraries are:

1. Makerspaces—integrated within existing library space or freestanding and sometimes mobile or pop-up
2. FabLabs—especially in Europe
3. Digital commons—often in academic libraries

They each have some distinguishing features worth understanding. The first two, makerspaces (and their close cousin, hackerspaces) and FabLabs, have a common ancestor in the European hacker collectives hailing from about the turn of the 21st century. One of the first of these, c-base, which opened in Germany in 1995, is still in operation, with more than 450 members. The garden-variety makerspace made its first appearance in about 2005, and became an increasingly popular concept when *Make:* magazine rose to prominence as the nation's premier do-it-yourself (DIY) magazine at about the same time.

Conceptually, makerspaces differ from hackerspaces in that they have a broader focus on a wide range of handcraft and less focus on electronics and programming. Makerspaces often have an educational focus aimed at youth and families. Hackerspaces tend to be more focused on large-scale machining and technological projects, and seldom make their way into the library vernacular. FabLabs[4] are a specialized space, more akin to hackerspaces with a focus on technology but part of an international association of spaces that agree to adhere to a set of protocols and standardized tools. They are popular in European libraries and common in university settings worldwide.

Traditionally, digital commons are repositories of academic research with the resources needed to access and use those repositories. In library Maker culture, the phrase can also refer to spaces like the one found in the Martin Luther King Jr. Memorial Library in Washington D.C., where the digital commons makerspace features, in addition to computers and related software, a 3D printer, a Skype station, SMART Boards, video conferencing capabilities, and collaborative space.[5] For our purposes, however, we'll look principally at the various manifestations of makerspaces.

We invited libraries worldwide that have had operational makerspaces of any category for at least two years to tell us more about their spaces, best practices, and recommendations for new spaces just starting out. About a dozen spaces shared thoughts in great detail, and a couple of makerspaces from our first book shared where are they now. The most successful spaces confirmed one common theme: Makerspaces are less about the equipment they're stocked with than the people who use them.

WHERE ARE THEY NOW?

Fayetteville Free Library FabLab, Fayetteville, New York (www.fflib.org/make/fab-lab)

We thought the best place to start was where it all started: Fayetteville Free Library FabLab. The Fayetteville Free Library (FFL) was first inspired to create a public makerspace when Lauren Britton Smedley impressed FFL executive director Sue Considine in 2011, with a graduate school project proposal on the idea of creating a makerspace within a public library. Considine liked the concept and hired Smedley to create the space, which formally opened to the public in 2013, with a focus on 3D printing.[6] Today, the Fayetteville Free Library FabLab (FFL FabLab) comprises about 8000 square feet overall and has expanded its offerings to include an Epilog Laser cutter, Shapeoko CNC Mill, vinyl cutter, sewing machines, hand tools, and more. We asked Considine a few follow-up questions about the FFL FabLab to see what has changed during the past couple of years and what Considine considers to be the greatest impact of the space for the library and patrons.

Said Considine,

> For us, back in 2010, when we first became aware of these disruptive technologies, and DIY was exploding and things were banging into each other, at that point our goal was not necessarily to create a space to put 3D printers in, but it was more understanding that the power of this revolution was the social aspect, that this brought people together in new and interesting ways. As a library, we were really excited about that part of this potential.

The first couple of years, recalled Considine, they spent learning what they didn't know about their community. She continued, "The transformative results of this exploration of what our community really wanted, what their goals are, was that we learned that all the expertise we really needed and wanted was right there."

That understanding, that the expertise they needed to provide the kind of programming and resources their community was interested in was right there in the community, was the lynchpin discovery that has powered the FFL FabLab ever since—creating the platform for neighbors to teach neighbors.

Considine added,

> In the past we'd have thought this was something a librarian would have been facilitating, but we're extremely grateful to give the reins back to the community. They have the talent, enthusiasm, expertise, and time. Once you flip the switch on the traditional volunteer idea and flip "What *we* need" to asking the community, "What do *you* want? What do *you* need?" and then saying, "Share it with your neighbor."

Now they have volunteers—whom they call community participants, leading repair series, robotics, and programming classes.

"We wouldn't have the staff or ability to do what we're doing, on our own," said Considine about the added human capital of the community participants.

The other result of that community commitment is that the library has found itself "integrating STEAM learning into everything" it does for every age group. Said Considine, "That's been a tremendous awakening for us at FFL." She continued, "All those STEM areas of learning for every age have become our mandate in a lot of ways. It's changed the way we prioritize our resources in how we train our staff and who we bring on our staff."

The FFL FabLab has also turned to hiring outside the library field, as have some of the other more community-focused library makerspaces. "For us one of our key hires outside of librarianship is a teacher," said Considine, adding,

> At the end of the day, we are not experts in curriculum design and lesson planning, and the different strategies to be effective teachers. It's not necessarily intuitive, so for us it was really important to get a teacher on board to develop those skills sets across the board.

> Opening our minds and our doors to these other professional elements—our challenges are so diverse and our community looks to us for more and more. The solutions are not going to come from those with a MLS (master in library science) degree.

Considine admitted this can be a tough sell to library administration more used to a different operational model. "There has to be an internal change," she declared, "a culture in place that is trusting, where communication about the direction that we're moving in and each individual's place in that conversation is critical."

It can be a hard sell sometimes, with people concerned that "this doesn't look like a library." When big ideas are pushed down from above, she said, the library has to go through an arduous process of buy-in. She suggests making it an organizational priority to think together on solutions and find a way to include everyone along the way, creating conditions where everyone, from staff to patrons, can feel and understand their piece about what happens next in the library. "We can't innovate and transform if our internal relationships aren't really strong or team relationships aren't strong and we aren't communicating together," she said.

The one thing that always makes Considine uncomfortable is when a library system gets a grant and

> puts together a kit and pushes it out to all their branches and members—ignoring the fact that each of those branches serves a different community and not working with those libraries and staff who are on the ground before they determine what that community is interested in and not having those conversations first.

That creates a lot of pushback, according to Considine, and can cause staff to feel nervous, scared, or threatened.

"One of the major challenges is getting down to the organizational, team level to help people prepare for innovation before they jump in," she related. Establishing regular communication links and chains is key to not scaring people along the way, Considine advised. "This understanding that the power of fabrication is the solution to the tech piece is obvious, but this social piece is so critically important. It's often the piece that helps change the mind of the people who are threatened by things that don't seem library appropriate."

It's important to help library administrators see and understand the power of makerspaces to bring people together and build community through relationship building, whether it's for coding, programming, or other activities, she said. "Then suddenly these little communities are developing within the community, and if not for the libraries creating these opportunities, these people would never have found each other."

The pivotal point for Considine in understanding the power of the community to make their library makerspace successful came from her participation in the R-Squared Conference in Telluride, Colorado, where she heard John McKnight, coauthor of *The Abundant Community* (2010), speak.

"It's a profound little book that changed everything for me," said Considine, continuing,

> What I learned was that every community already has within it what the community needs. From that idea, for me, it was a total eureka moment.
>
> I realized we need to turn this around and embrace this, and it allows us to have purposeful conversations with our community at every turn, whether at the circulation desk or out in the community, and ask those questions: What do you know? What do you love? What are you passionate about? And will you share it?

Integrating the passion of community members into a community makerspace inspires ownership of the space and its programs, and ensures the long-term sustainability and support of users, she explained. Commensurately, the library moved from seeking makerspace "volunteers" to a "community participant" model to better leverage community assets.

Today, the library's director of community engagement works with more than 90 volunteers. Interested volunteers fill out a community participant form, which is evaluated by the director, "who looks through them and considers opportunities for people to share what they know and love, does a short interview, and then determines how to create conditions here for people to share what they know and shepherds people into that position, and becomes point of contact."

FFL also stays active in both the library community and the community they serve, holding Friday FFL Innovation Tours for individuals, groups, museum staff, and anyone interested in learning more about what they do at the library and how it might be done in other public places, fulfilling yet another unique aspect of the maker movement: open collaboration and sharing.

"We run the gamut and have had visitors from all over the United States and worldwide, and feel so grateful to have the opportunity to share our vision as widely as we have," related Considine. "But it's a reciprocal thing, and we've learned so much from the people we're visiting with. It's this ongoing relationship we're having with individuals from everywhere."

The money question, of course, is whether these changes have impacted library patronage and space usage, and the library's bottom line in any significant, practical, and positive way. That's still a hard question for many libraries to answer, but Considine feels they're finding ways to provide the qualitative metrics they need to honestly assess the value of their offerings.

The library has definitely grown. In less than 20 years, their operating budget quadrupled, and they've grown from a staff of six to 34, with more than 90 volunteers, in a library designed to serve a community of 10,000 people. Clearly, the makerspace has added new dimensions to programming and growth in the last five years. There's some concern, she said, that they're growing too quickly.

"A large percentage of the community would push back on that. It's a very dynamic time," stated Considine, further commenting,

> The flip side is you can't be afraid you're going to face opposition. There will be a core group of people in every community that are going to push back when they see their tax dollars are going to things they have no interest in. The fine line we have to walk is an appreciation of that point of view, but we have to bring in that other group that wants it and be able to show why.
>
> The first year you can't point to any benchmarks, but now we're just getting to a place where we've developed assessment tools and are in the process of getting to that meaningful information.

It's easy to know how many people are certified on equipment use, a requisite for using equipment in the FabLab, and how many people are using printers and sewing machines. But to get a better understanding of impact, FFL developed a short survey that asks a couple of key questions: Did you get what you needed from this one-on-one learning or skills development opportunity? And, what Considine thinks is the most important question: What are you going to do with this knowledge and this new skill?

"From that we're starting to capture this new array of information about what people do with these skills," she declared. According to Considine, organizing that information into a meaningful format that shows the full picture of social impact is challenging, however.

"Right now, at the community library level, we're looking to see how we can incorporate the best of what's out there and make it work for us. We need to find ways to get to that goal of having the right information so we can communicate results effectively," she concluded.

The HIVE, Tampa, Florida (hcplc.org/hcplc/services/hive.html)

We also featured the HIVE library makerspace in Tampa, Florida, in our first book. Designed by my husband and me, the HIVE, at 10,000 square feet, is Tampa's largest public library makerspace and one of the largest in Florida. The makerspace has evolved differently than the free-spirited, community-driven space we originally envisioned, with more top-down programming and being more meeting space-oriented than user prescribed.

Equipment use is tightly controlled, with 3D printers, for example, only available for use in conjunction with a class. The lack of spontaneous, free-flow access to the facility, along with regimented tool access and limited spontaneous community engagement or independent usage of the space, presents obstacles to the HIVE in reaching its full potential as a center for creativity and innovation in the community; however, staff have worked within those constraints to maximize user experiences in ways they feel are effective and successful.

We reached out to the HIVE manager, principal librarian Megan Danak, to get her thoughts on the library's makerspace journey.

"Since the HIVE at John F. Germany Public Library opened in late 2014, the library has made a few changes to the layout, based on usage of the space," said Danak, continuing,

> For example, the Robotics Center was moved from the literal center of the floor, as use of the space was seasonal. The robotics field was moved into a workshop area, with easier access to tools. The center area, visible when patrons first exit the elevator, was then turned into an open exploration zone dubbed the "Makerdome." The HIVE had experienced an increase in walk-in visitors, especially younger patrons, who wanted to do or make something

> on the spot. In the Makerdome, visitors can sit down right away to work on rotating mini-projects and crafts, or to explore technology like the paper/vinyl cutter, MaKey MaKeys, and littleBits.

The library also made personnel changes in the last year, said Danak. The HIVE was launched and originally run by a department separate from the John F. Germany Library staff. After a training and transition period, the space is now fully integrated with the main library's scheduling and staffing, which has resulted in more public hours, better promotion, and a fresh group of talented and enthusiastic staff to lead programming and help customers.

Danak feels library usage has increased, especially after expanding operating hours to match regular library operating hours. "As a result, the library is able to offer more events and classes, as well as more public bookings for equipment and spaces, like the Recording Studio," she stated. The Recording Studio is one of the most popular and well-used features of the makerspace.

The effect of the HIVE has reached beyond the John F. Germany Library makerspace, according to Danak, influencing the development of variations on the main HIVE in branches systemwide:

> The space brought new users to the library, and through training and sharing equipment, many programs we launched there are now offered in many of our branches. Libraries without dedicated makerspaces (as most of our libraries do not have them) have been inspired to come up with creative, flexible ways to offer hands-on programming, which is always popular with customers. The Maker movement has energized library staff to explore new ways of engaging and educating their communities, and the response is overwhelmingly positive from our users.

"It's been a wonderful journey," said Danak, adding,

> but we most look forward to seeing the journeys our customers will take as they learn these new skills, discover new passions, or make new inventions at the library. That's the most exciting part—when given the tools, encouragement, and room to try something new, people can do amazing things. Libraries help make that happen, and it's awesome.

The HIVE measures usage through space use and program attendance statistics, as well as comment cards and program evaluation feedback from patrons. Plans are underway to reconfigure some spaces, including the area that currently holds the 3D printers, which they feel is underused, understandably so if people aren't permitted to freely use the printers. But that's also the beauty of a library makerspace—it should be flexible and adaptable to suit the reality of each space's needs and preferences.

iLab, St. Petersburg College, Seminole, Florida

On the other side of the size spectrum is iLab—the Innovation Lab at St. Petersburg College Seminole Campus, a library jointly managed by the college and the city of Seminole. Smaller than a classroom, the tiny space is efficiently stocked with 3D printers, soldering irons, and a variety of electronics. More importantly, it is the energetic heart of a campus library and the local creative community. Head librarian Chad Mairn caught us up on what's new at iLab.

"We have expanded what we offer with regards to emerging technologies," said Mairn, continuing,

> We also are offering more learning opportunities. In October 2015, the Innovation Lab received a $7,500 Curiosity Creates grant from the Walt Disney Company, in collaboration with ALA's Association for Library Service to Children, to expand our successful Maker Boot Camp series, which helps "promote exploration and discovery for children ages six to 14." The workshops have been offered to adults too and are extremely popular. In fact, they are always full. Imagination and originality, flexibility, decision-making, communication and self-expression, collaboration, and motivation are the critical components of creativity that our Maker Boot Camp program has integrated into the curriculum.

Moreover, the iLab continues to offer free video game design, robotics, 3D design/printing, circuitry/electronics, virtual reality, drone, video editing, Hour of Code, and introduction to sewing for cosplay workshops, which like the Maker Boot Camp workshops, Mairn says, are always full.

Mairn is also spearheading more advanced workshops and other learning opportunities, saying,

> We were recently awarded eight Finch robots from Birdbrain Technologies, a product of the Carnegie Mellon University CREATE Lab. As a result, we partnered with FLASTEM, a collaborative, community-based, and volunteer-led STEM outreach program with focus in robotics, computer programming, and technology for K-8 after-school education enrichment and technology learning outcomes for all, to offer a workshop at St. Petersburg College that showed participants how to program robots to move, compose music, change color, sense temperature/light/movement, play pong, and more. The Programming Finch Robots curriculum, with a video and pictures, is available at bit.ly/iLabRobots. Students, Innovation Lab volunteers, parents, faculty, and staff are all encouraged to share, so they can learn how to cogently present their complex ideas and end products.

Mairn said usage has definitely increased, and he expects no slowing of participation. In early 2017, iLab also received three Innovation Grants from the St. Petersburg College Foundation. They are "Microsoft HoloLens: Holographic Enhanced Learning" ($3,360), "Graphs and Geometry: Engaging and Illustrating Mathematics with 3D Printing" ($2,894), and "Virtual Reality: A Renaissance" ($2,000). The iLab will have more opportunities to partner with other academic disciplines at St. Petersburg College to develop a variety of tools to enhance learning and support overall student success. Mairn invites anyone interested in seeing copies of the grants to contact him at mairn.chad@spcollege.edu.

Said Mairn,

> The library has always been a place of discovery, but now with our Innovation Lab we are the epicenter for people to discover new and emerging technologies that most people don't have access to. We are a "technology playground" and offer a place for people to share and learn more about their dreams and aspirations, but also they have a space to make them come true. Our motto is "Dream.Think.Create," and I think we are still going strong but have a lot more to accomplish.

The iLab also collaborates with other businesses and college departments, and this helps bring more visibility to the library, according to Mairn.

Local inventors visit the lab inside the library to see their prototypes come to life via the 3D digitizer and 3D printer. The *Sandbox News*, St. Petersburg College's student-run newspaper, borrowed the iLab's 360-degree camera to do an immersive story about the Seminole Campus's Nature Trail, narrated by Maura Scanlon, associate professor of natural sciences.

Mairn added,

> I am proud to say that what we are doing in the Innovation Lab, with our Maker Boot Camp and other workshops, is not to prepare students for specific careers; instead, what we are doing is hopefully enabling them to adapt to whatever careers and to learn to successfully solve problems that might emerge in the future. The Innovation Lab, in partnership with the St. Petersburg College Seminole Campus Engineering Club, recently finished building a drone that includes a GoPro video camera. The iLab is in the process of building its own 3D printer, too.

THE MAKERSPACE LANDSCAPE: NEW CASE STUDIES

FabLabs

Technically, FabLab is short for Fabrication Laboratory, although some libraries use the phrase more colloquially, such as the Fayetteville Free Library FabLab. Started by Neil Gershenfeld at the Center for Bits and Atoms at the Massachusetts Institute of Technology Media Lab (http://cba.mit.edu/) in about 2005, formal FabLabs are typically guided by a Fab Charter[7] and stocked with a basic set of tools and instruments. Typically operated by nonprofit organizations, there are now FabLabs in more than 40 countries. The UTA FabLab at the University of Texas at Arlington Libraries, in Arlington, Texas, is a great example.

UTA FabLab, University of Texas at Arlington Libraries, Arlington, Texas (fablab.uta.edu)

At two years old, the UTA FabLab is an intergenerational academic library makerspace with work areas that include art, craft, and tech tools and related resources. The FabLab acts as a creative hub for students, faculty, and staff of the University of Texas at Arlington. It provides access to technologies, equipment, and training; opportunities for interdisciplinary collaboration; and access to inspirational spaces in support of invention and entrepreneurship. Katie Musick Peery, director of the UTA FabLab, says the FabLab is intended to be a platform for project-based, hands-on science, technology, engineering, arts, and mathematics (STEAM) experiential learning.

About the UTA FabLab The FabLab is funded through the library budget and grants, and charges materials fees. It is supported by the University of Texas and local government, with three dedicated staff to run it. The lab serves 35,000 people annually. It is stocked with tools and equipment, for example, sewing machines, hand tools, power tools, large-scale manufacturing equipment, 3D printers, electronic kits and supplies, vinyl cutters, laser cutters, screen printing tools, kilns, powder coating tools, and air brushing tools. Peery says the laser cutter is the most-used piece of equipment at the FabLab, with the 3D scanner the least used.

The facility holds equipment-specific workshops and sessions on crafts and different projects and safety, with an annual cosplay event.

The biggest challenge they've faced at the UTA FabLab, said Peery, is "staffing it with people with expertise to share on any given piece of equipment at any time that we're open." Their biggest achievement has been promoting student success and community within the space. "I'm incredibly proud of the students who come in with no background or familiarity with making and are able to not only learn, but [also] turn around and teach others," Peery stated, adding,

> Perhaps a lesson for me personally is the fact that if you start by building a strong community, the help and expertise you need will fall into place! People will begin helping each other and offering to teach workshops and lessons out of their own passion and excitement. Leadership in the space doesn't need to be the experts or architects of all these activities.

If she could have done anything differently, she said they would have aimed for greater diversity within their staff at the start of their FabLab effort. She also feels it would be better to recruit student staff from a greater variety of majors "so that all of our student population see themselves reflected in the staff of the space."

"Each of our survey respondents was asked what they'd consider a best practice," Peery said, continuing,

> With courses using the FabLab for assignments, we have made it standard to give students a tour of the space so that we can explain the equipment, ease their anxieties, and set some ground rules to make sure they're using the lab properly and having an enjoyable learning experience. We also have a standardized system for creating "tickets," whereby we are able to track usage statistics and keep track of jobs people are making in the lab, making it easier for us to track payments and pickups later.

Peery's greatest personal pleasure, she says, is seeing the students "(particularly our student employees) learn and grow! I've seen them develop not just their technical skills, but [also] their confidence, teaching abilities, and creativity."

Among her favorite recollections:

> A student recently brought one of his FabLab creations to a job fair on campus so that he could demonstrate his practical knowledge and application of manufacturing skills. Before he had used the FabLab, he had theoretical knowledge of principles he'd learned in his computer science courses but had not applied them outside of the lab or integrated them with other technologies. He remarked that he didn't have access to the tools we offered from any other place. As an underclassman, other campus labs have restricted access and a different set of tools.
>
> By being able to have open access to FabLab equipment, he was able to iterate his design for an automated teddy bear until each component met his vision and standards. He used the sewing machine to make the bear, the electronics bay to automate its eyes and sounds, and the laser cutter and 3D printers for support structures. This student procured an internship after showing off his creation, and that internship was later extended because of the amazing work he was doing for the company! We were proud to have contributed to his professional success.

Makerspaces are more than just 3D printers, said Peery, a truism noted by many of our survey respondents and librarians we've spoken and worked with during the last few years. "They are more than any of the individual pieces of equipment in the space," she said. "They are about community and creativity. Make sure you or your staff are willing to gain some troubleshooting expertise on whatever you buy, and let your users guide your decision-making process. Use data-driven decisions to provide the tools and programming they want most."

Makerspaces

The most common form of creative space in public and school libraries is the type identified by the catchall term *makerspace*. These spaces can vary widely in style, inventory, focus, and intent. They can be huge or modest in size. They can be mobile or pop-up, youth-oriented or aimed at older adults. The spaces here include all of the above and a few things in between.

Johnson County Library Makerspace and FabLab, Johnson County Library, Overland Park, Kansas (www.jocolibrary.org/makerspace)

The Johnson County Library Makerspace is a three-and-a-half-year-old dedicated space for makers, tinkerers, and learners of all types to create and learn how to make digital and physical artifacts. Maker librarian Meredith Nelson shared insights and best practices from this model makerspace, which serves 160 people daily, with more than 2,300 youth coming in for their Makerspace Summer Passport projects in 2016. Despite having Makerspace in its name, Nelson identifies the space as a FabLab on the basis of the type of equipment it contains and its ability to support both digital and manufacturing enterprises.

The space is currently funded by grants, with an annual operating budget of $24,500, and it enjoys support from both the local library community and local government. The facility has at least three dedicated staff and one volunteer, and serves mostly adults age 50 and older, followed by teens and young adults (mostly male).

About the Johnson County Library MakerSpace The Johnson County Library MakerSpace has a wide array of tools and resources, including sewing machines, hand tools, power tools, large-scale manufacturing equipment, 3D printers, electronics kits, vinyl cutters, and laser cutters. The laser cutters and 3D printers are the most-used equipment in the space. The library also hosts a variety of workshops, including Beginner's Night for new users, summer programs, meetups, teen club, and demonstrations. Annual events include a cosplay event and an anime event.

Their biggest challenge, said Nelson, is the high demand created by the space. Their greatest success she reflected, is their summer programming for youth, and one of the things they're most justifiably proud of is their super-efficient reservation system for equipment.

Nelson's advice: Start small, measure demand, and get staff.

PUBLIC LIBRARY MAKERSPACES

The Foundry, Land O' Lakes Branch Library, Pasco County Library Cooperative, Land O'Lakes, Florida (www.pascolibraries.org/about-us/land-o-lakes-makerspace)

The Foundry is a physically small space with large-scale engagement in an active and forward-thinking library community. Like the HIVE, the Foundry was designed in consultation with Eureka! Factory, run by my husband and me, but comes closer to the community-driven model we feel is vital to a successful library makerspace experience. The Foundry consists of a workshop built into a repurposed computer lab that includes a wood and metal working area used by hobbyists and the library's *FIRST* Robotics Competition[8] team, the Edgar Allan Ohms. Another repurposed space in the library supports a light arts and crafts section to teach and host sewing, jewelry work, painting and children's arts and crafts.

Pasco County Library administrator Sean McGarvey, who also coaches the *FIRST* Robotics Competition team, shared an overview of the space and some best practices.

About the Foundry

The Foundry is funded through the Pasco County budget at $5,000 annually, as part of the library's overall budget for materials and programming. The library charges no user fees and serves 1,200 people annually. All users must sit through an orientation session and complete an annual hold harmless agreement. The majority of users are from 30 to 60 years old. McGarvey feels the library Maker initiative is well supported by the library and local government.

Foundry equipment includes sewing machines, art supplies, hand tools, power tools, 3D printers, electronic kits, vinyl cutters, a band saw, a drill press, a miter saw, and lathes. The lathes are used the most, thanks to an active woodworkers group that meets at the Foundry, and the 3D printers are least used, said McGarvey. The space has at least three assigned staff plus three or more volunteers who help with the makerspace.

The biggest challenge they've encountered with their makerspace program, said McGarvey, is the legal aspect of being able to run the programs they offer, necessitating a lot of time with county attorneys. The Foundry's biggest success: "Community woodworking and wood-turning programs have offered people of all ages the ability to learn skills they never knew they had," related McGarvey.

McGarvey stresses the importance of "asking what the community wants *before* constructing the space. Hire and recruit volunteers from in the community, not from companies. And make sure you have a plan for storage space before you start."

His favorite experience, is seeing people who have never used a particular item or tool make a cut, paint, or sew for the first time. He finds the teen robotics team particularly inspiring. Stated McGarvey, "I am the head coach on (the library's) *FIRST* Robotics Competition team, and suffice to say the proudest moments have all been watching the students work diligently in the makerspace til late at night on robot after robot."

His best advice to any library interested in exploring makerspace development: "Always involve the community; a makerspace is not the tools in the shop. It's about the people who want to use those tools, so if you don't have the right ones, no one will come."

Hazel L. Incantalupo Makerspace, Palm Harbor Library, Palm Harbor, Florida (phlibkids.wixsite.com/phlchildren/makerspace)

Kiki Durney, head of Youth Services at the Palm Harbor Library in Pinellas County, Florida, describes the Hazel L. Incantalupo Makerspace as a "zero-tech, art-themed makerspace for children ages five to 12." The space is integrated into existing public library space, carved out of a small corner of the children's library section, and funded through a generous local benefactor who gives to the space as needed. There are no user fees. Durney says both library administration and local government are supportive of the youth makerspace, which has two dedicated staff members and serves more than 3,500 people annually.

About the Hazel L. Incantalupo Makerspace

As a makerspace focused on children's art, the center is stocked largely with Perler beads, modeling clay, and paint, which are among the most popular resources for participating youth. Least used in their inventory, said Durney, are the embroidery and scrapbooking supplies. The space provides no classes or workshops. It's all "open make," providing unstructured opportunities for children to make whatever they'd like during their time in the makerspace. An annual cosplay event and an anime event are hosted each year at the library.

The biggest challenge they've faced at the Palm Harbor Library, said Durney, is balancing staff time to manage the makerspace during other programs. Their biggest success, she declared, is "changing the perception of how people think of libraries."

Durney recommends having children and their caretaker sign a behavior contract before entering the space and limiting the child's time in the space but not limiting materials. Her best piece of advice for makerspace newcomers: Remember location, location, location. "A makerspace can be anything you want it to be," she stated. "Determine what your community needs and provide it."

3D Printing Incubator for Children and Youth, Rijeka City Library, Rijeka, Croatia

The 3D Printing Incubator for Children and Youth at the Rijeka City Library in Rijeka, Croatia,[9] includes laptop computers equipped with 3D design software, 3D printers, and a 3D scanner, as well as Raspberry Pi mini-computers. Kristian Benic, associate for marketing and projects at the library, explained that the library is developing training programs for children and youth as old as age 24 to learn to use 3D design and modeling software and operate the printers. The library also holds demonstrations of 3D printing for schools and the general public.

The 3D Printing Incubator serves 200 people annually. It was initially funded by the Electronic Information for Libraries (EIFL) Public Library Innovation Program[10] and is now funded by the main library budget and some user fees. Benic said the library is very supportive of the project, which has one full-time staff and several volunteers to help manage it.

About the 3D Printing Incubator

In addition to the 3D printers and related software, the space also includes art supplies and electronics kits. The makerspace also offers regular 3D modeling workshops and hosts an annual Maker festival. Their biggest challenge, said Benic, has been space and budget. Their biggest success: "lots of special 3D printing projects and children's enthusiasm." Benic has been most surprised by the different kinds of usage of 3D printing.

If he could have done anything differently when they started their project, Benic said they would have first ensured a place for the project in the overall library strategy. While their program is successful, he said the space they have now is too small to accommodate the need.

Benic related that their best practices include fielding lots of creative ideas, doing demonstrations for kids from local schools, and participating in regional public events. He most enjoys the experience of reinventing the library and loves the success stories that come out of their program:

> A college student has developed and printed a prototype of a spray bottle holder for a local business; our workshop groups 3D printed medals for a children's race; children are making objects inspired by books. For example, one 10-year-old made a bookmark in the shape of a ghost that was featured in a story he read. All of these experiences were really emotional and interesting.

His best piece of advice, "Ensure that your library really wants to develop this service, not only for marketing purposes."

Library Makerspace of VTL, Valley of the Tetons Library, Victor, Idaho (facebook.com/VTL-Makerspace-546906075486261/)

The Library Makerspace of VTL (Valley of the Tetons Library) is a youth makerspace housed in a separate space within the library and also includes a branch library that uses adaptable creative space that transforms as needed. Rasheil Stanger, programs director for the makerspace, shared an overview and best practices from VTL.

"Our makerspace movement consists of Maker Monday, Tech Club, and Open Build Days all through the week," she explained. The space is funded through the library budget and Friends, and operates on a budget of $3,000 for both libraries. The library charges no fees and has support from the library community, as well as limited support from local government. The spaces operate with two dedicated staff and a small corps of volunteers.

About Library Makerspace of VTL

The library handles risk management through on-site supervision, special lockout devices on more sophisticated equipment, and age requirements for tools and materials. The facility serves more than 200 people annually with their makerspace programming, mostly families, teens, and young adults.

The space is stocked with sewing machines, art supplies, hand tool, power tools, 3D printers, electronic kits, and supplies. The items that get the most use at VTL, said Stanger, are hand tools, glue guns, Arduino, and Raspberry Pi. Art supplies aren't used as much, but they're planning to integrate more programming into that area. The makerspace is already chock-full of programming, including 3D printing classes, workshops on Arduino, tech clubs, open-build sessions, robotics programming, LEGO builds, filmmaking, paper making, coding, computer gaming, girls and coding, Japanese dirt balls, summer of code, sewing, and virtual reality programs.

The biggest challenge they've faced, declared Stanger, is "educating the public to what makerspaces are and reaching them." They're biggest success, he said, is the program itself. It was such a success, she said,

> we hired a designated Maker librarian, and we have kids coming in after school to "make" and have a fun at our library. We have a small community,

> and this is amazing. We participated in the Jackson Hole Maker Faire, (where) our remote control car run by a hat was met with tons of praise. We are growing every year.

The biggest surprise she found was "how much enjoyment the kids have with making with their own hands." She added, "Some kids said they weren't even allowed to touch hammers at home. Well, not in our space! And no gender biases: Boys love to use the sewing machine, and the girls love the hand tools. No stigma attached."

About the only thing she'd have done differently when they started was to have marked their space more boldly in the beginning.

Stanger considers adaptability among their best practices, saying, "We are open to change and open to molding the curriculum to fit the users at will."

She loves how people experience the space. Among her favorite stories is the following:

> A girl came in to the library at Christmastime and 3D printed her mom a Christmas gift she found on Thingiverse. Saved her money for the print, $3, and had her dad help her so it was a surprise. She was so proud; I was so excited. I'm not ashamed to say there was a tear in my eye. Another experience last week, two boys came downstairs, saw what we were doing, looked at each other: "We can come? Is this free? Now?" High five! "We are so LUCKY!"

The best piece of advice Stanger has to offer is, "Take your time, be organized, and research, research, research . . . and you don't have to do *everything*! Do what you can do well, the rest will come. And use your community. I realized I don't need to be an expert at everything, Someone else already is."

PUBLIC SCHOOL MAKERSPACES

The Inquiry Zone, Discovery Canyon Elementary School, Colorado Springs, Colorado

The Inquiry Zone is a two-year-old do-it-yourself creative space in the Discovery Canyon Elementary School library in Colorado Springs, Colorado, where students gather to reflect on their International Baccalaureate Units of Inquiry and create a project that demonstrates their understanding of their grade-level unit. Irene MacLean, elementary teacher-librarian and digital learning coach, shared insights and best practices from her library makerspace.

"Students experience the entire design-thinking and problem-solving process, and are encouraged to reflect on their conceptual understanding, creation, and skills," said MacLean. "This empowers them to take charge of their own learning. Risk-taking is celebrated, since the experience is the true goal, rather than the product. Projects range from glue and craft sticks to coding."

The school library budget covers the cost of such consumables as glue and tape, and most of the other supplies and tools have been donated. MacLean said there is a great deal of support from the school but little from local government. The space is managed by two dedicated staff and several volunteers, and serves more than 500 people annually, mostly families, teens, and young adults.

About the Inquiry Zone

The makerspace stocks sewing machines, art supplies, hand tools, and iPads, and runs robotics and coding programs from the facility, with its largest focus on arts-related projects. MacLean said she feels the biggest success in the program is creating students who are empowered by the creative process and continue to create outside of school. Students can choose to work independently or collaboratively and select their own projects.

MacLean related that she enjoys watching students fail "and then try again until something works, listening to them solve a problem together."

Among her favorite experiences at the school makerspace is a conversation she overhead between two fifth graders.

"Did you know Ms. MacLean has a SAW?" one student asked.

"Yes," replied the other, "and she's not afraid to use it, either."

"That's what scares me!" said the first.

MacLean's best piece of advice: "The value gained by allowing students to take charge of their learning by far outweighs any headaches or mess. Whether you have actual storage space or have to work out of bins, find or make a way to include this in your library program!"

G.E.N.I.U.S. Hour (Generating in Education New Ideas and Understandings for Students) School Library Makerspace, Bay Shore Middle School Library, Bay Shore, New York (tackk.com/bsmsgeniushour)

The G.E.N.I.U.S. Hour makerspace program at Bay Shore Middle School Library in Bay Shore, New York, is managed by Kristina A. Holzweiss, school library media specialist, and is now more than two years old. The program, said Holzweiss, is an "exploratory time for anywhere from a week to three weeks." She continued,

> It is mostly for sixth grade students, to acclimate them to the critical thinking required for middle school-level learning. Students develop communication and collaboration skills. The makerspace is open to all students during their free periods (lunch and study hall). This year we will be instituting a new techspert program for students to serve as technology mentors and managers of the makerspace.

The makerspace, which is integrated into existing library space, is funded through grants, fund-raising through book fairs, and DonorsChoose. There is no annual operating budget allocated, although school administration is supportive if local government is less so. Beyond Holzweiss, there is no other dedicated staff, but there are several volunteers. The space serves 500 students annually.

About G.E.N.I.U.S. Hour

This school makerspace is stocked with sewing machines, art supplies, 3D printers, robotics kits, iPads, LEGOs, scrapbooking materials, and a paper cutter. The most-used items, according to Holzweiss, are the robotics kits, iPads, and LEGOs. Programming consists largely of student-driven activities and events like SLIME (Students of Long Island Maker Expo) and similar programs.

The biggest challenge they face at G.E.N.I.U.S. Hour is managing materials with only one part-time staff member. Their greatest success, Holzweiss said, is that "students love visiting our library and have learned how to have fun learning again." She added, "You never know what kids are going to like to do until they are given the opportunity to try different things."

Holzweiss encouraged "controlled chaos," allowing students to learn at their own pace and be creative without fearing failure.

She said if she could have done anything differently with her school library makerspace when she started, it would have been to begin with student staff and then focus on getting resources. She feels more student input would have been helpful. She also would have invited parents and the community into the space to help them better understand and use it.

Holzweiss loves how the space reinvigorates a joy of learning in students. "I have the opportunity to connect with students in ways that other teachers can't. In our program, it is truly learning for learning's sake," she related.

One of her favorite experiences at the makerspace involves the school's Teen Tech Week. Stated Holzweiss,

> Teachers signed up their classes to learn how to create video games using Bloxels. There were classes from all grade levels (6, 7, and 8) from a variety of classes. I was thrilled that my ESL students and life skills students (handicapped, Down syndrome, autistic, etc.) were able to be active participants and enjoy the lesson as well.

Her best piece of advice: "Like the Nike slogan, 'Just do it!' You have to learn how a makerspace works for you by working through it. After reading and researching, eventually you just have to dive in and try it. There are so many people to help you on Facebook and Twitter." Holzweiss offered up her own websites as a resource as well: www.bunheadwithducttape.com, www.slimemakerexpo.com, and bsmslibratory.weebly.com

POP-UP MAKERSPACES

Maker Boxes, Yolo County Public Library, Woodland, California

Maker Boxes is a project of the Yolo County Public Library in Woodland, California, now in its second year. Managed by library associates Gail Stovall and Sue Billing, the project is formally called "S.T.E.A.M.ing Ahead with MAKER BOXES." The Maker Boxes feature pop-up makerspace-in-a-box-style programming, with mobile Maker stations or equipment made available for open builds or classes.

Initially funded with a $5,000 grant from the California State Library system, funding now comes from Friends groups as needed. There is some support from the library community but none from local government. The program is run with three staff and some volunteers, and serves 150 people annually, mostly families and teens.

"Maker Boxes are action based," Stovall and Billing explained. They further commented,

> They encourage experimenting, inventing, testing, and reinventing, whether individually or in groups. They facilitate long-term program planning and provide for last-minute programming changes. Maker Boxes appeal to and can be adapted to different venues—single program or Mini Maker Camp. Different objectives—active or passive. Different presenters—expert or neophyte. Different audiences—children, teens, adults. They are about lessening worries about "subject expertise" and expanding outreach, learning, and library influence. They are about teaming with library and community partners to present captivating programming more quickly, more effectively, and more effortlessly. And all of this in a little itty bitty box.

"Well, maybe not itty bitty," they admitted.

About Maker Boxes

The idea was launched in October 2013, when Yolo County Public Library staff, teens, and partners worked with Jess Munro of Entrepreneurs by Design, to experience and experiment with the Design Thinking process developed by the Stanford d.school and IDEO Consultancy. According to Stovall and Billing,

> Our primary goal was to determine what teens wanted in their library. One "wish" was Maker Spaces. Due to financing issues, Maker Spaces became a Maker Truck, which then evolved into the less expensive Maker Boxes—portable programming in a box. We were awarded $5,000 in seed money from a grant awarded by the California State Library. Subsequent funding has come from Friends groups and from donations of items from staff.

Yolo County libraries worked with teens to develop programming of interest to the students, beginning with a Rocketry Maker Box. Participants researched types of rockets, the history of rocketry, and the physics involved in rocketry. They developed puff rockets, stomp rockets, air rockets, and fuel rockets.

Said Stovall and Billing, "Following similar techniques, the staff and teens at the Yolo branch developed an Electricity and Circuitry Maker Box. In each case, participants presented the programs in different venues. Subject experts volunteered their time to enhance the learning and excitement."

Staff developed 20 additional boxes. While the first boxes were developed with teen interests in mind, subsequent boxes were designed in a multitude of themes and used in branch programing for participants of all ages. The staff continues to develop Maker Boxes, reviewing, revising, and expanding the library's programming resources.

Equipment included with the Maker Boxes consists of art supplies, hand tools, power tools, and electronics kits. There tends to be a greater interest in the arts and crafts components than technology, but the library hosts STEAM-related programs with the Maker Boxes, plus annual events like STEM fairs.

Their biggest challenge, said the librarians, is reorganizing, reordering, and restocking the boxes, a time-consuming task. They also observed that there is a strong Russian and Spanish community in Yolo County. Yet, they have few Russian and Spanish speakers participating in their program. Stovall and Billing see a "need to have extra staff to meet these needs." They were also surprised by how messy the program can be.

Their biggest success so far, however: "A seven-box Mini Maker Fair!"

If they could have done anything differently when they started, Stovall and Billing said they would have created check-off sheets for reordering and created and labeled boxes within the main box so they could put things back in order and reorder more easily.

Although at first they promoted the program only to teens, they lamented, "We found out it's most successful when multigenerational."

The librarians continue to be surprised by the variety of creations that weren't anything they'd come across when they developed the boxes or had suggested in sample materials. One example they recalled was as follows:

> Emma came to story time early. She stopped by Appendage Art, where I expected her to create a "creature" or two from a handprint, footprint, or

fingerprint. Instead, she took one look at the ink pads and used them to create designs in colorful squares for one solid hour! She refused to go to story time. She was about three years old!

Their best advice:

Organize the boxes for each repacking, reordering, and restocking. Be sure to know what needs copyright credit. It's a bear to go back and redo. Ask customers what themes they are interested in and create first boxes to their preference. Nurture your Makers in small steps if you want them to learn a particular skill. For example: Making rockets and learning about the history and physics behind rocketry is a multiprogram endeavor.

Also, take advantage of the skills of your customers and partners. It's a win-win to have them present a program they are expert in. We even had one partner develop the entire box. Use your teens; train them to be facilitators. Let them learn how to speak in front of a group. Use experts. For example, we had a NASA employee speak at one rocketry meeting.

Make It @ Your Library, East Bonner County Library District, Sandpoint, Idaho

East Bonner County Library District has been providing a different type of "pop-up" makerspace programming for the last three years. Young adult services librarian Morgan Gariepy explained how their program works: "Children and teens are introduced to robotics, coding, engineering, embroidery, crochet, and other STEAM concepts during a one-and-a-half-hour weekly program. We also offer adult and teen 3D printing workshops twice monthly."

The program was initially funded by the Idaho Commission for Libraries, to support training and supplies. Additional funds now come from the Young Adult programming budget. The program, which serves 600 patrons annually, is managed by one full-time dedicated staff and several volunteers, and enjoys support from both the library community and local government. Users are largely families and individuals age 30 and older (mostly males).

About Make It @ Your Library

The mobile resources include sewing machines, art supplies, 3D printers, electronics and robotics kits, and LEGOs. The most-used resources, according to Gariepy, are the Fischertechnik robots and LEGOs, with Arduinos among the least-used resource.

The library offers a weekly children and teens program, plus two monthly 3D printing workshops. Their biggest challenge has been engaging older teens with advanced tools. Their greatest success: "Engaging younger children with STEAM concepts, such as problem solving, attention to detail, and teamwork." Gariepy continued, "We have many kids that consistently come each week since our first year."

"I'm surprised at the level of commitment that some children have for the program. I hope that they will consider careers in a STEAM profession in the future," said Gariepy.

If she could have done anything differently at the start, Gariepy said, "I would have had separate children's and teen's programs from the beginning."

Gariepy said she loves watching students' faces light up when they successfully complete a project. She related,

> I have one participant who began coming with his grandfather early in our first year. The two used it as quality bonding time. The grandfather would help his young grandson complete projects. As time went on, the boy became one of our most accomplished robotics kids we had. He moved from needing his grandfather's help to being the first line of help for other kids.

Gariepy advised, "Makerspaces are informal, and mentors are guides, not instructors. Let the kids explore, create, and troubleshoot on their own, asking peers for help. Only step in if a peer can't help."

Makerspaces, she also pointed out, "are loud, messy, and full of energy. Shouts of excitement, paint spilling on the floor, soldering bits falling onto the table, and other such messes are inevitable. Plan your space accordingly."

MOBILE MAKERSPACES

Mobile makerspaces can refer to either in-house mobile carts or stations,[11] or a larger-scale mobile space, like a bus or van.[12] The two mobile spaces shared here represent both in-house mobile stations and a vehicle-based makerspace.

Discovery Lab, Mamie Doud Eisenhower Public Library, Broomfield, Colorado

Discovery Lab at Mamie Doud Eisenhower Public library in Broomfield, Colorado, is a series of weekly after-school programming for students ages nine to 18, offering hands-on learning from a librarian, science expert, or teen volunteer. The subject focus of these exploratory programs is science, technology, engineering, art, and math. Additionally, artists and Makers are invited to set up a three-week residency and use the space as a studio, an extension of the Discovery Lab titled Maker-in-Residence. These sessions are offered for all ages and provide an opportunity for artists or Makers to use the space to work on a project, as well as interact with the public through observation, conversation, and experiential learning.

The program has been around for two and a half years and is managed by Pauline Noomnam, librarian II, Teen Services. Discovery Lab, she said, is a combination of intergenerational and mobile makerspace. The physical space can be manipulated to incorporate tables and chairs or no furniture. Supplies are rotated on shelving for public use and kept in locked cabinets in the room when not in use.

The program is funded through an annual programming fund and a science and culture grant. It is staffed by three librarians and two volunteers, with support from the library system. More than 5,200 patrons are served annually, mostly families, teens, and young adults, and more females participate than males, Noomnam noted.

About Discovery Lab

Discovery Lab inventory includes sewing machines, art supplies, hand tools, 3D printers, culinary resources, electronic kits, a scanner, a green screen, iPads, rockets, and soldering irons. Arts and crafts resources are the most used, and culinary arts resources are least used. Programs offered include such STEAM-based topics as cooking and music.

Their biggest challenge, said Noomnam, is that some sessions are offered as drop-in, with no registration required. "It is difficult to determine the quantity of supplies needed to accommodate all participants. On the other hand, when registration is required, sometimes we will have a no-show, and people on the waiting list lose the opportunity to attend," she elaborated.

Their biggest success, Noomnam said, is "participants returning on a weekly basis. Participants who came to a science-based program and return to attend an art/music-based program because of the quality of programming and presenter. The increase in curiosity and exploratory-based interest in learning."

Her biggest surprise, she said, was learning "you can have the most successful program (based on attendance, returning participants, feedback) with very little planning. On the other hand, a program that may take months to plan can have a less-positive outcome (little interest/attendance, unplanned obstacles)."

If she could have done anything differently, she said she would "dedicate a staff person to the development, volunteer coordination, partnership outreach, and facilitation of the programming series." And she would involve other departments in the development and implementation of the program.

Noomnam continued,

> The Teen Services Department was the sole entity in the library offering makerspace programming. After two full years, the Adult Services Department has begun to offer programming. We now have a Makerspace Team that incorporates teen and adult librarians.
>
> Best practices: Staff who are open to test ideas and engage in unfamiliar topics. A strong volunteer pool (to develop and/or facilitate activities). Dedicated time in the day/week/month for short- and long-term planning.

Noomnam's greatest personal enjoyment is experiencing the knowledge and curiosity growth of their patrons.

One of her favorite stories illustrates what patrons can do given resources and freedom:

> We had a Recycled Instruments session with our tweens on a Tuesday and offered a GarageBand (iPad app) session on a Thursday. A few of the participants brought back their instruments from the Tuesday session to record

> music on the Thursday session. This showed our staff that if we provide the resources, our patrons will explore and create beyond our expectations.

Her best advice: "Say yes. If you are okay with failure and are willing to try again (or ditch the idea completely), you can discover new abilities within yourself and your patrons."

Make It @ Your Library, Community Library Network at Hayden, Hayden, Idaho

Make It @Your Library is a four-year-old program at the Community Library Network in Hayden, Idaho, managed by youth services specialist Nick Madsen. The mobile makerspace involves simple robotic, engineering, and coding programs brought to outreach sites and library events, taking tools and resources into the community.

The program is budgeted through the Library Friends Group, the library budget, and national initiatives. The library system is somewhat supportive, Madsen said, with no support from local government. The program is managed by two dedicated library staff and serves 950 people annually, mostly families, teens, and 30-somethings.

About Make It @ Your Library

The mobile makerspace is stocked with sewing machines, art supplies, 3D printers, culinary resources, and robotics kits. Most used are the Bluetooth-enabled robots, the 3D printer, and building toys, and least used are the high-level robotics and 3Doodlers. The mobile makerspace offers the following classes and workshops: 3D Printer Orientation, Make a Movie in Four Hours, MaKey MaKey Music, and Explore Simple Robotics.

The program faces quite a few challenges, said Madsen, including a shortage of storage, lack of time to create new programs, lack of local Makers and resources, funding challenges, insufficient library space, and minimal staff buy-in.

Their biggest success, however, puts things in perspective. Said Madsen,

> Even years after the events took place, young people still remember us bringing a 3D printer into their school and showing them how it works. Having the

> resources to give technological exposure to students that might not have had the opportunity or the interest otherwise is very rewarding.

If he could have done anything differently, Madsen reflected, "I would have started by gaining staff and administration support, and making co-workers aware of the tools that were and are available." If he could change anything now, he said, "I would strive to offer tools for in-library checkout, home use, and classroom use, so they are used to their full potential, instead of waiting for a library staff member to use them."

Madsen recommends leveraging community resources as you plan and implement your makerspace or program. "Partnering with local organizations is priceless."

He also observed, "Technology is only one way to have a person experience Maker principles. You don't need a dedicated space to do Maker-style programs."

Madsen said he enjoys watching students and educators look at a challenge in a different way, discussing projects with members who are passionate about them, being part of a project that many people do not associate with libraries, and starting conversations about how libraries have evolved.

Asked about his favorite story, Madsen related,

> I recently had the chance to present low-tech making ideas to a group of school librarians. Hoping to incorporate the collaborative and enjoyable nature of making, I asked small groups of librarians to draw a line on a piece of paper in as many steps as possible. The idea was based on Rube Goldberg machines and chain reactions.
>
> This group of professionals embraced the challenge. Some built pendulums, some built slides, and some shot candy from a rubber band to start a chain reaction. But all of them had experienced the joys of relying on your team, coming up with unique ways of solving a challenge, and being proud of your finished product.
>
> Following the training, many of these professionals shared their enjoyment in the project and stated they wanted to bring similar projects to the students at their schools.

Madsen's best piece of advice: "Focus on equipping people to think for themselves instead of focusing on getting the latest and greatest tools out there. Sometimes a 3D printer can assemble an epiphany, but sometimes it is as simple as blowing a marshmallow through a small piece of PVC pipe."

BEST PRACTICES RECAP

By now it should be pretty evident what most of these successful library makerspaces have in common. Whether a higher education FabLab library, K-12 library makerspace, public library pop-up, or mobile or integrated makerspace, these libraries have the following characteristics:

- *Community-based focus:* They take into serious and principal consideration the needs of the community they serve, whether it's the students attending their schools or the patrons using their services and programs.
- *Intentionality:* They take the time to plan their designs and programs, conferring with library administration, community members, volunteers, and staff.
- *Adaptability:* The most successful spaces can pivot quickly, adapting to the changing needs and interests of users, new technologies, and available expertise.
- *Ability to empower:* Libraries with the most robust Maker programs empower those who run the spaces, from volunteers to staff, to exercise creativity and originality in running the space and the programs.
- *Willingness to fail forward:* Don't be afraid to fail. Write it into your strategic plan if it helps. Makerspaces are designed to allow for mistakes, from which new things arise. That's just as true in the design and facilitation of a makerspace as it is for those using the spaces. Few things will derail a library makerspace effort like excessive risk aversion.
- *Expectation and acceptance of noise and mess:* Makerspaces are messy. If you want a makerspace, you need to accept what comes with the innovation and creation process—noise and mess—and plan accordingly through scheduling, design, and space-use protocols.
- *Use of the expertise of the community:* Everything and everyone you need are right in your community, as confirmed by library after library.

> There's no need for library staff to be experts in everything or even anything. Once it becomes clear what the community wants in a makerspace, you can go to the community to find out who wants to share what they know and then help them do that.

Armed with library makerspace basics and the experience of these great spaces to guide you, we can now turn our attention to some best practices in makerspace architecture to help with the design and implementation process.

NOTES

1. "A Map of Library Makerspaces." *Google Fusion Tables*. Accessed October 27, 2016. https://fusiontables.google.com/DataSource?docid=1ur0ifo-RvglbfzwRPu0KMYAM9-XNyFFIf6U2hTeL#rows:id=1.
2. "Makerspaces in Libraries, Museums, and Schools." *Google*. Accessed October 27, 2017. ww.google.com/maps/d/u/0/viewer?mid=1wKXDd1rOs4ls1EiZswQr-upFq7o&ll=42.9439004719218%2C-111.44518153922797&z=7.
3. "Ray Oldenburg." *Project for Public Spaces*. Accessed October 27, 2017. www.pps.org/reference/roldenburg/.
4. "FabLab FAQ." *FabCentral*. Accessed October 27, 2017. http://fab.cba.mit.edu/about/faq/.
5. "Digital Commons." *District of Columbia Public Library*. Accessed December 10, 2017. www.dclibrary.org/labs/digitalcommons.
6. McCue, T. J. "First Public Library to Create a Maker Space." *Forbes*. November 28, 2014. Accessed January 27, 2017. www.forbes.com/sites/tjmccue/2011/11/15/first-public-library-to-create-a-maker-space/#4004aac079cf.
7. "The Fab Charter." Massachusetts Institute of Technology.. Accessed October 25, 2016. http://fab.cba.mit.edu/about/charter/.
8. Miller, Daylina. "Robotics Team Builds One for the Books." *Suncoast News*. April 30, 2014. Accessed January 17, 2017. www.tbo.com/su/list/news-pasco/robotics-team-builds-one-for-the-books-20140430/.
9. "3D Printing Project Transforms Public Library into City's Premier 'Makerspace.'" *Electronic Information for Libraries*. February 15, 2016. Accessed February 20, 2017. www.eifl.net/news/3d-printing-project-transforms-public-library-citys-premier-maker-space.

10. "Public Library Innovation Program." *Electronic Information for Libraries*. Accessed March 2, 2017. www.eifl.net/programmes/public-library-innovation-programme.

11. Johnson, Mica, Brittany Witte, Jennie Randolph, Rachel Smith, and Karen Cragwall. "Mobile Maker Spaces." *School Library Journal*. May 3, 2016. Accessed March 2, 2017. www.slj.com/2016/05/technology/mobile-maker-spaces/#_.

12. "The MakerBus." *MakerBus*. Accessed March 15, 2017. https://dhmakerbus.com/.

4

MAKERSPACE ARCHITECTURE

Don't forget that you're a makerspace—if all else fails you can make your own benches and tables! Make the building of the makerspace furnishings the first makerspace project.

—Chuck Stephens, Maker librarian,
Pasco County Library Cooperative, Florida

Chapter 3 provides a look at a variety of library makerspace models that will hopefully inspire some ideas for new spaces. But ultimately, the best library makerspace model is the one that works for your community, with an eye to accessibility and inclusivity, and within the working parameters of your library system.

Chuck Stephens is a former tradesman and an artist, hired by Pasco County Library Cooperative in Florida to bring his Maker sensibilities to bear on the Pasco Libraries' developing makerspaces and creative programs. He also helps coach *FIRST* youth robotics teams in the Pasco County libraries and is a great example of Sue Considine's recommendation, and our own, to hire outside of traditional library roles to better leverage community expertise in the development and management of makerspaces and related programming. His ideas about makerspaces are practical and based on years of real-world experience in construction and handcraft.

"The allocation of space and the floor plan are some of the most important factors when designing a makerspace," said Stephens, continuing,

> Consider the goals of your space and create a layout that complements those goals. If we aim to foster a creative community in the makerspace, it needs to be comfortable and inviting. We want to provide a safe environment where things are secure, spacious, and uncluttered. We want people to be productive, so tools need to be accessible; benches and work surfaces need to be clean, and basic materials and hardware need to be stocked. We want to be flexible, so fixtures and furnishings are designed to be multipurpose, easy to move, and modular. As patron demands change, the space should be malleable and accommodating. The goal is to create an open, inviting space where people feel comfortable to create and share. They need to see it as their space.

To that end, while libraries vary widely in size, scope of services, and staffing, there are some basic rules of thumb that should guide your design and build-out process:

- *Accessibility and usability:* Workshop areas should allow 75 to 100 square feet of independent work space per person so people don't get in one another's way, maximizing safety and productivity, and all work spaces should ideally be accessible directly from common traffic areas without the need to pass through other rooms and spaces, as well as inclusive in design and furnishings and accessible by those with physical disabilities when possible. For libraries in the United States, this means compliance with the Americans with Disabilities Act (ADA).
- *Lighting:* Appropriate lighting for close work or working with machinery and tools is important. You want bright, even lighting that doesn't produce distracting shadows.
- *Power distribution:* There should be plenty of easily accessible power receptacles distributed throughout your makerspace areas, with dedicated circuits for power-hungry electrical equipment.
- *Storage:* Many of the makerspaces that participated in our survey said they wished they'd taken storage into consideration earlier in their planning stages. Consider storage solutions for everything from consumables to tools.

- *Safety and security:* Spaces need to be designed with safety in mind, allowing for 25 to 35 percent open floor space, required by most fire codes, with easy access to first-aid stations and exits, and good signage throughout.
- *Adaptability:* The most successful spaces pivot easily, adapting to the changing needs and interests of users. Thus, it is important to build with adaptability in mind, rather than rigid permanence.

We'll also take a brief look at mobile makerspaces, with respect to mobile Maker stations, as well as vehicular-based makerspaces. This section also assumes that libraries have done their homework and are building the space their community wants, not putting in a room full of 3D printers when patrons are more interested in music or cooking, or vice versa. We'll only briefly touch on tools and equipment in this chapter, with chapter 7 being your go-to section for those.

Your mileage will vary on final makerspace designs, as actual usage determines what works and what doesn't, and will likely necessitate some tweaks. As Ralph Waldo Emerson said, "A foolish consistency is the hobgoblin of little minds." And that's just as true in a library makerspace as with anything else. It will probably take at least a year before your new space settles into its most useful groove, and then you might discover that what you started with is not necessarily what everyone ended up enjoying or using the most. Listen to your users, and adjust accordingly.

ACCESSIBILITY AND USABILITY

Whether your library makerspace will be 500 square feet or 5,000 square feet, there are certain basic makerspace design principals that can be employed when building or adapting your creative space. The first thing you need to do is identify the type of space you're designing. You can ask the following questions:

- Are you integrating makerspace functionality into existing library space?
- Are you repurposing other separate spaces?

- Are you designing a "dirty" facility, where things are actually being made, or a "clean" facility, where people are mostly designing, or some combination of both?

The answers to these questions will help guide your design process.

Integrated Space

If you're integrating creative design space into your current floorplan by adding 3D printers or high-end computers with design software, or just carving out a corner of existing space to add a workbench or arts area, you'll probably want to stick to "clean" activities. Noise and traffic are two of the main things to take into consideration with an integrated space. Some of the benefits of integrated space are that they don't require any significant construction and provide ease of access and high visibility of offerings and resources to better inspire engagement and interaction among patrons.

However, integrated spaces require thoughtful placement and management. 3D printers are quieter than they used to be, but they still hum and rattle, and can run for several hours, depending on what's being printed. They can also pose minor hazards with the hot filament nozzles and baseplate. Some things you can do to ameliorate sound issues from a 3D printer

Hazel L. Incantalupo Makerspace. ***Hazel L. Incantalupo Makerspace***

might be to put the printer in an enclosed room, only operate it during certain times, or position it somewhere away from quiet reading and study areas.

The same thing holds true for integrated craft areas. Aside from the mess of craft leavings from vinyl cutters or paper craft, art and craft areas typically inspire a lot of conversation, which is an important part of the experience and shouldn't be discouraged. Hence, integrating an arts area into existing library space also calls for thoughtful scheduling and organization.

Repurposing Space

If you're repurposing study, meeting, or computer rooms, or other closed off, separate areas, there is a lot more leeway for creativity and functionality. The square footage you have to work with will determine what you can reasonably build within your repurposed space. You'll also have to establish whether you want to do physical structural changes or upgrades,

Land O'Lakes Library Foundry makerspace. ***The Foundry***

for example, adding new lighting or power and ventilation, or whether your build-out is largely based on furnishings and equipment that don't require any physical changes to the space.

Most of these decisions will be guided by the type of space you're designing. The shorthand descriptors are "dirty" and "clean" types of programming and equipment. In an article about designing makerspaces, *Make:* magazine defines "dirty" equipment as things like drill presses and saws, which produce dust and debris, and "clean" equipment as things like 3D printers, laser cutters, and vinyl cutters.[1] Those definitions generally hold, but we would adapt those descriptors a bit for libraries to take into consideration the debris or fumes from cutters and hand tools, and noise as well. The bottom line is, you don't want to have machines or tools that produce sawdust, for instance, next to computers used for design or things you want to keep clean, like textiles or electronics.

INCLUSIVITY AND ACCESSIBILITY

You also want your space to be inclusive and accessible. "The Maker Movement should not just be about rich, white males and the toys they can build and buy," says Sylvia Martinez, coauthor of *Invent to Learn.*[2] She is referencing a 2013 study by Leah Buechley, a former Massachusetts Institute of Technology Media Lab professor, who analyzed every *Make:* magazine cover between 2005 and 2013—36 covers total—and found that this premier magazine about making leaned most heavily toward such male-dominated interests as electronics (53 percent of covers), vehicles (31 percent), robots (22 percent), rockets (8 percent), and music (5 percent).[3]

One of Martinez's recommendations involves creating surroundings that appeal to a wide range of individuals, as your community interests dictate, but with an eye to being inclusive. Even if the general interest group involves woodworking, consider showcasing or displaying woodworking projects that appeal to everyone, in a variety of colors and textures. If your space is technically focused, for instance, things like "smart clothes" that integrate microcontrollers, sensors, and lights might be a more appealing way to engage a broader demographical range of your community than just showcasing robotics.

Martinez also recommends providing incentives—"multiple on-ramps, praise, and glory for all kinds of making." An easy and attractive way to do that is to showcase a variety of work, actual and potential, in display cases, which helps people see what's happening in the space and serves to inspire and encourage everyone to get involved. Using a device like the electronic Silhouette cutting tool, as opposed to 3D printers, can better engage older patrons in technology as they use the programmable paper, vinyl, and textile cutter for such traditional crafts as scrapbooking or quilting. As a result of a craft session that employed the Silhouette cutter, said Stephens, about a third of participants—mostly older women—wanted to learn to use the machine and have access to it.

Accessibility is another important aspect of makerspace design, especially in libraries where everyone should have an opportunity to get involved, enjoy creative programs, and use tools and resources. Accessibility doesn't just refer to ADA-type access, with appropriate access for wheelchairs and other assistive technologies. It also involves making a space accessible to those with cognitive, visual, and other impairments.[4] Accessibility also extends to patrons on the autism spectrum, as well as those with developmental disabilities who can be better accommodated through staff awareness, quiet make sessions, and special sensory projects.

The University of Washington Access Engineering program has developed a set of "Guidelines for Accessibility and Universal Design" for makerspaces. The guidelines call for creating a "culture of inclusion and universal design as early as possible," ideally during your planning and design process, making it an intentional part of your library makerspace design. Some key considerations during the planning stage are as follows:

- Include people with a variety of disabilities in the planning and setup of your makerspace.
- Provide a way for people to give feedback and recommendations on adaptive and accessible equipment.
- Have detailed, well-organized documents in accessible formats, including large print, describing the rules and best practices for the makerspace.
- Ensure that websites and other publications include images of users from diverse backgrounds and abilities.

Some things to consider with respect to the actual spaces you're designing:

- Ensure that pathways and entrances are wheelchair-accessible and clearly marked, and connected via an accessible route of travel.
- Make sure signage and equipment labels are high-contrast and in large print, especially for information related to safety.
- Plan for aisles that are wide and clear of such obstructions as wires and cables for people with mobility or visual impairments.
- Include safety procedures for users with hearing, visual, or mobility impairments.
- Whiteboards and other tools should be accessible from a seated position. Consider painting the makerspace walls with whiteboard paint so the walls become an accessible creative surface.
- Tables should be height adjustable, but at the very least there should be resources for making tables and workspaces accessible. Wheels on mobile furniture should lock into place.
- Ensure that tools are usable by both right- and left-handed people, and that power cords, including those suspended from the ceiling, are out of walkways and easily accessible and adjustable.
- Include magnifying lenses and desk lamps in your design.
- Make sure storage for projects and supplies is clearly labeled and easily accessible.

When evaluating tools and equipment for your space, take the following into consideration:

- Users should have easy operational access, for example, hand- or switch-operated sewing machines for people who can't use pedals and accessible print surfaces on 3D printers and laser cutters, along with easily readable instructions and information related to equipment.
- Keep hand tools organized and clearly labeled, with rubberized grips and plastic guards on sharp tools.
- Electronics components storage should be organized, easily accessible, and clearly labeled.
- Avail your space of assistive technologies for computers whenever possible, with things like trackballs, alternative keyboards, screen readers, and speech-to-text software.[5]

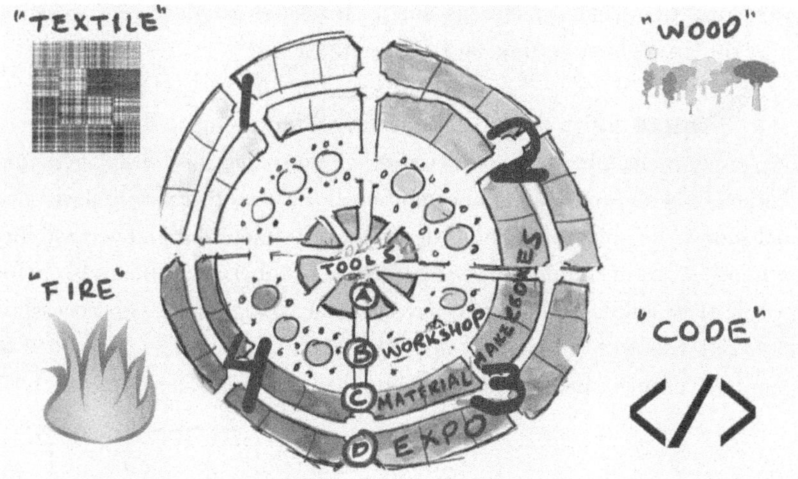

Ambient signage. ***Åke Nygren***

Other design principles to take into consideration involve the basic ambiance of a space, writes Åke Nygren, project leader at the Digital Library at the Stockholm Public Library in Sweden. "All kinds of 'stuff' is loaded with symbolism and connotations in terms of intentions, gender, and culture," Nygren contends in the working paper *Digital Interfaces and Material as "Signage" in a Library Makerspace.*[6]

His design recommendation

> takes as a starting pointing the insight that material/stuff is very much linked to culture and that a library makerspace needs to create environments that bridge the gap between different creative cultures. The idea of the design is to bring different creative bubbles closer to one another, open up for unexpected meetings across interest groups, foment crossover interaction, and thereby facilitate innovation.

Essentially, Nygren suggests grouping by affinity:

- Textiles, with related materials, equipment, and activities
- Wood and related items and activities
- Code, or computer- and Internet of Things-related equipment and activities

- Fire, or meltable materials and heat-related activities (e.g, plastics, soldering, laser cutting, and 3D printing)

This type of design thinking, while visually appealing and socially inviting, requires planning for the separation of "dirty" versus "clean" activities that might be in proximity to one another. But it's another way to design for inclusion. The great thing about designing with inclusion and accessibility in mind is that everything that helps people of differing abilities also helps people of all abilities. Good space layout, clear signage, and easily accessible tools and resources are good for not only people with special needs, but also people of all ages, shapes, heights, cultural backgrounds, and so forth.

BEST PRACTICES

A great way to inspire community engagement and a sense of ownership by users, suggested Stephens, is to employ the Tom Sawyer effect:

> We turned the painting of our makerspace into a class on the patching, prep, and painting of walls. Several patrons came in on a Saturday, and a professional painter volunteered to teach the basics of painting while they practiced on the room. We got our space painted with professional oversight, our patrons had an educational opportunity, and we saved some money.
>
> Our workbenches were designed and built as an Eagle Scout project by a young library patron. Even the assembly of our makerspace furnishings was done as a service project by our robotics team. Many of the jobs associated with the makerspace build-out can be turned into learning experiences for your patrons and give them a sense of agency in the makerspace process. Crowdsourcing promotes a sense of community.

With respect to makerspace build-out, Stephens said, "Most libraries, whether they're county branches or part of a school, will have to work closely with some other department for any major changes in their space. How we relate to those other departments will have a great impact on the development of our makerspace." He recommended doing your homework so you can communicate your needs clearly to facilities personnel and setting realistic goals and expectations. There's also a lot to be said for employing makerspace staff that hails from outside the traditional library staff and MLS (master in library science) community. When one of the Pasco County Libraries wanted a recording studio built, it turned out to be outside the scope of what the county facilities department had ever done. There was some discussion about using a local general contractor, but that was outside budget feasibility.

Nonetheless, when the library cooperative hired Chuck Stephens, they were able to tap into his real-world tradesman skills, and he was able to lead the design of the new studio, in conjunction with Facilities Maintenance, turning the design ideas of the musicians into off-the-shelf solutions the tradesmen understand.

The Magic Triangle

There are some great resources for pre-build-out research in the do-it-yourself (DIY) community—hobbyists, home builders, and crafters who pursued home improvement and garage mechanics long before being a "Maker" was a thing. Among the most basic of best practices is the idea that the most efficient workspace design is triangular, with the most important workstations at the three corners of the triangle.[7]

In the case of a workshop that might handle wood and metal, for instance, you'll want your raw materials near your largest equipment in one "corner" of your triangle so things aren't being carried across the workspace. The second point of your triangle would be a workbench or work area to design or assemble. The third point would be a finishing station, with appropriate tools and equipment, including any necessary special ventilation. Organizing your space, regardless of its size, in a way that minimizes cross-traffic and makes appropriate workspace easily accessible will also make it easier to maintain and consequently safer, more inviting, and better used.

DESIGNING FOR TOOLS AND TOOL USE

Tools occupy two types of space in a workshop:

1. Stationary physical square or cubic footage required for storage, as in the case of hand tools, or standing floor space, in the case of things like drill presses or laser cutters

2. Operational space, which expands according to the size of materials being used with the tools or machinery

Thus, while a drill press might take up about five square feet, if the material being worked on is a few feet long or wide, you'll need to reserve at least that much more space plus space for the tool operator for safe and comfortable room to work.

It's also important to consider the differences between freestanding and benchtop tools. In one respect, benchtop tools give added functionality to a workbench, but in another, they reduce workbench space, because of their benchtop footprint and the loss of space at the bench if someone is using one of the tools; however, benchtop tools can also be configured for easy removal to store away when not in use.

Stephens reminded us that, ideally, makerspace furnishings will be determined by the interests of your user community:

> If your makerspace has an emphasis on woodworking, solid workbenches and tables will be necessary. If it's sewing and fiber arts, lighter-duty furnishings will suffice. The biggest concern is the best use of space. . . . Be creative in sourcing your furnishings. One county I work with has a Central Stores warehouse full of old furniture and equipment that they are using to furnish their new makerspace. Another branch had the workbenches in their makerspace built by a patron as his Eagle Scout project. Don't forget that you're a makerspace—if all else fails you can make your own benches and tables! Make the building of the makerspace furnishings the first makerspace project.

Stephens said not to forget "chillspace"—a place where users can gather outside the workspace to help facilitate creativity and sharing, which is the point of the Maker movement:

> Furnishings will help define the culture of the space. Paint things. Cover them in stickers. Add a giant stenciled logo to all the tabletops. Theme it to look like a pirate's den or a spaceship. Use furniture, lighting, layout, and decorations to create a space that promotes creativity, provides access to tools, and reflects the user base. Have fun and trust your patrons to take co-ownership of the space.

LIGHTING

Good lighting in a work space of any kind is important, but it's also an often-overlooked part of makerspace development in libraries. Rich with fluorescent overhead fixtures, most libraries are usually pretty well set for good overall lighting. But once workbenches and cabinets are in place, or fabric on cutting tables, the need for more specialized lighting often becomes apparent.

"Room lighting defines the space and provides illumination for general-purpose activities in the space," said Stephens, adding,

> Work lights are typically job-specific, but a variety of fixed and temporary lighting fixtures are vital. Permanent work lights include recessed halogen or LED spots under cabinets, track lights above benches, and amiable ceiling fixtures. Temporary lighting fixtures include hanging work lights, gooseneck lamps, Anglepoise desk lamps, portable halogen work lights, and a bunch of those cheap clamp-on lights with the stamped tin reflectors.

If you want to get into the nuts and volts of appropriate lighting in a workshop space, the experts say a typical hobby workspace should be evenly lighted to 50 or 100 foot-candles (fc), depending on the age of those using the workspace: 50 fc for those age 25 or younger and 100 fc for older patrons, who naturally have more visual challenges (even if they say they don't). And 3,500-kelvin lamps give the most neutral lighting.[8]

Moreover, not all lighting is illumination, Stephens reminded us:

> Plan for projectors, interfaces, and screens. Built-in projectors are useless if they're aimed at a workbench or need a ladder and adapters to plug anything in. Consider placement and lightfastness of any UV sources—lasers, screen-print exposure lamps, safety goggle sterilizers, welding arcs, etc. Also consider natural light from outside. Can the windows be covered to show a video or use a projector?

And use what you've got or at least what you're becoming. "You're a makerspace," said Stephens. "Make some cool decorative lighting fixtures! Sculptural lamps in your lounge area or a junk chandelier over your entrance create an opportunity to showcase creative talent in your space and help promote a unique makerspace culture that reflects the patron base."

POWER DISTRIBUTION

Power is king in a makerspace and needs to be a key part of the design and build process. When we designed the John F. Germany Public Library makerspace in Tampa, we were delighted by the wealth of power available throughout the third-floor space, which was being repurposed for the HIVE. Huge columns span the length of the 10,000-square-foot space, with multiple outlets on each so that almost anywhere something needed electricity it was possible to supply it. Obviously, while amazingly fortuitous for the HIVE, abundance of power to that degree is a rarity.

Most library makerspaces are going to need to plan for additional power. And even in the case of the HIVE, with its abundant power, they only had standard outlets. Some tools draw a lot of power and require a dedicated 220-volt circuit, which would require a visit from facilities.

"Here's the rule for running power in a makerspace," Stephens declared:

> Figure out exactly how many receptacles you will need and double it, with provisions to expand it further later. While most makerspaces will start out in a repurposed room and use the power that's available, it's best to start over fresh with exposed conduit and surface boxes. This allows the power distribution to be expanded, modified, or changed later without having to tear open walls or resort to rats' nests of extension cords. This is how real shops do it.

Indeed, professionals outfitting real shops recommend diagramming a solid electrical plan as you design your workshop to help determine the locations of electrical outlets, dedicated circuits, receptacle heights, and so on.[9] While things like small power tools can be plugged into a safety-type GFCI (ground-fault circuit interrupter)-equipped outlet, big equipment like table saws or drill presses should have its own dedicated circuit.

Outlet placement is also important. In a workshop, it's helpful to have outlets located higher on a wall than usual to make access from workbenches or work tables easier. Many libraries also have flush mounted floor outlets that can be effectively used in a makerspace. The more easily accessible the power, the less need there will be for extension cords, which can pose both safety and organizational challenges.

Stephens also pointed out that there are more options than the standard three-prong outlet, relating,

> Add USB charging ports, GFCI safety outlets, bench-mounted strips, and hanging, retractable outlets. No one has ever complained about having too many open receptacles!
>
> Consider backup/alternative power. You may not be able to run your entire space on solar, but what about a charging station powered by a single panel? Add a battery or two and use it to power emergency lighting in your space. Don't forget basic UPCs (uninterruptable power supply) for your computers in case of a power outage, too.

STORAGE

Almost every library we've worked with has experienced the challenge of storage. Storage is already an issue in libraries without makerspaces, for collections, program materials, computers, arts and crafts supplies, and so forth. If you're adding a makerspace to your facility, your storage challenges just increased—a lot. But this also presents a great opportunity to evaluate what's actually used and what's just eternally stored. One library we worked with had a long, endless storage closet—easily 20 feet deep, with only one door at a far end. No one had been to the back of that closet in years. Our recommendation was to add a door at the other end and start excavating.

If you're going into the makerspace business, it's time to learn to curate. "Curation is making the decision of what comes and what goes," Stephens stated. He continued,

> This is making sure there are not 20 Philips screwdrivers and only two slotted. Curation is giving a firm "no" to the guy wanting to donate a "classic" green phosphor CRT monitor. It's ensuring you don't have 30 crates of yarn and no knitting needles. Curation is also deciding when things need to go. The one-year rule is handy: If it hasn't been used in a year and there's a better use for the space, then it goes. Curation can be broken up by departments or set by policy, but it has to happen or you'll be overrun in no time.

The importance of making storage a primary part of the design process and planning for good storage well in advance of building your makerspace and starting programming cannot be overstated. But storage also isn't an exact science.

In an excellent report called "Creating Space: The Impacts of Spatial Arrangements in Public Library Makerspaces," developed by Shannon Crawford Barniskis in the School of Information Studies at the University of Wisconsin–Milwaukee, Crawford Barniskis describes the experience of visiting a small library makerspace in upstate New York:

> When I arrived in the space, craft and electronics supplies were visible in open wire bins. These bins contributed to a sense of "storage room," which confused patrons wondering whether they were able to come in. The bins also showcased the variety of creative activities possible in the space.

Two weeks later, she returned to find the bins replaced with cabinets in an apparent attempt to better organize the space and keep sawdust and other debris out of the "clean" Maker projects, and better secure supplies. Writes Crawford Barniskis,

> While the cabinets solve parts of this problem, they present another: How will people know that they can use the equipment in them? Some users said they would open the cabinets, but others said they would not feel comfortable doing so. One library user said that, even with signs, she would not open the cabinets. The cabinets reduce clues about what types of making might be possible in the space.[10]

Chuck Stephens had some suggestions for addressing this common human behavior:

> Organization covers tool placement and storage, as well as materials storage and accessibility. An open storage plan, where everything is accessible, visible, and inviting, encourages spontaneous creativity and exploration. Patrons are more likely to pull a tool off a shelf than out of a closed cabinet.
>
> Placing common tools on a pegboard with silhouettes and labels makes tool inventory easy, teaches patrons the names of the tools, and encourages clean work surfaces. All storage needs to be accessible and labeled to ensure that tools and materials get used. Make tool storage self-evident to ensure

> patron cooperation. Silhouettes give a visual feedback that something is missing. I like the *Mythbusters* approach—a wall of steel shelves with labeled Rubbermaid containers. This makes it clear what you have while taking the least amount of space possible.

In "Workshop Design Part 3," master woodworker Phil Rasmussen notes that most of the workshops he has seen don't have enough storage space or maximize possible storage space within their facilities, and his advice for home workshops applies just as readily to the library makerspace.

> Fixed benchtops usually have cabinets underneath them. In some shops, there are also wall cabinets spread around the shop; however, most of these wall cabinets are limited, small, and do not go to the ceiling. This is a big mistake not only in kitchen design, but even more so in the workshop. The open space above the cabinets is a dust accumulation paradise. Often, the top has molding around it, and if things are placed on the cabinet top they are soon forgotten. When constructing wall cabinets make them tall enough to go to the ceiling, thus providing extra storage space and reducing dust accumulation.[11]

He also notes that other potential storage space often goes underutilized.

> Open and closed storage shelves and drawers can be easily constructed to fit under the workbench. A moveable cabinet on wheels can be made to fit under the table saw extension. Under the bottom shelf of most bench cabinets there is storage space for all those plastic cases that your power tools come in.

Good labeling and signage is also important. "Label everything," exhorted Stephens. He elaborated,

> Organize things by discipline: woodwork, metalwork, electronics, art, sewing, etc. Add signs to designate storage areas for specific things. Be very clear about what goes where.
>
> Develop your Jawa instinct! Junk comes and goes. Some junk is awesome. Anything old and mechanical is great for a deconstruction event with kids. Some old organs are full of amazing things if you have musical Makers in your community. A stack of old hard drives provides the materials for a variety of cool projects. Make the hard decisions about the balance between the value of the stuff versus the value of its footprint.

> Don't store anything; transfer it. If it's not going to a class or a specific project, then it better be pretty awesome! Institute a "free" table for things that have been around too long. Offer something weird and bulky as a "design challenge." Get creative.

And also have a written policy about supplies and materials, and how to handle consumables—things like 3D printer filament, fasteners, paints, and textiles. Decide before you build your space how you want to handle donations, because people will donate everything they've been saving in their garage as potentially useful once they see a makerspace in place. If you don't want to see old electronics dropped off at the library or crates of yarn and boxes of old tools, make sure you have signage to that effect and a written policy that outlines donations protocols clearly, and how and when to dispose of unwanted items.

SAFETY AND SECURITY

Signage and good documentation also figure significantly in the safety and security department. It is important to make sure makerspace users are well versed in safety protocols regarding the use of any library makerspace tools or equipment, from sewing machines to shop tools and 3D printers, as well as creating a generally safe space where everyone is welcome and included. You also want to make sure your patron users feel secure when they're in the space, that their projects can be protected, and that the library's tools and resources are maintained in a secure fashion. The last thing you want is for expensive tools and equipment to go walking out the door.

The *Makerspace Playbook*, designed to aid in the creation of school makerspaces, has a great section on safety and a number of other recommendations that are equally applicable to library makerspaces. To paraphrase from the playbook, there's a fine line between informing users about the potential dangers inherent in a makerspace and discouraging them from or frightening them about using or supporting the makerspace. The same holds true for the library's risk management department, except the line seems even finer.[12]

As a matter of fact, the playbook points out, "While accidents happen when the proper steps aren't taken, many millions, perhaps billions, of

Good signage. ***Theresa Willingham***

people make with dangerous equipment every day without incident."[13] If you plan ahead, codify safety and security protocols, and message clearly with accessible, written policies and prominent and plentiful signage, your library makerspace will likely be free of any incidents.

The key is creating a "culture of safety" from the beginning. Creating a culture of safety starts with having a codified makerspace safety policy that includes adequate training and cleanup protocols, plus bold signage that reinforces and reiterates safety and security best practices prominently and often. It's also important to enforce those policies, because letting things go makes things go south pretty quickly.

Some basic best practices with respect to maintaining safety and security, as well as accommodating inclusivity and accessibility, are as follows:

- Design with safety and security in mind, taking into consideration the build-out best practices discussed earlier in this chapter, including clear access to workspaces, separating "clean" and "dirty" Maker areas, appropriate ventilation, adequate storage, and documented use policies.
- If you'll have large tools, be sure to use lockout devices or provide adequate supervision and protocols for using equipment.

- Use clean, clear, specific signage—not handwritten signs, but digital signage on monitors, wherever possible, and laminated signage with large type that identifies tools and their intended uses, requisites for using tools or equipment (e.g., required classes or orientations), cleanup policies (and consequences for not following them, e.g., probationary usage of space),[14] and common safety rules.[15]
- Label everything clearly, from tools and their storage places to first aid supplies.
- Ensure that safety equipment (e.g., fire extinguishers and alarms) is well identified and can be accessed by people in wheelchairs or with other physical challenges.
- Make sure safety gear is prominent, clearly labeled, and accessible (e.g., first aid stations, safety glasses, and hearing protection dispensers), and ensure such reusable items as safety glasses are regularly cleaned and disinfected.
- Ensure that staff is trained to enforce safety policies and that they themselves adhere to those protocols.

MOBILE MAKERSPACES

Some libraries will call pop-up or mobile Maker stations within their facilities "mobile makerspaces." But there are also mobile library makerspaces akin to book mobiles—a vehicle stocked with some assortment of Maker gear that goes on the road and transports creative tools and resources to citizens in the community. We'll take a brief look at both options.

Mobile Maker Stations

As detailed in an excellent *School Library Journal* piece by librarians in Knox County School District in Knoxville, Tennessee, they used a $50,000 grant to develop a series of themed mobile Maker carts.[16] They created four different types of mobile Maker stations, which consisted of appropriately stocked carts in the areas of art, STEM (science, technology, engineering, and math), production, and 3D printing. The Knox County librarians used large-wheeled totes and flexible "wagons," but you can also use rolling metal carts and wheeled work and storage benches designed for everything from sewing to cooking.

Maker carts or mobile activity stations are great for libraries that don't have space to repurpose into physical makerspace or just want to gauge community interest. They do require their own level of organizational planning with respect to inventory management and maintenance but can be a good solution for smaller libraries or those with limited Maker content interest in their communities.

Mobile Maker Vehicles

Actual mobile makerspaces, built into buses or vans that travel around, are less common in the United States than in Europe, but the development process for a mobile makerspace is about the same as for an in-house makerspace, plus some transportation safety and security consideration, and a different level of risk management. But it serves the admirable mission of bringing the Maker experience to those who are remote from library makerspaces or lacking transportation to get to one.

FryskLab[17] was Europe's first mobile library-powered FabLab, developed by Dutch librarian Jeroen De Boer, a contributor to this book and coauthor of our previous book, *Makerspaces in Libraries* (Rowman & Littlefield, 2015). FryskLab was initiated by a public library service organization (Bibliotheekservice Fryslân), in close collaboration with team members with scientific, educational, and technological backgrounds. As a FabLab, FryskLab is equipped with the standard FabLab resources, including 3D printers, laser cutters, vinyl cutters, and hand tools. FryskLab also has 3D doodler pens, MacBook Airs, and electronics kits like MaKey MaKeys and littleBits, with such related software as Scratch, Doodle3D, Cura, and more. The mobile FabLab hosts related programming on digital fabrication and media and Web literacy for educators.

In the United States, the best example of a mobile library makerspace is San Jose Public Library's Maker[Space]Ship.[18] The customized bus, funded through grants, is Wi-Fi equipped and stocked with 3D printers, a laser cutter, A/V equipment, induction cooking elements, science gear (e.g., microscopes), and much more. The Maker[Space]Ship operates 15 hours a week at public and private locations ranging from schools to senior centers.

The San Jose Public Library has helpfully published a *Mobile Makerspace Guide*[19] to help other libraries interested in developing a similar program.

Key considerations in the development of physical mobile makerspaces like FryskLab or Maker[Space]Ship are, of course, the type of vehicle to be used and related investments in securing the vehicle, insurance and maintenance expenses, and properly equipping and securing said equipment in the vehicle, as well as staffing.

ADAPTABILITY

We'll end this chapter where we started, with a reminder that the main thing to design for in a library makerspace, stationary or mobile, is really adaptability and flexibility, because the best makerspaces are never really "finished" and should be considered works in progress as patron interest and usage varies throughout time. As people become accustomed to the idea of making and get better versed in available equipment, some will want new challenges and more sophisticated equipment. In some cases, things people were initially interested in, for example, 3D printing, may become less popular as the novelty wears off. Design so you can pivot easily, and be willing and able to change up everything from space layout to program offerings and tools and equipment. Some good practices for building with adaptability in mind include the following:

- Use movable workspaces and tables with locking wheels.
- Track tool and space usage closely to have a real-time measure of use and interest.
- Solicit user feedback regularly and, more importantly, listen to it. Recruit Makers from the community to share what they do as part of your regular programming, which can help drive and inspire new interests,
- Conduct an annual internal evaluation of your makerspace to gather feedback from staff and volunteers.

Now we're ready to look at programming ideas for your well-planned, flexible library makerspace.

NOTES

1. Baddock, Alex. "Six Essential Tips for Designing Your Makerspace's Layout." *Make:*. September 22, 2016. Accessed April 6, 2017. http://makezine.com/2016/09/23/6-tips-makerspace-layout-design/.

2. Martinez, Sylvia. "Making for All: How to Build an Inclusive Makerspace." *EdSurge*. July 10, 2016. Accessed April 6, 2017. www.edsurge.com/news/2015-05-10-making-for-all-how-to-build-an-inclusive-makerspace.

3. Quattrocchi, Christina. "MAKE'ing More Diverse Makers." *EdSurge*. October 29, 2013. Accessed April 6, 2017. www.edsurge.com/news/2013-10-29-make-ing-more-diverse-makers.

4. Klipper, Barbara. "Could a Child with a Disability Use Your Makerspace?" *Association for Library Service to Children*. July 31, 2014. Accessed April 6, 2017. www.alc.ala.org/blog/2014/08/could-a-child-with-a-disability-use-your-makerspace/.

5. "Making a Makerspace? Guidelines for Accessibility and Universal Design." *DO-IT*. 2015. Accessed April 6, 2017. www.washington.edu/doit/making-maker-space-guidelines-accessibility-and-universal-design.

6. Nygren, Åke. *Digital Interfaces and Material as "Signage" in a Library Makerspace*. Working paper. N.p.: n.p., n.d. Print.

7. "The Workshop Triangle." *DIY Network*. March 24, 2015. Accessed April 6, 2017. www.diynetwork.com/how-to/skills-and-know-how/workshops/the-workshop-triangle.

8. Lindsey, Jack. "Lighting the Small Workshop." *Sawmill Creek Woodworking Community RSS*. Accessed April 6, 2017. www.sawmillcreek.org/content.php?146-Lighting-the-Small-Workshop-by-Jack-Lindsey.

9. "The Ultimate Workshop: Lighting and Electrical Layout." *DIY Network*. March 14, 2015. Accessed April 6, 2017. www.diynetwork.com/how-to/skills-and-know-how/workshops/the-ultimate-workshop-lighting-and-electrical-layout.

10. Crawford Barniskis, Shannon. "Creating Space: The Impacts of Spatial Arrangements in Public Library Makerspaces." Proceedings of the 2016 World Library and Information Congress. The Hague, Netherlands: International Federation of Library Associations and Institutions.

11. Rasmussen, Phil. "Workshop Design Part 3: Storage Options, Electricity, and HVAC." *Wood News Online*. 2014. Accessed April 6, 2017. www.highland-woodworking.com/woodworking-tips-1401jan/workshopdesign.html.

12. *Makerspace Playbook: School Edition*. *MakerEd.org*. Spring 2013. Accessed April 6, 2017. https://makered.org/wp-content/uploads/2014/09/Makerspace-Playbook-Feb-2013.pdf.

13. *Makerspace Playbook*, 13.

14. "Safety in School Makerspaces." *Make:*. October 23, 2015. Accessed April 6, 2017. http://makezine.com/2013/09/02/safety-in-school-makerspaces/.

15. "Common Safety Rules." *Make:*. August 2013. Accessed April 6, 2017. http://cdn.makezine.com/uploads/2013/08/commonsafetyrules.pdf.

16. Sutton, Roger, Amanda MacGregor, Elizabeth Bird, Brigid Alverson, Karen Jensen, Roger Sutton, Robin Willis, and Travis Jonker. "Mobile Maker Spaces." *School Library Journal*. May 3, 2016. Accessed April 6, 2017. ww.slj.com/2016/05/technology/mobile-maker-spaces/#_.

17. "FryskLab/FabLabs." *FabLab Network*. Accessed April 6, 2017. www.fablabs.io/labs/frysklab.

18. "Maker[Space]Ship." *San Jose Public Library*. January 9, 2017. Accessed April 6, 2017. www.sjpl.org/makerspaceship.

19. Berman, Erin, and Parker Thomas. *Mobile Makerspace Guide. San Jose Public Library*. Accessed April 6, 2017. www.sjpl.org/sites/default/files/documents/MobileMakerspaceGuideBook.pdf.

5

MAKERSPACE PROGRAMMING

The Possibilities Are Endless

A "Maker program" should "allow, generate, or foster an output of new ideas, a physical product, or a new skill learned."

—Brian Pichman, Evolve Project[1]

Whether you build out a full makerspace facility or simply carve out some auxiliary spaces for creative programming via passive, pop-up, or mobile makerspaces, the types of programming you offer can either complement or diminish your makerspace efforts. If your programming is top-down, library-created content, there's no incentive or inspiration for building a strong, community-owned user base. But if you don't offer at least some Maker-style programming related to your makerspace, it's hard to introduce people to your space and the tools and resources available to them or help them see the possibilities.

Makerspace programming is a balancing act of content, frequency, and focus. It's tempting to incorporate every children's programming session into your makerspace, and if you have an arts and crafts or youth science and tech-focused space, that might not be a bad idea. But if you're trying to appeal to a broader audience or your community fact-finding has suggested a totally different type of programming, rolling regular library programming into your makerspace will only water it down.

A "Maker program" says Brian Pichman of the Evolve Project, which works with libraries throughout the world to create makerspaces and

FabLabs, should "allow, generate, or foster an output of new ideas, a physical product, or a new skill learned."[2]

Ideally, your programming should reflect the community driving the development of your makerspace and be provided equally by makerspace users and library staff and volunteers. The more your programming can be driven by those who use the space, the more robust your community support will be, which is good for alleviating work stress on staff and securing year-round funding. But staff-driven programming can be invaluable for introducing concepts, tools, and ideas that participants will then feel empowered to pursue on their own.

While libraries often categorize programming by age range—preschool, elementary, tween, teen, and adult—that can be a bit arbitrary, since what appeals to a 20-something is not likely to appeal to an 80-something. Pichman also recommends separating by skill set, rather than age, particularly with educational programming, and avoiding stereotypes for participants in promotional materials, showing, for instance, both males and females knitting for a textiles program.

In this chapter, for our purposes, we're going to look at programming based on different categories of user interest.

- Hobby programming (the different things people like to do that aren't work related, from woodworking and quilting, to music and hobby electronics projects, to arts, including handcraft, A/V, and graphic arts)
- Professional programming (including skills development and entrepreneurial programming)
- Educational programming for adults and youth (including skills development)
- Youth-specific programming
- Civic programming (e.g., community gardens and other community projects, like Habitat for Humanity, Little Free Libraries, and a variety of civic or community engagement projects)

At the end of this chapter, we'll look at some tools and resources for making it as efficient and effective as possible to provide programming.

HOBBY PROGRAMMING

We'll start with hobbies since that's one of the key interests served in library makerspaces and, indeed, with much of modern library programming, ranging from cosplay costuming to cooking. Hobbies are big business in the United States, with the Association for Creative Industries (AFCI) valuing the industry at $43 billion in 2016.[3] According to AFCI surveys, the crafts with the highest levels of household participation in 2016 were:

- Painting and drawing (41.0 million)
- Edible (culinary) arts (39.7 million)
- Kids crafts (37.0 million)
- Paper crafts (36.5 million)
- Sewing and fabric crafts (32.2 million)

The report also found that 63 percent of U.S. households participated in at least one creative activity during the period surveyed, and 60 percent of females and 40 percent of males make up the overall participation in most crafts.

These categories also neatly sum up the major categories of Maker interest in libraries. But there's more to it than knowing that drawing and painting are the top hobby interests and putting in easels and paints, and calling it a day. The fact is, regardless of national trends, the only trends that matter when it comes to library makerspaces are the trends and interests in your own library community. Thus, before you embark on any hobby-related programming, make sure you know what interests your community the most.

That information will come from the focus groups you hopefully conducted earlier. But even then, stay nimble. The things people say they want may (and likely will) change as they try out or learn about new things. Hence, plan on regularly reevaluating interest in and the effectiveness of your programming.

Types of Hobby Programming

That's exactly what Idaho Libraries did in Boise when the Boise Public Library launched a series of winter Maker programs designed for adults and then surveyed participants for their feedback.They focused on a broad range of topics using community experts to provide the sessions, holding one program a month for five months. To reach the most people possible, they chose a different branch each month and varied the date and time of workshop sessions. The real payoff was what they learned after the sessions.

According to Sarah Chase of the Idaho Commission for Libraries,

> Based on surveys and attendance, we learned that adults in our community between the ages of 24 and 68 are looking for both hands-on programming and interactive conversations about maker-type hobbies. We are expanding our offerings this fall and actively finding new partners.[4]

Through a careful selection of programs, rolled out for a limited time frame at different libraries, the Boise Public Library was able to get a good pulse on patron interest and plan accordingly to provide the types of hobby programming their users indicated most interested them. Some eye-catching examples of Boise's offerings are as follows:

- "Intro to Home Brewing"
- "Intro to Soldering"
- "Intro to Arduino"
- "Tiny Houses"

"Intro" classes are excellent for introducing patrons to some of the tools and resources in a particular makerspace. There are also "stealth" ways to introduce new tools and skills. In a card-making class, Maker librarian Chuck Stephens, of Pasco County Library Cooperative, used the Silhouette electronic programmable craft cutter. People simply interested in the craft activity were introduced to a tool most of them knew nothing about and probably wouldn't have come to a dedicated class to learn about; however, Stephens reported that a third of the group became interested in learning more about the Silhouette cutter as a result of the craft class. Mission accomplished.

Look at programming that's a little more sophisticated than the usual arts and crafts fare, something beyond Perler beads and pasta necklaces, to things that introduce some science or technology, new skills, and tools.

Library voice. ***Theresa Willingham***

CraftLab, at the Library Makers blog (http://librarymakers.blogspot.com/search/label/CraftLab), offers some great examples, including the following:

- Pasta maker printing (repurposing pasta makers to make cardboard prints)
- DIY screen printing
- Paper making
- Needle felting

Along those lines, crafts like wool painting, making musical instruments (e.g., box drums and kalimbas), cartooning, graphic arts, making electronic wearables (e.g., clothing that integrates LEDs or conductive thread), special cooking programs, and ham radio can take library programming to another level beyond the traditional offerings.

Engaging Patrons

There are a couple of schools of thought on scheduled programming. On the one hand, having a scheduled, "open make" kind of access makes it possible for people who happen to be on-site during a workshop to indulge in spontaneous engagement. On the other hand, you usually have to know how much you need in the way of program supplies and materials to host an effective session. If you have experts from your community teaching classes or workshops, you also don't want to waste their time if no one shows up for an event, so preregistration is a good way to ensure you get at least the minimum to make it worth a guest teacher's time.

Some good ways to hedge your bets on active participation in Maker programming are:

- Listen to user feedback to make sure you're offering what patrons are interested in and have requested.
- Publicize early and often. Leverage social media, as well as printed materials, and post throughout your library.
- Engage local experts to teach and share their crafts and skills, from woodworking groups to local folk musicians and textile artists, and so forth, which can inspire participation and encourage others to share their skills as well.
- Show off publicly, in glass cases and on walls and shelves, what was made in other sessions so participants can see the results of programs.
- Tie in related books and other media from your collection in special displays leading up to sessions.
- Take photos and share the activity as it happens and afterward via social media, articles, and blog posts.
- Try the same idea a couple of different ways. For instance, there are lots of ways to approach print making. Try a few different versions and see which one engages people best.
- Keep asking for participant feedback, and keep listening to it.

Prepped for Success

For hobby-related programming especially, it's important to be prepared. That means doing the following:

- Have more supplies and materials than you think you need.
- Have workstations set up for participants with the materials they need for the program, with the relevant tools on hand.

- Know how to do the activity or program being offered. Whether it's you, a volunteer, or a guest teacher, whoever leads a program must be well versed in the project at hand. Don't offer something you don't understand or if you can't find someone knowledgeable to teach it.
- Make sure you have relevant safety measures in place, including things like safety glasses and the right tools in good shape for the project at hand.
- Start and end on time.
- Factor in time for questions and show and tell afterward so everyone can see what everyone else did or made.

Hobby programming in your makerspace can be a great way to introduce patrons to new tools and resources for their hobbies, and new ways of doing traditional handcrafts, resulting in powerful community building. Cosplay, for instance, can become an intergenerational learning opportunity when older people with skills in sewing and textile design and craft join together with younger people interested in creating their own cosplay costuming. Hence, it is important to take the time to understand the types of hobby programming your patrons are interested in and consider creative ways to serve those interests that will result in new skills development and awareness.

Digital Badges

One fun and useful way to encourage program participation is through a digital badging system. Digital badges (and actual ones if you want to get creative) can be incentivizing and motivating with respect to the subjects at hand, not to mention a useful way of identifying those who have completed orientations on different types of equipment, tools, or space use. Digital badges can also be tied directly to patron records, making it easier to see who is cleared to use spaces and equipment that might require training or orientation.

According to the Association of College and Research Libraries,

> Badges provide an opportunity for students to chart their goals and visualize their progress with incorporated feedback from faculty and peers. When students have the ability to customize their learning experience, it can amplify motivation by allowing for more autonomy over their educational path.[5]

The same holds true for patrons of all ages, helping move people toward competency based experiences that provide some visual measurement of achievement, which can also provide a metric for libraries measuring the impact of their programming.

PROFESSIONAL PROGRAMMING

Another type of programming service libraries can provide is more professional in nature: certifications, skills development, and training. There's a little overlap here between educational and professional programming, since some of the same types of programming—coding, for instance—can qualify for both categories. But for our purposes, we're talking about more high-level professional development that results in either certifications or a level of knowledge and experience that specifically relates to or produces some career benefit or workforce readiness.

According to a 2012 Online Computer Library Center report that appeared in an *American Libraries* story on the topic, public libraries provided small-business services to owners and employees 2.8 million times every month.

> One study estimated that the Free Library of Philadelphia (FLP) alone provided almost $4 million in direct support to local businesses in 2010—and that did not include the exponential return to the community in new revenues generated by the 8,700 businesses that FLP aided, as well as the ripple effects of the spending of those businesses' suppliers and employees in the local economy.[6]

Libraries already offer a great deal of professional and educational content, but the type of professional "Maker" programming we're talking about here includes not only things like Microsoft certification, but also Autodesk computer-aided drafting (AutoCAD) certifications, machine skills development, coding, and similar offerings. It also ramps up the technological aspects of offering this type of programming, for example, using library webinars or podcasts.

Certifications

Some libraries, for instance, Seattle Public Library, offer free Microsoft Office Specialist (MOS) certification exams, in their case as a part of the Microsoft IT Academy program. Certifications are available in MS Access, Excel, OneNote, Outlook, PowerPoint, SharePoint, and Word. The Microsoft Imagine Academy (www.microsoft.com/en-us/education/imagine-academy) provides libraries and their patrons with access to online courseware for technology training at no cost. The market value for Microsoft certification exams is typically about $120 per exam. Thus, providing opportunities for this type of professional skills development has a clear return on the investment in terms of quality library services and the actual economic impact of those services.

Other skills and workforce development programs can include training and professional development programs provided through collaborative partnerships with groups like SCORE, an association of volunteer business counselors, local Code for America groups comprised of civic-minded programmers and others. It's also important to appeal to young professionals, as well as older individuals, including veterans. Arlington (Virginia) Public Libraries (http://library.arlingtonva.us/explore/for-young-professionals) offers a wide range of programming aimed at young professionals, including such social opportunities as game nights and networking, interspersed with professional development opportunities. Digital badges can play an equally important role in professional and educational programming.

EDUCATIONAL/SKILLS PROGRAMMING (ADULT AND YOUTH)

Educational programming is also something with which libraries are typically quite familiar; however, the addition of a makerspace or Maker-style programming can put a new, exciting twist on the standard educational offerings, whether they're basic literacy skills or simple knowledge-based projects for the sake of knowledge itself. Makerspaces add to educational programming to potentially help users embrace everything from learning computer-aided drafting (CAD) to developing sewing skills or learning how to use anything from hand and power tools to customized graphic arts or video editing software and designing for 3D printing

3D Printing

When *Makerspaces in Libraries* came out in 2015, 3D printers in libraries were still new and relatively untried. Fayetteville Free Library FabLab, the nation's first library makerspace, was designed around the 3D printing phenomenon. Three or four years ago, 3D printers were an expensive novelty. Thus, having access in a public library was especially exciting and a great public asset. Today, they're fairly common in schools and libraries. As a matter of fact, the first sign of impending Maker programming in many libraries, for better or worse, is the appearance of a 3D printer.

However, while they're more common than they used to be and certainly far less expensive, and it's predicted that 50 percent of homes will have their own 3D printer by 2030,[7] there is still a fairly steep learning curve to designing a print, which hampers more wide-scale adoption at this point and makes libraries a perfect entry point to the device. Teaching 3D printing design is where libraries can provide the most useful programming here, in addition to providing the printing services themselves.

There are several common tools for teaching 3D printing, the most often used of which is Tinkercad (www.tinkercad.com/), which is relatively easy to master and includes a wealth of educational resources and online tutorials, as well as ready-made files for a variety of projects. 3D printing classes should also be an orientation requirement for anyone wishing to use library printers. There are also vast collections of 3D printing libraries, where files of existing designs can be found and reused.

In the spring of 2017, Dutch startup 3D Ninja launched iFind3D,[8] an online search engine with access to more than 740,000 3D designs. The search engine acts like the Kayak of 3D printing, bringing together all the online 3D design libraries, for example, Thingiverse, Shapeways, and many others, using 100 different variables running on IBM's Watson supercomputer to build the library. As of this writing, iFind3D can search 70 percent of online libraries and repositories, and expects to have 90 percent of the worldwide 3D printable designs indexed by the end of 2017, with the goal of making it easier for people to find printable 3D models across a wide range of needs and interests.

3D printing will remain a limited-access resource for most people, but teaching patrons how to use a 3D printer can empower them to use these high-end tools at the library for everything from small-scale hobby projects to household repairs, and open the door to such sophisticated tools as 3D scanners and related resources.

Drones

A few years ago, drones were a thing of science fiction and the Department of Defense. Today, you can buy little multicopters like the Whoop and big multirotor machines like the Phantom online. The machines are largely used for hobby and recreational fun, but they are in the educational category because there are some Federal Aviation Administration (FAA) rules and regulations of which users need to be aware, as well as various possible certifications. An additional educational component is building and programming drones, as well as learning to fly them.

Arapahoe (Colorado) Libraries has a robust tech program that includes drones. In an article for *Public Libraries Online*, Arapahoe's coordinator/supervisor of programming, Anthony White, says it's important to "really focus on what you are trying to accomplish with your program" if you decide to provide drone programming in your library.[9] It's especially important to

Drones. ***Theresa Willingham***

understand the various types of drones and what might be the most effective for your program.

Arapahoe uses Parrot's AR.Drone 2.0, which White says is one of the most widely available drones on the consumer market. One of the main things that needs to be taken into consideration is liability issues for injuries or damage, although the Parrot's rotors are small, plastic, and stop on impact. It's important to have trained staff and volunteers assisting with any program like this, be familiar with FAA regulations, and understand how drones work and how to fly them well.

Simulators

People don't often think of simulators in the context of public libraries, but they're there. The Dorothy Lumley Melrose Center (http://tic.ocls.info/simulation/) in Orlando, Florida, which we covered in *Makerspaces in Libraries* in 2015, is home to one of the largest public library collections of simulators, including the following:

- Triple screen flight simulator
- Touchscreen cockpit display
- Cockpit driving simulator
- Hydraulic excavator

That's a pretty expensive off-the-shelf collection, at approximately $10,000 per machine. Fortunately, there are also cost-effective ways to provide this unique offering, if there is interest in your library. Martin County (Florida) Library System librarian George Seaman works in the technology labs at the library, where using Microsoft Flight Simulator X and various Saitek controllers and radio panels, he created a desktop flight simulator for the library at a cost of about $5,000.[10] Today, he teaches six lessons every Friday to students ranging from three to 90-plus years old. The simulator is incredibly popular and housed in the center of the library, where anyone, at any time, can have access to it. Seaman reports that at least one of his students has been inspired to pursue a career in aviation as result of learning on the simulator.

Flight simulator. *Theresa Willingham*

Cafés

The "café" concept works well with this type of programming, and there are several existing models to work with, or you can create your own, unique to your library community. One concept worth considering is the café way, informal get-togethers with a particular focus or topic, with a resident expert acting as a kind of informational barista.

Science Café

The Science Café (www.sciencecafes.org/) concept grew out of NOVA PBS programming and consists of events that take place in casual settings—like coffee shops or libraries—and are open to the public. They feature an engaging conversation with a scientist about a particular topic and can also incorporate Citizen Science programming and topics, which are more hands-on and action oriented. The Science Café is not intended to be a long lecture program, but rather an interactive, dynamic experience between scientists and the public that empowers participants to learn and become more involved. They're a great fit for a public library makerspace.

Tech Cafés

Sewickley Public Library in Pennsylvania (https://calendly.com/tech-cafes-at-spl) hosts a series of Tech Cafés. The library lets patrons make one-on-one appointments with a variety of experts on any of several possible dates. The experts help provide tech and educational support across a range of platforms, from smartphones, tablets, and e-readers to small consumer electronics. This is also a good opportunity for reverse mentoring by engaging teen and young adult volunteers to help older patrons with their tech challenges. Similarly, older patrons can provide tech support for things like sewing machines and other traditional technology that younger people may find challenging. "Tech" doesn't just mean computers and cell phones. Tech cafés can also address tech literacy through hands-on mentoring and support.

Repair Cafés

The Repair Café[11] concept has been around for a few years, and now there is a robust Repair Café network where people can list Repair Café locations for others to find. Repair Cafés are free meet-ups focused on repairing things together. The operative word is "together." The idea isn't to bring in a broken item and have someone else fix it for you, but rather to use the opportunity to learn how to fix the item yourself and pick up a few new skills in the process.

Hosting a Repair Café in a library makerspace is a natural fit, bringing community members into your space to learn practical use of tools and gain a better understanding of the household equipment that may need repairing. Repair Cafés can focus on any repairs for which you may have resident experts or expertise, including repairs to clothes, furniture, electrical appliances, bicycles, toys, or other household items.

On the designated repair day, participants bring in their broken items and, working with local experts, learn to make repairs. Guests can also just hang out to learn about the various types of repair. You can also have coffee or tea available for the full "café" experience. Repair Café's also offer a great opportunity to highlight different book collections, ranging from DIY collections to volumes on repairing things and different types of handcraft skills. The official Repair Café website has a series of "house rules" for makerspaces and other organizations that want to host events in alignment with their protocols, but you can also just do it your own way, customized to your library and community needs and resources.

Other educational programming can include partnerships with organizations like Coder Dojo (https://coderdojo.com), which provides programming education for youth; *FIRST* youth robotics programs (FIRSTInspires.org); Instructables projects, either making projects from the Instructables.com website or Make It @ Your Library, or creating new ones for those websites; and High Low-Tech (http://highlowtech.org) projects, which integrate high and low technological materials, processes, and cultures to engage diverse audiences in designing and building their own technologies, developing tools that are culturally relevant and democratize engineering.

YOUTH-SPECIFIC PROGRAMMING

While much of the educational and hobby-related programming discussed so far can be adapted for all ages, youth-specific programming is a major part of any library program, and no less so with makerspaces. As a matter of fact, a library makerspace makes it possible to kick up youth programming, in particular, to an especially engaging level. Story time, for example, can now have the added component of related Maker time, giving youth an opportunity to experience hands-on activities related to their stories. Storytelling can roll over into podcasting or video production. History can come alive with the help of local artisans with traditional handcraft expertise. And interest in anime and cosplay can become hands-on opportunities to learn graphic design, 3D printing, sewing, and prop making. What follows are just a few possibilities for incorporating Maker programming into youth programming.

Cosplay

Cosplay can be a little baffling to the uninitiated. Cosplay is a mashup of the words "costume play." It started out as a form of performance art in which people—known as cosplayers—dressed up as different anime, science fiction, or super hero characters at conferences, live-action events, or other special events, for instance, anime conventions. Throughout time, cosplay

Cosplay costuming. ***Theresa Willingham***

morphed into a cultural subset of fandom, and cosplayers found almost any remotely connected event, for example, Maker festivals, an opportunity to dress up. During the last few years, many libraries have embraced cosplay as a way to appeal to the teen and young adult community. Library ComicCons or cosplay events are fairly common and can be a complementary component of makerspace programming.

Author, librarian, and cosplayer Elyssa Kroski, director of information technology at the New York Law Institute, has written a book on the topic, called *Cosplay in Libraries: How to Embrace Costume Play in Your Library* (Rowman & Littlefield, 2015). Kroski feels cosplay is a good fit for libraries, incorporating math, science, engineering, technology, and art, and providing a way for libraries to engage patrons of all ages in everything from instruction and design to the literary connection with comics, graphic novels, manga, and science fiction.

It's true that cosplay can be an avenue to makerspace programming through sewing and prop-making workshops and classes. Hosting cosplay sewing programs can be an effective intergenerational opportunity, a way to bring together the finer elements of textile work, from pattern making to sewing, and the older people who have used these skills for more traditional uses, and younger people interested in making their own costumes. The same is true of such handcraft skills as woodworking or sculpting, with respect to making some of the props used in cosplay. Technology can be integrated, too, with the use of 3D printing for costume accessories or elements.

Cosplay Caveat

But there's another element to cosplay in libraries that is seldom addressed but should be considered. Cosplay can become an inadvertent opportunity for cultural appropriation and insensitivity, sexism, obscenity, harassment, and exclusion, and it's important that libraries exploring cosplay programming be aware of some of the related issues so they don't creep into otherwise creative, inclusive programming.[12]

Scott Ertz, editor in chief at PLuGHiTz Live, who has spent a lifetime in the cosplay community serving as a podcaster and providing event coverage, says there are four different types of costuming today: costuming itself, cosplay, cosplay burlesque, and nerd-fandom stripping.

"All four are very different from one another," he explains. "Costuming is the art of making and wearing a costume. Cosplay takes it a step farther and involves the person becoming the character they are dressed as. The last two are what they sound like." For the purposes of a public space embracing cosplay, Ertz says, "Normal cosplay is character- and story-driven costuming."

It's important to keep any programming inclusive, appropriate, and welcoming, and having the facts about cosplay can help you make the most of this creative opportunity. At heart, Ertz says, cosplay is about becoming a character you admire. "If a girl or boy wants to be Batman or a girl or boy wants to be Harley Quinn, we should be empowering them to embrace whatever it is about that character that they feel connected to and not to focus on the scale, scope, or lack thereof of a costume for themselves."

That sums up the best of cosplay and provides a great rule of thumb for libraries exploring engagement in the cosplay community as a way to update programming and appeal to millennials. Ertz recommends deciding on what your culture will be, defining that clearly, and adapting programming accordingly. We'll explore some of these parameters further in chapter 6, with respect to events, and chapter 9, regarding risk management. For now, suffice it to say that, developed intentionally and thoughtfully, cosplay can have some useful elements for a library makerspace when focused on costuming, design, and prop making. If you decide to do a cosplay event at your library (see chapter 6), set your parameters early and adhere to them.

Robotics

Robotics is an increasingly common part of library programming and works particularly well in libraries with makerspaces. Youth robotics programs like *FIRST*, VEX, or Sumobots scale well to any size makerspace and can provide valuable STEM content for your library. *FIRST* LEGO League, especially, is a highly attractive and engaging program to incorporate into a library makerspace. Additionally, the LEGO Mindstorms kit used for *FIRST* LEGO League is also highly adaptable to a number of other robotics and engineering projects.

FIRST (FIRSTInspires.org), in general, is a particularly robust youth robotics program to integrate into library programming because it's scalable and has both visual appeal and measurable impact. *FIRST* LEGO League Jr. is a great programming option for youth ages six to nine years old. It's inexpensive and, rolled out among branch libraries, creates the opportunity for an interlibrary *FIRST* LEGO League Jr. Expo, which is essentially a little trade show for children in the program. They exhibit their season build and a simple show-and-tell project. This is a great way for the public to see

FIRST* Robotics Competition team Edgar Allan Ohms, Land O'Lakes Library, Pasco County. *Theresa Willingham

libraries in a new way and provide enjoyable Maker-style programming for families.

FIRST LEGO League is a competitive robotics program for youth in third through seventh grades and can either be rolled out as noncompetitive "community" program, where a library system uses previous season games to teach and hold informal interlibrary events, or as part of the local competitive program, where children on the library team compete with other community teams. The latter acts as a great promotional tool for libraries, helping the public see library learning opportunities for children in a new light.

FIRST Tech Challenge and *FIRST* Robotics Competition are middle school and high school-level programs with more challenging engineering builds but commensurately higher rewards for youth, including more than $50 million in scholarship availability. Pasco County Library Cooperative in Florida is home to the nation's only *FIRST* Robotics Competition team, the Edgar Allan Ohms,[13] which has proven a boon for the Land O'Lakes Branch Library, where the team is headquartered, functioning as a draw for other Maker-style programming and collaborative relationships with other user groups. One of those groups, a woodworking club, became a principal program provider at the library.

FIRST robotics programs can open doors to additional funding as well. The Haslet Public Library in Texas was awarded a Loleta D. Fyan Grant in the amount of $5,000 annually to "support a project that will develop and/or improve public library services, effect changes that are innovative and responsive to the future, and have potential for broader impact and application beyond a specific local need."[14] The Pasco County, Florida, team typically receives county support and recognition as well, because of the positive public image it inspires. Many libraries also routinely offer LEGO robotics camps during the summer, which are a great way to use makerspaces and introduce people to the variety of resources available.

Filmmaking

This is another of those programming options that can be intergenerational but is especially appealing to youth. Library movie screenings are old hat. Now you can incorporate actual filmmaking into your programming with great resources for stop-motion animation using everything from clay to LEGOs to iMovie.[15] The great thing about filmmaking today is that you don't need anything more than a smartphone and movie editing tools, many of which are free or extremely low cost.

Filmmaking introduces a number of important concepts and skills, from exercising language arts skills to design thinking and promoting critical media consumption.[16] You don't need a fancy recording studio for a filmmaking program. You can do something as simple as painting a single wall in green chroma key paint for a green screen and using tabletop sound equipment you can make yourself, for example, a DIY tabletop reflection filter,[17] for recording sound and a simple tabletop studio.[18] You can also use a variety of higher-end editing software, depending on the focus of your programming and your budget, which brings another level of learning and skill building to your programming.

Gaming

The American Library Association's (ALA) Games and Gaming Round Table site (www.ala.org/gamert/public) identifies three basic types of "gaming" for public libraries:

1. Circulating games, where patrons check out games and play them at home
2. Game-based events, like game nights or RPG (role-playing games) groups, where patrons play games at a specific time in the library
3. At-will gaming, where patrons can freely play games at any time (e.g., readily available gaming tables for chess or console games)

The ALA also gives a nod to a fourth option, game making, which fosters the creation of games through game-design workshops or clubs and is more in line with makerspace and creative programming. While gaming at all levels can serve both youth and adults, it's more likely to appeal to the teen and young adult crowd. When we talk about game making here, we're also looking at the development of board games and computer games, both of which have large followings for different reasons.

Minecraft (https://education.minecraft.net/), in particular, is an amazing resource for teaching programming to youth and allows for a wealth of creative opportunities, from design to storytelling. The New York Public Library got especially creative with game making in 2016, when Mauricio Giraldo, a designer with the New York Public Library (NYPL) Labs, created a video game that incorporated some of the library's own public domain collections, a unique way to bring together the old and the new.[19] The game, Mansion Maniac, allows users to travel through actual early century floor plans of New York City homes and apartments, adding historical layouts as you travel and allowing users to save and print out the floorplans.

NYPL Labs hosted a hackathon-like "Remix Residency" to create programs similar to Mansion Maniac, inviting the public to create more interesting projects with the public domain resources they make available. The key message, they believe, is "You can do it yourself," which should be the key message of all Maker-related activities offered to the public.

CIVIC PROGRAMMING

Libraries have a long tradition of civic engagement, acting as polling centers, hosting community engagement programs and panels, and providing services to patrons needing assistance with everything from taxes to job forms.

Libraries with makerspaces and Maker programming can elevate their civic engagement programs to another level with things like community gardens, Little Free Libraries, public arts projects, partnerships with groups like Habitat for Humanity, and a host of other active civic programs.

Civic projects present important opportunities for making that matters, bringing together people, tools, skills, and resources to improve or enhance everything from neighborhood blight to the library environment itself, both indoors and out. With respect to engagement of girls and women in science, tech, and making in general, studies have shown that women typically prefer to engage in projects that have a meaningful social purpose.[20] Creating opportunities for civic engagement is a great way to create Maker projects that are inclusive and attractive to women, and to men for whom meaningful making is also important.

Other civic Maker projects can include making items for those in hospitals, from knitted caps and blankets for newborns to toys for children in long-term hospital stays or foster homes; enrichment toys for animals in shelters; contributions to public works projects; and just about anything that would improve a neighborhood or community. Partnering with local civic agencies like homeless shelters or youth agencies can help identify useful projects and create powerful collaborative partnerships that help residents see libraries in new and vital ways. There are also civic events you can host, for instance, hackathons, which we'll discuss at greater length in chapter 6.

INCLUSIVE PROGRAMMING

We talked in an earlier chapter about designing inclusive makerspaces and programs that are welcoming to people of all abilities. Just as there are ways to design for inclusivity and diversity, there are some best practices to consider with respect to providing accessible programming. The ALA highlights a program model on their website called "Library for All."[21] The Jefferson County (Colorado) Public Library runs the program, which is held once a month at the four branch libraries. The program has a do-it-yourself (DIY) focus and welcomes adults of differing abilities to make crafts, create art, play games, and explore the library. Each participant has the opportunity to make something to take home. In addition to the ALA website, there are some great inclusive-program projects at DIYAbility.com.

Programs serving people of different abilities need to take into consideration the need for small-group programming, sufficient staff and volunteer support for programs, tools that are easy to use or equipped with adaptive devices, and large-print instructions, and plan for longer programming sessions than the usual 30 minutes to an hour. The Jefferson County sessions are 90 minutes long.

In designing inclusive programming it's also important to take into consideration the right way to appeal to African American patrons, women, and perhaps local area cultural groups to ensure that programming is relevant and meaningful. The Minority Male Maker Program,[22] sponsored by Verizon, is one such offering. The program serves middle school students and has been hosted at four Historically Black Colleges and Universities since 2015. The goal of the program is to "empower a new generation of minority men by giving them lifelong technology and entrepreneurship skills to build future innovations and create brighter futures for themselves and their families." Programs like this are most effective with library leadership and instructive teams that look like and understand the community being served. Sourcing volunteers for Maker programs from that community is the best way to provide meaningful and appropriate programming that meets the needs and interests of participants.

TOOLS AND RESOURCES

Makerspace programming provides new avenues for creative content delivery but also some new challenges due to the scope and complexity of some of the new possible offerings. Fortunately, there's now a wealth of resources for libraries looking at these innovative new programming options.

Space

In the *School Library Journal* article "Where the Magic Happens: Library Maker Programs,"[23] Tim Carrigan, senior library program officer for the Institute of Museum and Library Services, says, "Don't wait for a perfect space—or frankly, any space. . . . Doing so could take valuable programming from students and patrons." Adapt the space you have to the programs you want to offer, and don't worry if you don't have a built-out dedicated makerspace to offer Maker-style programming.

In the article, Cindy Wall, head of children's services at Southington (Connecticut) Library and Museum and coauthor of *The Maker Cookbook: Recipes for Children's and Tween Library Programming* (2014), says that with a more fluid environment, projects can be flexible. "The positive of not having a Maker space is that [you don't] depend on what's there," she states. "If you have a space with a bunch of 3-D printers, then you're going to do a lot of 3-D programming, because that's what you have." Conversely, if your spaces are open and adaptable, your programming can be also.

Guidelines

In the terrific resource the "Let's Make Guide" (www.letsmakeguide.com), developed by the Bill and Melinda Gates Foundation for libraries interested in developing makerspaces, there's this sage piece of advice:

> Every library should compile rules and guidelines for the general use of their makerspace or a media lab by its users, and/or for the use of specific tools (for example: 3-D printers, digital cameras, musical instruments, sewing machines). The public should be warned of any danger, assume responsibility for their actions and use of the tool(s), and be advised on how to behave in the makerspace (in addition to receiving adequate and proper training to help them safely and properly use the tools).
>
> Some general best practice guidelines:
>
> - Children under the age of 12 must have a parent or legal guardian with them.
> - No open-toed shoes.
> - No loose-fitting or dangling pieces of clothing.
> - Tie back long hair.

Some other recommendations from the site:

- Start small and be flexible—communicate regularly with users.
- Reassess such existing services as technology training classes, craft workshops, or hobby groups, and if they're "Makery," you can build on them.
- Use language people understand, as opposed to colloquially using "Maker" or "hacker" when advertising a new service; people may not recognize them, so focus on what users will be doing or creating in a space or class.
- Keep equipment portable and mobile so equipment and materials can be moved into different locations as needed.
- Use special events to advertise what you do in your makerspace or media lab (see chapter 6 for ideas).[24]

Prepare for Success

The most successful programming will be planned out well in advance, something most libraries are already well versed in doing; however, with Maker-style programming, in addition to space and programming guidelines, it's also helpful to make sure you have the appropriate tools and consumables, and, most importantly, that programming staff understand the project or program they're delivering. If you don't fully understand 3D printing, don't try to teach a program about it. The same goes for things like Arduinos, robotics, game making, A/V production, and similar projects.

It's often a good idea to try a higher-end Maker-style program with staff and volunteers first, before offering it to the public, at least if your topic isn't already an area of expertise. You also need to make sure you have enough staff and volunteers on hand for Maker-style programming, which often requires a little more one-on-one time with participants than traditional library fare. Thus, it is important to plan ahead to make sure you're properly staffed for Maker programs and that you're prepared with equipment, resources, and knowledge before hosting. These aren't the types of programs you want to "wing," by any means.

Good Programming Resources

You'll find an extensive collection of tools and resources in chapter 7, as well in the appendix, but some good programming-specific resources include the following:

- The Programming Librarian, a website of the American Library Association: www.programminglibrarian.org/programs
- Maker and DIY Programs Wiki, from the Young Adult Library Services Association: http://wikis.ala.org/yalsa/index.php/Maker_%26_DIY_Programs
- Makerspace Resources and Programming Ideas, by Colleen Graves: https://colleengraves.org/makerspace-resources-and-programming-ideas/
- Special Needs and Inclusive Library Services, resources from Illinois youth services librarians: https://snailsgroup.blogspoty.com
- Program Ideas, Activities, and Events, from the Idaho Commission for Libraries: http://libraries.idaho.gov/page/program-ideas-activities-and-events
- Let's Make Guide: www.letsmakeguide.com

Next up, we'll look at some great ways to highlight, celebrate, and invite more engagement in Maker programming through public Maker events.

NOTES

1. Pichman, Brian. "Creating Library Programs That Work" Accessed May 22, 2017. https://drive.google.com/file/d/0B7-TbEK4D5B5al9EN2hzblFFZUJnOGx-uZHU0NjRfRjlTaHRj/view.
2. Pichman, "Creating Library Programs That Work"
3. "Association for Creative Industries Reveals Size of U.S. Creative Products Opportunity is $43 Billion." *AFCI News*. Accessed May 22, 2017. www.craftand-hobby.org/eweb/dynamicpage.aspx?webcode=cha_news&key=FA50D125-9C58-4805-BD45-2408BB8929F8.
4. Chase, Sarah. "Maker Programs for Adults." *Idaho Commission for Libraries*. July 16, 2014. Accessed May 22, 2017. http://libraries.idaho.gov/blogs/sarahchase/maker-programs-adults.

5. Pagowsky, Nicole. "Keeping up with . . . Digital Badges for Instruction." *Association of College and Research Libraries.* July 21, 2015. Accessed May 22, 2017. www.ala.org/acrl/publications/keeping_up_with/digital_badges.

6. Collins, Bradley. "How Public Libraries Are a Boon to Small Business." *American Libraries.* March 4, 2016. Accessed May 22, 2017. https://americanlibrariesmagazine.org/2012/08/13/how-public-libraries-are-a-boon-to-small-business/.

7. Krassenstein, Brian. "Over 50 Percent of All Homes to Have 3D Printers By 2030, Market Worth $70 Billion Annually." *3DPrint.com.* February 10, 2014. Accessed May 22, 2017. https://3dprint.com/915/over-50-of-all-homes-to-have-3d-printers-by-2030-market-worth-70-billion-annually.

8. Flaherty, Nick. "Startup Uses IBM Watson to Build World's Largest Search Engine for 3D Printable Models." *EeNews Europe.* May 16, 2017. Accessed May 22, 2017. www.eenewseurope.com/news/startup-uses-ibm-watson-build-worlds-largest-search-engine-3d-printable-models.

9. White, Anthony T. "Drones @ the Library." *Public Libraries Online.* January 6, 2016. Accessed May 22, 2017. http://publiclibrariesonline.org/2016/01/drones-the-library/.

10. Seaman, George. "Girl Power." *Naflod.* Accessed May 22, 2017. www.naflod.me/flying/girlPower.

11. "What Is a Repair Cafe?" *Repair Café.* Accessed May 22, 2017. https://repaircafe.org/en/about/.

12. "Cosplay." *Geek Feminism Wiki.* Accessed May 22, 2017. http://geekfeminism.wikia.com/wiki/Cosplay.

13. Miller, Daylina. "Robotics Team Builds One for the Books." *Suncoast News.* April 29, 2014. Accessed May 22, 2017. www.tbo.com/su/list/news-pasco/robotics-team-builds-one-for-the-books-20140430/.

14. Boyer, Katie. "Robotics Clubs at the Library." *Public Libraries Online.* June 16, 2014. Accessed May 22, 2017. http://publiclibrariesonline.org/2014/06/robotics-clubs-at-the-library/.

15. Jensen, Karen. "Take Five: Five Tools for Movie Making in Your Makerspace." *School Library Journal.* May 18, 2015. Accessed May 22, 2017. www.teenlibrariantoolbox.com/2015/05/take-5-5-tools-for-movie-making-in-your-makerspace-quarto-week-makerspace/.

16. Desler, Gail. "A Case for Filmmaking in the Classroom." *Digital Is.* October 28, 2010. Accessed May 23, 2017. http://digitalis.nwp.org/resource/1325.

17. Caleb, A. J. "Microphone Reflection Filter." *Instructables.com.* May 13, 2016. Accessed May 23, 2017. www.instructables.com/id/Microphone-Reflection-Filter/.

18. Curbelo, Alex. "Make Your Own Object Photography Soft Light Box." *Instructables.com*. May 12, 2016. Accessed May 23, 2017. www.instructables.com/id/Make-Your-Own-Object-Photography-Soft-Light-Box/.

19. Kotzer, Zack. "The New York Public Library Hopes You'll Make Video Games." *Motherboard*. February 14, 2016. Accessed May 23, 2017. https://motherboard.vice.com/en_us/article/the-new-york-public-library-has-free-public-domain-documents-for-game-devs.

20. Hoopes, Laura. "Are Girls and Women Just Not Interested in STEM?" *Nature News*. April 28, 2011. Accessed May 23, 2017. www.nature.com/scitable/forums/women-in-science/are-girls-and-women-just-not-interested-19620118.

21. Douglas, Stephanie. "Library for All." *Programming Librarian*. April 19, 2017. Accessed May 23, 2017. www.programminglibrarian.org/programs/library-all.

22. "Middle School Boys Learn Coding, 3-D Design in Pioneering New Program from Verizon and KSU." *Kentucky State University*. July 21, 2015. Accessed May 23, 2017. http://kysu.edu/2015/07/21/middle-school-boys-learn-coding-3-d-design-in-pioneering-new-program-from-verizon-and-ksu/.

23. Barack, Lauren. "Where the Magic Happens: Library Maker Programs." *School Library Journal*. May 1, 2015. Accessed May 23, 2017. www.slj.com/2015/05/programs/where-the-magic-happens-the-maker-issue/#_.

24. Bill and Melinda Gates Foundation. "Let's Make Guide." Accessed May 23, 2017. www.letsmakeguide.com.

6

MAKER EVENTS

The Library Makerspace as Community Hub

You do have to try, learn, and improve. You do have to put yourself out there and risk failure. But in this new world, you don't have to go bankrupt if you fail because you can fail small. You can innovate as a hobby. Imagine that: a nation of innovation hobbyists working to make their lives more meaningful and the world a better place. Welcome to the Maker revolution.

—Mark Hatch, *The Maker Movement Manifesto: Rules for Innovation in the New World of Crafters, Hackers, and Tinkerers*[1]

With the creation of a makerspace comes the opportunity for hosting great events at your library that both showcase the making going on in it and promote your resources and programs to the larger community. Library makerspaces are not only an empowerment tool for patrons, but also a promotional tool for libraries, providing an engaging way to let the community know about resources available to them. Libraries can design their own events or get on board with such national campaigns as Engineering Week (E-Week), National Day of Civic Hacking, National Day of Making, and other high-profile events that will let people know what you're doing in your makerspace and invite them to be part of the empowering fun.

High school Maker librarian Colleen Graves has crowdsourced a great collection of public events, some well-known and some more obscure but equally worthy, on her blog, Create+Collaborate Innovate,[2] an excellent resource for all things related to making at the library. Her "National Maker Events" list includes things like Fair Use Week in February, National Robotics Week in April, National Week of Making in June, the Global Cardboard Challenge in September, International Games Day in November, Computer Science Week in December, and a wealth of show-and-tell celebration opportunities in between.

The process for putting together any celebratory public outreach event is about the same. Whether you're looking at hosting a library Maker festival, an E-Week event, or a pitch event, you'll need a few essential things:

- *A planning team:* Every good event needs a good event-planning team. Source team members from among staff and volunteers who really like the things you'll be doing at the event—artists, crafters, musicians, and people with interests in technical and mechanical things. Or, conversely, do the things at your event that interest team members who would love bringing those things together.
- *A good date and sufficient planning time:* If you want people to come out to your event, you don't want to conflict with other area goings-on. Give yourself plenty of planning time—at least six months or more—especially the first time out, and depending on the size and scope of your event.
- *Space:* Depending on the size of your event, you may want to use both indoor and outdoor spaces. Depending on your location and the time of year of your event, consider whether you'll need canopies for shade outdoors and where you'll have access to power.
- *Collaborative partners:* This is a great time to call on community partners to be part of the event and perhaps help produce different aspects of it (e.g., a ham radio club organizing an amateur radio section or the local robotics team showcasing their work).
- *Entertainment and presentations:* Make it fun and educational with local performers and workshop sessions featuring some of the Maker programming you do at your library.
- *Promotion, promotion, promotion:* Leverage social media, websites, local news, radio, and Internet tools. Run website features leading up to your event, highlight programs and partners, and generally make a big deal of your event so that people won't want to miss out.

For the purposes of this chapter we're going to look at a variety of public events and celebrations you can host, from small-scale hyperlocal events to collaborative events with other libraries or organizations. We'll explore the following:

- Maker festivals
- Coding events
- "Open make" events (including build contests)
- Pop-culture events (e.g., cosplay, gaming, comic and anime festivals)
- Entrepreneurial and product/service pitch events (e.g., 1 Million Cups, Alligator Zone)
- Other special events (e.g., youth robotics events, deconstruction, fix-it clinics, TEDxLibraries, webinars, community service projects)

MAKER FESTIVALS

We'll start with the most obvious potential offering: a library Maker festival. First, it's important to understand that there's no one "right" way to host a

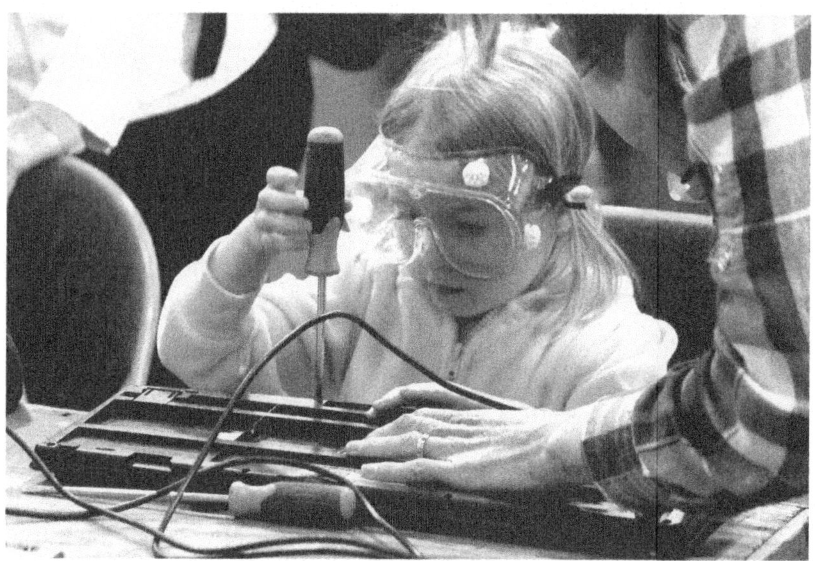

Young Maker at Gulf Coast MakerCon 2015. ***Theresa Willingham***

Maker festival. While *Make:*-branded Maker Faires are pretty familiar to a lot of folks now, if you want to host a Maker Faire with the "e" at the end, there's an associated licensing fee and a host of requirements for running a franchised event. There are several Maker Faires hosted at libraries, including San Antonio Mini Maker Faire, Maker Faire Westport, and Colorado Springs Mini Maker Faire.

The organizers of the Colorado Springs Mini Maker Faire (coloradospringsmakerfaire.com), hosted by the Pikes Peak Library District and now in its third year, have put together an overview of their first event and what it took to produce it. Says librarian Rebecca Cruz, in the Public Library Association article about the event,

> The application process requires quite a bit of information, including several short-answer questions, letters of support, and budgetary information. Once accepted, certain aspects of the Faire have to be handled in particular ways, like publicity being approved and specific websites being used.[3]

In their case, they felt the branding and relationship with *Make:* magazine was important to the library. For the purposes of most libraries, however, a do-it-yourself (DIY) Maker festival is a far more cost effective and less labor-intensive way to go, and just as rewarding. We hosted a public Mini Maker Faire for a couple of years before deciding to produce an independent event in 2014, called Gulf Coast MakerCon.[4] We've enjoyed the creative freedom of crafting an event tailored to our local community and interests, and the budgetary flexibility that entails. Gulf Coast MakerCon remains the oldest and biggest community Maker festival on the Florida Gulf Coast. For our 2018 event, we're partnering with St. Petersburg College Seminole Public Library in Largo, Florida, combining our event with their popular Pinellas ComicCon and MakerCon event, to pool resources for a more robust event for both groups.

The Tampa Bay Library Consortium in Florida hosts their own Library MakerFest (librarymakerfest.org) each spring, where consortium libraries come together to showcase their growing Maker programs. That event is targeted at other libraries as a best-practices event, where libraries can learn from one another and get ideas for their own programs.

The Portland (Maine) Public Library (PPL) hosted Makers@PPL, an event highlighting the importance of the STEAM subjects (science, technology, engineering, arts, math) and showcasing "workshops and presentations that not only teach, but are fun and engaging." The library's website continues, "Regardless of your background or expertise, this event will show you that everyone is a Maker; after all, humans have been inventing and experimenting for hundreds of years."[5]

In the Netherlands, the national government is entertaining the idea of an education-oriented Maker event, intended to be the first big Maker festival in the country.[6] The Netherlands has also hosted a Maker Party,[7] a public event organized by the Kennisland (Knowledge Land) company and Mozilla, bringing together issues of copyright, Maker culture, and librarianship. The event invited artists, authors, activists, educators, coders, and entrepreneurs to learn "how to connect outdated copyright law to our modern Maker culture."

For a complete "how-to" on hosting a Maker festival, check out our Eureka! Factory Instructable on the topic: www.instructables.com/id/How-to-Make-a-Maker-Festival/. The information is scalable to any size event by any hosting organization. The most important thing to remember with a Maker event is to keep it fun, both to produce and to attend. Keep the scale of your event within the scope of your staff, volunteer, and community partnership capabilities to give it the best chance of becoming a successful annual event that will help grow your library community and programs.

The following are some tips for preparing to host a Maker festival:

- *Start small.* You can use both indoor and outdoor spaces to display crafts and demonstrations, but don't go bigger than you can comfortably manage with volunteers and staff, especially the first time around.
- *Collaborate.* Invite community groups from the area, from knitting clubs to drone hobbyists. The more engagement you have from community collaborators for your event, the more engagement you'll have from them between events.
- *Keep it interactive.* Make it fun and interactive, instead of relying on static displays. Maker Festivals, by nature, are active and hands-on experiences.
- *Have entertainment.* Bring in local talent or look within your stacks for library musicians. The more you can showcase out-of-the-box talent and expertise sourced right from the library, the better.

- *Promote, promote, promote.* Promote early and often, right up to the day of the event. Be generous with signage both inside and outside your library, and promote outside the usual channels in ways that reach people interested in arts, computer sciences, technology, trades, and so forth.
- *Large or small, celebrate it all.* Make it a party from start to finish.

CODING EVENTS

While libraries have offered basic computer literacy classes for years, only recently has coding become a big part of those offerings. In *Makerspaces in Libraries*, we include a section in the projects chapter on how to host a hackathon in the library and why hackathons are good for the library community and the library. Today, libraries throughout the world offer coding classes, programs, and events. In 2016, to mark European Union (EU) Code Week, and as part of the "New Skills Agenda for Europe," Public Libraries 2020 hosted "Generation Code: Born at the Library" at the European Parliament.[8] The goal of the interactive exhibition was to demonstrate "how Europe's public libraries are meeting the digital age." The exhibition included several

Hackathon t-shirts. ***Theresa Willingham***

interactive stations showcasing a wide range of digital projects underway at EU libraries, including coding, robotics, 3D printing, virtual reality experiences, tech advice workshops, and digital making, where participants could explore a new digital skill and experiment with new technologies.

There are lots of great public coding events that feed into library programming in the United States and abroad. Hour of Code, organized by Code.org, is a particularly popular and effective event for introducing coding to the public and a great platform from which to build a more robust coding program for patrons. In the 2016 webinar "Coding for Everyone: How Your Library Can Help Anyone Learn to Code,"[9] presenter Kelly Smith, founder of Prenda, a company dedicated to helping libraries start coding clubs, gave three good reasons why coding and libraries naturally go together:

1. Libraries are a community resource and thus a trusted place for families.
2. Libraries are open to everyone and everyone is invited to learn for free, which equalizes opportunity through tech skills.
3. Libraries exemplify 21st-Century Learning, putting no obstacles between learner and information.

Florida's Orange County Library System (OCLS) in Orlando has one of the most robust and comprehensive selections of computer courses around,[10] a direct response to the growing tech community in the Orlando area. As interest grew in the field, and in response to patron demand, OCLS began offering coding classes in Spanish and Haitian Creole, and expanded their offerings to online classes, as well as in-person sessions, to help meet the needs of working patrons who couldn't get to the library for classes. The library system does a lot of back-end work to determine demand and need, and regularly reassesses their offerings through patron surveys, to ensure they're providing the type of computer literacy programs patrons want and the most updated programming possible.

Learn before You Teach or Host

While coding programs and libraries may be perfectly compatible, coding education isn't the kind of thing you can or should fake your way through.

While it's not as big as an issue to learn alongside children in a programming class using Scratch (ages eight to 15) or Scratch Jr. (ages four to seven) (scratch.mit.edu), trying to teach older teens or adults C# or Java requires at least the basic knowledge you're trying to impart to students. It's almost always obvious to anyone age 13 or older when a teacher doesn't understand the material, which is helpful to neither those in a class nor the library itself, since participants don't get anything out of an experience because of an inadequately prepared instructor.

Thus, the rule of thumb is, don't take on anything more than you understand or are willing to learn yourself beforehand. Better yet, find experienced members of the community to lead programming classes or events, for example, members of your local CoderDojo or Code for America Brigade, diverse and inclusive groups like Black Girls Code (blackgirlscode.com), Girls Who Code (girlswhocode.com), or local programmers willing to share their skills and help organize events.

Different Types of Coding Events

You can host your own library hackathon for a small-scale local project, either for the library itself or as a community service project. Chattahoochee Valley Libraries hosted an event called Hack the Library, with the goal of applying technology to improve the library's community engagement.[11] Or you can jump into any of several national events. Participating in national events is a great way to leverage publicity for the library and help people see the bigger picture of the library as a community engagement hub, with the potential for wider social and economic impact. The following are some larger national events and the time of year they typically occur:

- *Code Week EU (European Union):* This event typically occurs in October. In 2016, almost 1 million people in more than 50 countries participated. The event is supported by the European Commission, with the aim to boost digital skills for all ages and demographics. Visit codeweek.eu for more information and to register an event.
- *National Coding Week (United States and international):* Aimed at adults, National Coding Week usually occurs in September. Visit codingweek.org to get involved.

- *Code Day (United States):* This event occurs in November and invites student programmers, artists, musicians, actors, and the general public to get together and build apps and games. It lasts 24 hours. Like a youth-focused National Day of Civic Hacking event, Code Day welcomes students 25 years of age or younger of all skill levels and includes workshops and mentoring support for participants. Visit codeday.org to register your event. The site also has great examples of event-day agendas that can help guide in the creation of your own library event.
- *Hour of Code:* Organized by Code.org and typically occurring in December, during Computer Science Week, Hour of Code was highlighted by the Obama administration as a model introduction to coding. The event now reaches tens of millions of people of all ages in more than 180 countries. One-hour tutorials are available in more than 45 languages. With massive freely available educational content (hourofcode.com/us/learn), Hour of Code also provides Beyond an Hour of Code (hourofcode.com/us/beyond) content for expanding educational opportunities beyond the introductory event. This is a great event to host, even for those with limited coding knowledge, since Code.org provides the tutorials and related educational materials.
- *Scratch Day:* This event is a youth-oriented coding event that usually occurs in May. As the name implies, the event celebrates Scratch, the free coding platform and online community for teaching coding to young children. Learn more at https://day.scratch.mit.edu/.
- *National Day of Civic Hacking:* Organized by Code for America and Second Muse, until recently the event was held in the summer but in 2017 moved to September. Code for America is a civic coding organization that specializes in uniting local governments and professional "software developers, citizens, and entrepreneurs to collaboratively create, build, and invent new solutions using publicly released data, code, and technology to improve our communities and the governments that serve them." The intent of National Day of Civic Hacking is to demonstrate the power of collaboration to strengthen government, and as a government agency, it is a natural fit for libraries.[12] The events can be themed and focus on a particular local challenge that needs a solution or explore any number of national or federal projects offered

up for public consideration. Visit codeforamerica.org for more information.

Coding Event Basics

Whatever coding event(s) you decide to try, none of them require much beyond tables, chairs, and access to power and Wi-Fi. But there are some technical details that are helpful for making your coding event successful and enjoyable for participants. The Hack Day Manifesto (hackdaymanifesto.com) outlines what makes a great hackathon great. Here's a summary:

- Wi-Fi should be easily accessible and reliable. Keep in mind the more Wi-Fi users, the less reliable most Wi-Fi can be.
- The system should be open and accessible, with minimal firewalls.
- There should be an Internet backup in case of power failures.
- There should be Ethernet availability, preferably with extra cables.
- Every programmer's seat should have access to power at the rate of 1.5 power sockets per seat.
- There should be A/V support for presentations.
- For civic and local hackathons, access to data sets and APIs (application program interfaces, the sets of routines, protocols, and tools needed for building software applications) is vital.

And have food. Libraries sometimes seem challenged when it comes to allowing food inside. But any kind of real integrated makerspace programming requires access to food. People like to eat and drink when they're creating, and while electronics, computers, mechanical equipment, and tools obviously need to be protected and kept clean, reasonable rules about food and drink go a long way in improving event success and enjoyment for participants.

Hackathon Best Practices

In addition to the technical basics, there are some basic best practices for hosting a hackathon of any size that will make your event easier to plan and host.

- *Set clear rules of conduct and participation.* Event guidelines should include the goals of the event, hours, and the data sources participants will have access to during the event, as well as a basic code of conduct. Participants should receive a copy of the guidelines when they register, and they should be reviewed with everyone at the start of the event.
- *Recruit attendees early.* The coding community is typically an active and engaged one, but it is usually comprised of full-time working people who need time to prepare to attend an upcoming event. Once you have an idea of your space and focus, reach out via social media or with sign-up sheets at your library. Hosting a pre-event meet-up will help build out the event agenda, as well as generate buzz and fresh ideas from stakeholders. Reach out to local coding groups through MeetUp, IEEE, and other professional associations; Microsoft coding groups; and so forth. The more people you can bring into the early planning stages the better, since only about 60 percent of event registrants typically attend.
- *Set an Agenda and registration.* Once you've selected your event date, put together an event schedule that includes break times or meal times. Multiday hackathons are often held on weekends. Consider work schedules, and if you're doing a weekend event, look at other possible competing events or hackathons in the area.
- *Promote the event.* Promoting the event creates the energy that makes it exciting for participants and increases library visibility in the tech community. It's ideal to have a freestanding webpage for the event, but promoting via the usual library social media channels, with flyers and news, is also effective. If your event is part of a bigger one, like the National Day of Civic Hacking, it's even easier to surf the tide of national promotion, leveraging bigger organizations' social media and website resources.
- *Facilitate networking and collaboration on event day.* People who know each other may form immediate affinity groups that become teams, and even strangers meeting for the first time can usually pair up pretty easily. Teams can consist of a couple people or several people, with the sense of community inherent in most hack groups lending itself to collaboration with little guidance. Coffee and bagels or donuts

Sample Hackathon Schedule

Saturday

9:00 a.m.: Check in and meet and greet with coffee and bagels or donuts.

9:30 a.m.: Welcome and event overview. (Present the agenda, rules, and the code of conduct.)

10:00 a.m.–11 a.m.: Scrum time! (Get out of the way while teams brainstorm ideas and strategize their approaches. Allow at least an hour.)

Noon: Lunch.

1:00 p.m.–5:00 p.m.: Team projects resume.

5:00 p.m.: Wrap up day one, dinner optional.

Sunday

10:00 a.m.: Hacking resumes.

12:30 p.m.: Lunch.

1:30 p.m.–2:30 p.m.: Hacking stops; project pitches honed. (It's fairly standard practice, with or without judging or prizes, to have a stopping point midday, at which point teams will prepare their "pitches" for their projects to share with one another.)

3:00 p.m.: Project pitches. (Some projects won't be finished, which is fine. Teams can still talk about their effort and goals.)

4:30 p.m.: Sum up. (If a panel—perhaps of library staff or community leaders—will be identifying top projects, make awards at this time, or just call it a fun weekend and celebrate with some pizza and beverages.)

can be effective icebreakers during the morning meet and greet prior to the event kickoff. Keep in mind that the point of a hackathon is to provide an opportunity for networking and collaboration, with bonus points for the development of a useful app, website, or digital tool that provides a solution to an identified problem. If most participants can come out of the event with a sense of camaraderie and some new knowledge, the event has been a resounding success

- *Stay connected.* The best hackathons are a starting point for not only participants, but also the library, helping establish a new gathering place for coders, developers, and other technical groups. After the hackathon, reach out to participants with regular opportunities for meet-ups and networking, and invite groups and individuals to make use of the library for their events and programs. It's also a good idea to archive hackathon projects and results on your library's website or blog so participants can enjoy some recognition and their projects can get continued use.

OPEN MAKE EVENTS

Open makes are great fun for the public and provide a terrific way to get people in the door for what is essentially free play for Makers. During open make events, which can be one day or even one night a week, the community is invited to come in and use makerspace resources or tools (within limits set by the library) to work on their own projects, whether it's art, handcrafts, design projects, video or game making, or some mechanical or other technical project. Open make events are not "programming" events, with guided learning and preestablished goals or outcomes, but rather user-driven experiences with appropriate library staff supervision. You're not going to want to let people loose on band saws and drill presses, of course, but this is a great opportunity for people to enjoy the freedom of independent creation.

Open makes can become an incentive for completing tool and equipment orientations and classes, giving participants access to the more sophisticated equipment, for instance, power tools, 3D printers, engravers, laser cutters, or recording and video equipment. If people know they'll have free and open access at certain times if they complete the necessary training, they'll be more likely to do so.

Open makes can also be enhanced with physical hack or build projects, like those found at Instructables.com or Hackaday.com. During the summer, Instructables.com typically hosts a summer makerspace contest with generous prizes. The contest is open-ended, a numbers game that challenges participating makerspaces to create as many "how-tos" in any category they'd like, from recipes to art projects, with prizes being awarded to makerspaces with the most total projects and most featured projects. It's a fun, free contest and provides a great way to engage a library makerspace community and highlight your library in the process.

Similarly, Hackaday offers a Hackaday Prize for "creating for social change in order to transform the world." The annual contest, which typically runs year-round in a series of challenges, tasks teams "using your hardware and programming knowledge, on top of your scientific, design, and mechanical abilities, (to) innovate to make an impact in peoples' lives."[13]

As you develop out your makerspace and users become more accustomed to tools and engaged in using them, contests and project events provide a fun way to build your library Maker community, as well as a way to start accruing performance metrics. Anything created at the library is a feather in your makerspace cap and good PR, and it provides good metrics for future funding and support.

POP-CULTURE EVENTS

Popular culture events include things like anime and cosplay festivals, ComicCons (conferences or conventions), gaming events, band battles, and similar festivals and celebrations. These are mostly entertainment experiences with limited literary or educational value, although with some advanced planning you can more effectively tie in such things as graphic novels, art, animation, music, and related literary opportunities. DC Comics, for instance, has a long history of engagement with public libraries, tying in things like Superman and Batman's 75th anniversary with related materials.[14] Each year libraries throughout the country participate in Free Comic Book Day (freecomicbookday.com) in May, distributing comic books and providing related literary content. Thus, a library ComicCon event is an easy fit.

A good resource for cosplay and comic events in the library is the aptly named website Cosplay, Comics, and Geek Culture in the Library (ccgclibraries.com), run by Ellyssa Kroski. As discussed in the previous chapter, however, it's important to set the right culture for these types of events before you start offering them. Cosplay and comic-focused events can easily become exclusive, trite, and problematically inappropriate if the right guidelines aren't set from the beginning. Libraries can take a page out of the playbooks of established events like MetroCon and similar big pop-culture festivals that have been around for a while and tackled some of the challenges.

MetroCon, a large anime and cosplay festival held in Tampa, Florida, cites public decency laws in their costuming guidelines section and requires that "all attendees wear clothing providing coverage equivalent to at least a nonthong swimsuit while in public." The convention also discourages "shock costumes, which have the sole purpose of offending and disrespecting other individuals, cultures, or religions in any way."[15]

Libraries can, and should, set guidelines early and adhere to them consistently. First and foremost, however, libraries interested in hosting comic, anime, and cosplay events should determine the goals of these events and what purposes they serve for the library. It's fine to have the goal of providing a fun, creative avenue of expression for participants and another way for the public to see the library, but make sure the public is seeing the library in a favorable light and that your pop-culture events serve your library mission and goals at a higher level.

The process for putting together a ComicCon, anime, or cosplay event is pretty similar to putting together a Maker festival or coding event, with some variations on the theme. Chad Mairn Innovation Lab manager and librarian at St. Petersburg College Seminole Campus Library, has hosted a ComicCon event at the library for the last three years. He shared these great tips:

- You don't need much money (if any at all) to have a successful ComicCon. Find sponsors to help provide food for special guests. Ask vendors to provide prizes to give away as raffles, which provides visibility for them.
- Ask other organizers what didn't work at their events and follow their advice.
- Create consistent branding. Have signs directing people around your event and use your branding.
- Use social media, and keep it current. Answer messages and comment in a timely/polite manner. Social media is a great promotional tool.
- Write a press release and submit it to various media outlets months before your event. Flyers and promotional videos (commercials) are fantastic, too.

- Use an online collaboration tool like Google Docs so everything is in one place and people can work on one "living document."
- Work closely with law enforcement, the fire marshal, risk management departments, and so on, so they know your plans before the event. These groups will make sure you are following safety protocols.
- Create a policy for vendors who sell unlicensed fan art. Have a license to play films in public, too. Make sure guests/vendors sign an agreement so they know the rules. Get a signed release for the children's costume contest.
- Send out surveys to vendors/attendees to see what worked and what didn't, and follow their advice/criticism.
- Figure out next year's date as soon as possible.
- Create a planning committee and assign responsibilities.

A few other considerations:

- Local comic book shops and gaming stores are your friends and can bring a lot of support and public engagement to your event. Reach out to local authors and artists, and consider recruiting local food trucks. If your event is science fiction-focused, which is actually a good focus for a library, since the science fiction genre is a rich and multifaceted one, there's usually a local 501st Legion (501st.com) in most communities, with people who enjoy Star Wars-themed costuming and will come out to any related event with advance notice. The biggest challenge in hosting events of this type is often having sufficient food on-site to keep people at the event. If they have to leave to find food, they're unlikely to come back. Having a variety of on-site food is a good community engagement opportunity and good for your event.
- Since some of the things you try may not work the first or even second time, it's important to be flexible. As with any creative programming, it's important to be adaptable and open-minded. Some things will work and some won't. Don't try to fit everything into your first event—keeping it sweet and simple is always a good rule of thumb—and be prepared to try something a couple times before deciding if it's something you'll keep.

- Engage your library community. Make it fun for everyone, including staff and volunteers. Encourage them to join in the costuming fun, within the established parameters, and lead creative activities and programs as interested.

Steampunk is another genre with strong Maker and literary tie-ins. Steampunk is essentially a Victorian era/science fiction/fantasy mashup. Think Jules Verne, H. G. Wells, and more modern writers like William Gibson and Bruce Sterling. Steampunk costuming is heavy in leather, gears, and brass. Like cosplay, it can easily cross the line and become inappropriate costuming. But again, setting your guidelines and culture early and enforcing them consistently will keep your steampunk event safe, fun, interesting, and inclusive.

A great way to keep the makerspace focus is to provide opportunities for people in advance of your event to work on costuming and props at your library makerspace and use the event as an opportunity to showcase what people made. This can include sewing costumes, 3D printing accessories or props, creating artwork and music, and more.

As with other library-hosted events, make sure that, in addition to identifying your purpose in holding these types of events, you've got a good planning team that includes members of the community, as well as library staff and volunteers, and promote early and often.

ENTREPRENEURIAL EVENTS

If your library makerspace program is more focused on small business or entrepreneurial endeavors, events like 1 Million Cups (1millioncups.com) or Alligator Zone (alligatorzone.org) might be more appropriate. 1 Million Cups (1MC) is a "free, national program designed to educate, engage, and connect entrepreneurs with their communities."[16] Developed by the Kauffman Foundation, the program is held every Wednesday morning in more than 100 communities throughout the country (as of 2016) and attended by more than 2,500 people. Coffee is the drink of choice, with the entire event hinging on the idea that entrepreneurs discover solutions and network over more than 1 million cups of coffee each week. Many libraries host 1 Million

Cups events, including the Westbank Library (1millioncups.com/austin) in Austin, Texas, Richland Library in Columbia, South Carolina, and the Madison Public Library in Wisconsin.

Sites interested in hosting a weekly 1 Million Cups event should apply at 1millioncups.com and, once accepted, are expected to adhere to basic event protocols, as detailed here:

- There should be ample weekly meeting space for 20 to 30 people, on average.
- Fresh coffee needs to be available.
- The room needs to be equipped with a projector and screen, and preferably recording equipment.
- Each week, one or two early stage local businesses, selected from applicants who apply to present at the 1 Million Cups website, present their companies and a particular need—funding, partners or investors, or some other challenge—to a local audience.
- Each business founder presents for six minutes, followed by a 20-minute question-and-answer session with the audience.

The events provide a great way for local businesses to network and learn more about one another and local business opportunities, as well as a means for young businesses to get helpful insights and support from older businesses and potential investors. If your library serves a decent-sized small business community, weekly 1 Million Cups events can be an excellent addition to a makerspace and related programming.

Alligator Zone is a similar idea, but with an interesting intergenerational twist: Intended specifically to be held at libraries, in the Alligator Zone format, businesses present to children. Started in 2014, in Florida, as of this writing, almost 100 startups have been showcased in live events held at public libraries to youth audiences in 10 cities in three states. Alligator Zone provides a great opportunity for startups to explain their businesses in a way that a seven-year-old can understand—a good exercise for anyone—and get insightful feedback from uninhibited young people. Moreover, it helps youth of any age get an idea of how business works and become inspired by the work of others.

Alligator Zone also provides opportunities for participating youth to receive coaching in different roles so they can independently run their own events, which adds another educational and experiential element to the program. To inquire about bringing Alligator Zone to your library, visit alligatorzone.org.

Libraries wishing to serve their business community might also look into doing their own "Shark Tank"-style events. Bridgewater Library in Somerset, New Jersey, hosted an event called "Teen Tycoons" based on the Shark Tank concept.[17] More than 20 students gave a one-minute presentation sans props, slides, or any other supporting materials, to a panel of judges on the lookout for original business concepts or interesting new variations of existing business concepts. Three top winners were awarded cash prizes from local sponsors. This type of event lends itself to an adult event as well, esppecially if you work with local business-support organizations like SCORE or your local small business administration office.

Pitch Event Basics

Most of the aforementioned planning basics for other events apply to holding a pitch event at your library, along with a few more event-specific guidelines. In the same way that cosplay and comic events depend on recognizable celebrity guests, pitch events depend on judges. Fortunately, recruiting judges for your pitch event is another powerful way to network in your community. Recruit from local businesses, IP (intellectual property) attorneys, chambers of commerce, and civic leaders to engage them as judges in your pitch event. Then you'll need to do the following:

- Decide on the type of pitch event you're hosting—product, service, community need, library project, and so forth—and what type of prizes will be offered (e.g., cash, trophies, networking and product development opportunities with area professionals).
- Determine how many participants you can accommodate based on the length of your event, space availability, and community support. Events like 1 Million Cups typically only have a couple of presenters, who are given about 20 minutes each to present their ideas. But 1 Million Cups is only an hour long. If your event will run two or more

hours, base your participant recruitment on how many people you think you can accommodate based on a 15- to 20-minute pitch presentation and about 15 minutes of follow-up Q&A.

- Recruit participants through local meet-ups, as well as library promotion.
- Recruit judges from your local community.
- Make sure participants are aware of predetermined judging criteria and rules. There are several sources for guidelines, including the free Logika Pitch Guide (logika-usa.com/pitchguide). But judging rubrics should be posted well in advance so participants know the parameters. Judges will look at the following:
  - Does the idea solve a real problem? That's the first critical question or what's the point of the event?
  - Was the product cocreated with the intended user? As with library makerspaces, every good idea with a presumed community client should engage that client in the development of the solution. There should be evidence that the person pitching the product went to the source of the challenge to arrive at their potential solution.
  - Is the purpose of the product clear? "It's about signal, not noise."[18] It's the judge's responsibility "to provide meaningful direction and to probe for a greater truth or increased clarity, and above all, to actively listen and seek to understand. It's really not about us—it's about the contestants and the pitches themselves. It's about signal, not noise," says Liz Anderson, director of engagement at Georgetown University.
- Before they sign up, make participants aware of the following:
  - Eligibility: Who can participate, including age limits or categories, if any?
  - Prohibitions on copyright infringement and requirements for original content.
  - Pitch format: The length of time for pitches, resources available for presentations, and so on.
  - Judging rubric: A typical pitch "deck" consists of five to 10 slides that include a business plan and venture idea. One way to weight judging can be a certain percentage for degree of problem identification, inclusion of information about marketing size, overall product

offering, market strategy, competitive differentiation, team recruitment and overall performance plan, financials, and credibility—how reasonable is it that this plan will work?[19]

Your pitch event can be a single round of judging with a single winner or two rounds if you want to make it a "playoff"-type event.

OTHER SPECIAL EVENTS

There are a variety of other Maker-style events you can host at your library that can engage and inspire your library community, including such things as community service project days, simulcast events or webinars,[20] robotics competitions, and presentation series like TEDxLibraries. Community service days are just that: special public events to kick off or work on a public garden or other community improvement project at or near your library. If your library is exploring A/V programming or employing a recording studio, webinar or simulcast events recorded at the library can be interesting event offerings.

Youth Robotics

Small-scale youth robotics competitions or showcases can be great public events, especially when tied in with something like National Robotics Week in April. Depending on the size of your library, you can provide space for small-scale *FIRST* LEGO League scrimmages for a handful of local teams and open the event to the public or host *FIRST* LEGO League Jr. Expos, which are essentially mini trade shows for children ages six to nine. *FIRST* LEGO League Jr. events are especially easy to produce, with a high return on the investment of time and space—perfect for libraries.[21]

FIRST LEGO Jr. teams are small—no more than six students each—and the expos consist of a tabletop presentation by participating children where they display a LEGO model they built and a research poster. The events last only a couple of hours and provide a friendly and welcoming experience both for participating students and their families, as well as the general public.

FIRST* LEGO League Jr. display.** ***Theresa Willingham

Deconstruction

Also known as "take apart" events, "deconstruction" programs provide an opportunity for youth and people of all ages to get hands-on experience with tools in an atmosphere where they don't have to worry about breaking anything because everything is already broken.

"One of the most fun and engaging programs we've done at the Regency Park Library in Pasco County, Florida, is the deconstruction," said Maker librarian Chuck Stephens. "The deconstruction is controlled chaos—we give kids tools and broken electronics and let them take things apart. We let them figure it out—I'm only there to make sure everyone leaves with the same amount of fingers and eyes with which they arrived."

A successful deconstruction event involves finding good things to take apart, having the right tools on hand, and properly disposing of the leftover parts from the dismantled items. Stephens offered these basic guidelines:

- *Collect interesting things to disassemble.* "Modern devices are marvels of miniaturization, but they can be kind of boring to take apart. Miniscule SMD components on dull green boards connected by wires and mounted in a plastic case won't grab a kid's interest the way all the gears, motors, and brightly colored circuit boards of a 1980s-era VCR will." Stephens recommended sourcing a variety of electromechanical devices, like VCRs, copiers, printers, fax machines, rear-projection TVs, and similar items, and combining electrical circuits with motors, gears, optics, and all kinds of things that move. This makes for a fun afternoon of exploration.

- *Have the right tools on hand.* Stephens's list included screwdrivers, pliers, wire cutters, scissors, hammers, and security bits and a hex bit holder to "give you access to all those devices held together with odd-shaped screws." For children, he prefers to avoid cordless screwdrivers so youth can get a better feel for hand tools. Hand tools, he said, "make the kids slow down and focus on the process, not just the goal of disassembly."
- *Practice safety first.* Research the devices you intend to take apart and plan accordingly. With no intent to discourage librarians from hosting a deconstruction event, Stephens recommended a healthy awareness. "The lens assemblies from old rear-projection TVs contain several pints of mineral oil that will make a slippery mess if you're not prepared to contain it. Remove all ink and toner from printers, copiers, and fax machines to avoid stained clothes and messes. Glass, mirrors and lenses can break and cause serious cuts. Gear trains, hinges, belts, and other mechanical linkages can pinch skin or even break fingers. Compressed springs and gas cylinders can cause serious injuries if handled carelessly. High-voltage capacitors from older TVs and other appliances can hold enough of an electrical charge to kill you. Also explain and enforce tool safety and the use of proper protective equipment."

Taking things apart is only the beginning, said Stephens. He continued,

> What will you do with the parts you have left over? Some things are easily recyclable, like circuit boards, glass, and metal, but plastic is another story. Plastic recycling is a labor- and resource-intensive activity. Since plastic is a petroleum product, production costs are tied to the price of oil. With oil prices lower than they've been in years, plastic recycling becomes more expensive than producing new plastic. This is an interesting talking point as you

discuss the trash cycle with the kids, but it's also a real concern when they go home and you're left with a pile of plastic debris. Do your homework!

Older electronics are great because they use larger, easy-to-identify components, which can be carefully removed and reused. Motors, stepper motors, servos, displays, and other visual and mechanical components can be reused in other projects as well. Working with an e-waste recycling company for your deconstruction event is a win–win for your library and the e-waste company.

Fix-It Clinics

In a sort of reverse deconstruction, the fixit clinic is an opportunity for libraries to address a community need in a creative and useful fashion. Developed with the idea of providing "education, entertainment, empowerment, elucidation, and, ultimately, enlightenment through guided disassembly of your broken stuff,"[22] fix-it clinics are being held in libraries throughout the nation, providing a new empowerment tool, quite literally, for participants. The idea is not to repair appliances or items *for* residents, but to teach them how to repair those items themselves.

Austin Public Library has run a Fixit Clinic program[23] for a while now and partners with Austin Resource Recovery, the Reuse Alliance, Texas Chapter, and Skillshare Austin to provide the program. The library offers Fixit Clinics the first Saturday of each month and each month features a different type of repair project—for example, clothing, small appliances, or toys—and helps participating patrons learn how to repair the broken items with the help of volunteer coaches. Visit fixitclinic.blogspot.com for information on how to start a Fixit Clinic at your library.

TEDxLibraries

While the TEDxLibraries program works just fine in almost any library, hosting a TEDx event in a library with a makerspace is a great way to bring people into your space in a meaningful and engaging way. TEDx events are localized versions of TED talks, independently organized and produced.

"A TEDx event can serve as a catalyst to broaden the definition of 'library' and create new ways to bring people and resources together," says the

American Library Association on their TEDxLibraries page.[24] Planning and implementing a TEDx provides a process that can support the move from "collection development to connection development."

While most TEDx events are held once or twice a year, TEDxLibrary events are typically recurring, held weekly, monthly, or quarterly. Libraries can feature local speakers and performers, as well show TED and TEDx films. To secure a TEDxLibrary license to host events in your library, you'll need to do the following:

- Read and understand the rules for hosting a TEDx event.[25]
- Adhere to the required naming convention: TEDx (LocationName) Library.
- Decide before you apply for your license how big of an event you can hold, how often you'd like to hold it, and if you're confident in your ability to consistently organize and produce the event.
- Once you've got all your ducks in a row, apply for your license at TEDx.com.

While the aforementioned list of events and overview is extensive, it by no means represents the full extent of special events you can host in celebration of your makerspace and related programming. Your imagination is the only limit to the types of events that can draw new visitors to your library and showcase the great work being done there.

NOTES

1. Hatch, Mark. *The Maker Movement Manifesto: Rules for Innovation in the New World of Crafters, Hackers, and Tinkerers*. New York: McGraw-Hill, 2014.
2. Graves, Colleen. "National Maker Events." *Create+Collaborate Innovate*. February 24, 2016. Accessed May 29, 2017. https://colleengraves.org/maker-event-calendar-for-libraries-and-makerspaces/.
3. Cruz, Rebecca. "A Mini Maker Faire at the Library." *Public Libraries Online*. March 23, 2015. Accessed May 29, 2017. http://publiclibrariesonline.org/2015/03/a-mini-maker-faire-at-the-library/.
4. Willingham, Theresa. "History." *Gulf Coast Makers*. May 24, 2013. Accessed May 29, 2017. https://gulfcoastmakers.com/history/.

5. "Makers@PPL 2017." *Portland Public Library*. Accessed May 29, 2017. www.portlandlibrary.com/events/makersppl-2017/#sthash.9wvwOHVv.dpuf.

6. Ministerie van Volksgezondheid, Welzijn en Sport. "Rural Makers Event for Education." *Subsidie | Dienst Uitvoering Subsidies aan Instellingen*. Accessed May 29, 2017. www.rijksoverheid.nl/onderwerpen/subsidies-vws/inhoud/subsidiere-geling-landelijk-makersevenement-onderwijs.

7. Kalshoven, Lisette. "Maker Party: Copyright and Maker Culture." *Read, Write, Participate*. Accessed May 29, 2017. https://medium.com/read-write-participate/maker-party-copyright-and-maker-culture-9bdbb198a489.

8. "Generation Code." *Public Libraries 2020*. Accessed May 29, 2017. http://publiclibraries2020.eu/content/generation-code.

9. Smith, Kelly. "Coding for Everyone: How Your Library Can Help Anyone Learn to Code." July 19, 2016. Accessed May 29, 2017. www.webjunction.org/content/dam/WebJunction/Documents/webJunction/2016-07/slides-coding-for-everyone.pdf.

10. Enis, Matt. "How to Talk Code | Digital Literacy." *Library Journal*. February 24, 2016. Accessed May 29, 2017. http://lj.libraryjournal.com/2016/02/technology/how-to-talk-code-digital-literacy/#_.

11. "Hacking the Library: 48 Hours to Better Libraries through Collaborative Technology." *GPLS NewsWire*. November 10, 2014. Accessed May 29, 2017. http://glean.georgialibraries.org/hacking-the-library-48-hours-to-better-libraries-through-collaborative-technology.

12. Davis, Robin Camille. "Hackathons for Libraries and Librarians." *Academic Works, City University of New York*. September 2016. Accessed May 29, 2017. http://academicworks.cuny.edu/cgi/viewcontent.cgi?article=1083&context=jj_pubs/.

13. "Hackaday Prize 2017." *Hackaday*. Accessed May 29, 2017. https://hackaday.io/prize.

14. MacDonald, Heidi. "How to Throw a ComicCon at Your Library." *Publishers Weekly*. April 18, 2014. Accessed May 29, 2017. ww.publishersweekly.com/pw/by-topic/industry-news/comics/article/61940-how-to-throw-a-comic-con-at-your-library.html.

15. "Rules, Policies, and Frequently Asked Questions." *MetroCon*. Accessed May 29, 2017. http://metroconventions.com/policies-faq-main/.

16. "About 1 Million Cups." *1 Million Cups*. Accessed May 29, 2017. www.1millioncups.com/about.

17. Makin, Bob. "Bridgewater Library Hosts 'Shark Tank'-Like Teen Tycoons." *My Central Jersey*. May 3, 2016. Accessed May 29, 2017. www.mycen-

traljersey.com/story/money/business/2016/05/03/bridgewater-library-hosts-shark-tank-like-teen-tycoons/83890102/.

18. Makin, "Bridgewater Library Hosts 'Shark Tank'-Like Teen Tycoons."

19. "Judging a Pitch Competition." *Beeck Center*. Accessed May 29, 2017. http://beeckcenter.georgetown.edu/judging-a-pitch-competition-tips/.

20. "Creating Effective Webinars." *Association for Library Collections and Technical Services*. August 26, 2016. Accessed May 29, 2017. www.ala.org/alcts/confevents/upcoming/webinar/081716.

21. "Junior *FIRST* LEGO League." *STAR_Net*. Accessed May 29, 2017. www.starnetlibraries.org/portfolio-items/junior-first-lego-league/.

22. "Our Mission/Contact Us." *Fixit Clinic*. Accessed July 25, 2017. http://fixitclinic.blogspot.com/p/bring-your-broken-non-functioning.html.

23. "Why Buy New? Fix What You Have! Fixit Clinics Coming to the Library's Recycled Reads Bookstore." *Austin Public Library*. Accessed July 25, 2017. http://library.austintexas.gov/press-release/why-buy-new-fix-what-you-have-fixit-clinics-coming-librarys-recycled-reads-bookstore.

24. "About TEDx and Libraries." *Libraries Transform*. June 10, 2013. Accessed May 29, 2017. www.ala.org/transforminglibraries/tedx-libraries.

25. "TEDx Rules." *TED.com*. Accessed May 29, 2017. www.ted.com/participate/organize-a-local-tedx-event/before-you-start/tedx-rules.

7

MAKERSPACE INVENTORY

A Closer Look at Tools and Resources

Makerspaces are loud, messy, and full of energy. Shouts of excitement, paint spilling on the floor, soldering bits falling onto the table, and other such messes are inevitable. Plan your space accordingly.

—Morgan Gariepy, young adult services librarian, East Bonner County Library District, Sandpoint, Idaho

As libraries turn to the big game of construction—from art and handcraft to filmmaking and more—the tools of the makerspace trade need to be considered carefully with an eye to the goals of your space, user needs and preferences, and available space in which to use them. Makerspace inventory essentially comes in two basic flavors:

1. Tools and equipment
2. Materials and supplies

Tools and equipment are not consumed but need to be tracked for security and maintenance reasons. Materials and supplies are inventory that are consumed and need to be kept stocked for library programs and projects. There are a number of different ways to manage these two categories of inventory, and the best time to make decisions about equipment and its management, storage, and maintenance is before you start accruing it—not after.

Equipment in the first category can have serial numbers or bar codes, or simply be outlined on a peg board or identified on lists in toolboxes or cabinets. Maintenance and safety inspection schedules should be prepared for any equipment that requires regular maintenance or has safety features associated with it, for example, blade guards, power locks, safety shields, and so on. Items in the second category, materials and supplies, need a more dedicated inventory management process since use and turnover will be more regular and items need to be restocked proactively before they are exhausted. If you're venturing into tool lending, lendable resources need a serial number or some identifying code that uniquely identifies them and connects them, like a book, to the person who borrows the equipment.

As you look at the different categories of tools and equipment, and related considerations for cost and budgeting, we recommend creating two price columns for your makerspace buildout: "$ Budget" and "$ Deluxe," since equipment prices vary depending on brand, supplier, source, model, and more. The two price columns can give you a visible budgetary range within which to consider each tool or piece of equipment. In this chapter, we'll take a look at the following:

- Basics: space, power, noise, and intent
- Common hand and power tools
- Specialty equipment for things like A/V programming, textiles, arts, 3D printers, etc.
- Large equipment
- Software and hardware
- Tool and resource lending.
- Tracking and inventory
- Maintenance

Keep in mind that everything shared in this section amounts to basic recommendations, and your own mileage may vary. Make your makerspace decisions based on what works best for your facility, with the budget and community needs and interests you have, which may not necessarily be the ones you want. Here we go!

THE BASICS

A great guide for getting started is *The Makerspace Workbench*,[1] by Adam Kemp, a special, freely available *Make:* magazine book available in PDF format that gets down into the weeds on everything related to physical makerspace needs. We'll draw on some material from *The Makerspace Workbench* here but recommend reading the book yourself to mine for applicable tips and ideas for your library space.

Another good resource is the 15-page "Make a Makerspace Worksheet,"[2] developed by Gui Cavalcanti and Molly Rubenstein at Artisan's Asylum (artisansasylum.com), a large, well-established public makerspace in Somerville, Massachusetts. While Artisan's Asylum is membership based and operates on a different model than library makerspaces, much of the process for developing a makerspace of either type is similar.

The worksheet starts with the same basic premise we've been repeating here: "You should know what your goals are for your space before you start this process. Why are you doing this? What are you looking to get out of both the process and the space?" The worksheet walks you through a variety of considerations, some more relevant than others for the purposes of a library makerspace, but most worth at least a summary evaluation.

A sander. ***Chuck Stephens***

The first things to consider as you begin to build out your space, tools, and equipment are the constraints within which you have to work and how people fit into those constraints when they go to use the resources in your makerspace. Once you've identified the type of makerspace you're designing for your library—based on the back-end work you did with focus groups and community asset mapping (chapter 2)—you can use the tool charts in *The Makerspace Workbench* to help you best allocate equipment and people within the space you'll be using. Things to take into consideration as you select your tools include the following:

- *Facility focus:* What's the intent of your makerspace and how was it determined? If it's top-down, be aware that what whatever you bring into your space should be as multifaceted as possible for variable uses and interest. If you haven't identified your user base, don't overinvest in equipment that may likely get little to no use. If, however, you have a good understanding of what your community wants, through extensive discussions and focus group analysis, you'll have a much better understanding of the types of tools and equipment your stakeholders will most value and use. Essentially, the better you know your audience, the more effectively you can stock your space and the better the return on your investment.
- *Power availability and allocation:* Do you have sufficient power access for hand or large-scale power tools, 3D printers, laser cutters, sewing machines, or other equipment that requires electricity? More critically, can the power distribution system in your library handle multiple draws on electricity?
- *Physical work space:* Kemp advises, "A good rule of thumb for determining a number of occupants in your makerspace is to allocate 50 square feet of space per person—that's roughly a 7-foot by 7-foot area. This allotment allows for safe use of floor space, especially as the occupants will be working in a lab environment." Also take into consideration accessibility for differently abled users.[3]
- *Noise issues:* You'll need to plan accordingly if your makerspace isn't sufficiently soundproofed or otherwise separate from other patron areas where people are reading or studying. You need to either plan for low-noise programming or schedule noisy activities so they don't

conflict with quieter times. Or plan the other way around and don't schedule quieter library activities when noisy things are going on in your makerspace.

- *Ventilation:* Plan ahead on ventilation. So many libraries we've worked with have stumbled on this issue. If you'll be using any kind of equipment that creates sawdust or other debris—metal shavings, dust, smoke or fumes, plastic or fabric residue—install the appropriate filtration and ventilation systems while you're building out your space. If you can't install outside ventilation, there are portable, freestanding units that can be attached to relevant equipment. Also consider dust and other debris when deciding on placement of such sensitive equipment as computers for computer-aided design (CAD) or digital editing and A/V equipment—and don't colocate the two.
- *Storage:* As library after library has told us (see chapter 3), storage is something many wished they also had taken into consideration earlier in their planning stages. Don't wait until you're knee deep in 3D printer filament, metal fasteners, and scattered hand tools to try to figure out where to store everything. Plan on appropriate storage for each piece of equipment and its related materials or supplies.
- *Safety:* As with storage, make safety an integral part of your makerspace planning and an unnegotiable part of your makerspace culture. We'll look more closely at best safety practices in chapter 9, on risk management. But it's important to mention this crucial aspect of your makerspace planning here so it's a top-of-the-mind issue going forward and a key component of the makerspace culture you want to establish. Be generous with signage throughout your space and the appropriate safety equipment, from easily accessible and well-maintained fire extinguishers, safety glasses, and hearing protection and first aid kits to solid orientation and training practices and relevant documents and user agreements.

HAND AND POWER TOOLS

"The overall goal of any tool purchase is to engage as many patrons as possible while providing educational and creative outlets to the community," said

Maker librarian Chuck Stephens, of the Pasco County Library Cooperative in Florida. Before purchasing a new set of tools, he recommended "testing the waters with a few related classes and workshops to gauge interest." He added,

> When a few patrons requested jewelry-making classes, our branch manager found some cool projects that required a minimum of tools. They were hugely successful, and now we're ordering a wider selection of jewelry-specific tools. We are taking a similar approach with our electronics classes, and it's working quite well. Allow the tool collection to grow with the patronage.
>
> You can't have enough basic hand tools—pliers, screwdrivers, scissors, wrenches, hammers, etc. When you're working with a group, everyone will inevitably want to use the vice grips at once. Have multiples of everything.

So, what's "everything"? That's going to vary a bit according to the purpose and intent of your space, but there are some basic hand and power tools that most good workshops should have, and that's as good a place as any to start in stocking up your basic tool inventory. A good guide to help you through the process is the MakerEd e-book *High School Makerspace Tools and Materials*.[4] Despite the title, the book is an excellent resource for understanding the different types of tools needed for different types of making, from electronics to woodworking, with basic costs to help you budget. The book is a few years old, but prices aren't significantly different and easy enough to update.

We also recommend sourcing tools and equipment independently, from good, reliable commercial or wholesale suppliers, rather than sourcing from makerspace package stores, so to speak—companies that promise one-stop shopping makerspace solutions. Prepackaged solutions are typically bundled with things you don't need and priced above normal retail, and certainly above wholesale prices you can get elsewhere.

But you also don't want to go the other route and underinvest in things that will get heavy use. While browsing Craigslist or accepting donations of equipment can be helpful, it's important that tools sourced are in good, reliable working order, for safety and optimum usefulness. With any tool purchase, you get what you pay for, said Stephens. "Cheap tools are never a bargain when you're trying to educate."

Drill press, Pasco County Library makerspace. ***Theresa Willingham***

There are good reasons you've heard of Dremel, Dewalt, Bosch, Milwaukee, and similar brands, he pointed out. For heavy public use, buy name-brand, trusted tools that are warranted and will last. It's important to note that there is no one correct and complete list of tools or resources for a one-size-fits-all makerspace, since every makerspace has different needs, circumstances, and clientele.

Perhaps the best way to think about tools is to consider what they're used for, which is a wide range of applications:

assembling
cutting
finishing
forming
fusing
gripping/holding
heating
imaging
impacting
lifting
measuring
pressure/vacuum
printing
prying
safety
testing
textile

Table 7.1. Tools Sorted by Category

Classification	*Category*	*Tool Name*
hand tools	assembly	socket sets
hand tools	assembly	torque wrench
hand tools	assembly	hex key sets, imperial and metric
hand tools	assembly	torx key sets
hand tools	assembly	mini hex drivers
hand tools	assembly	combination wrenches, metric and inch
hand tools	assembly	adjustable wrenches
hand tools	assembly	screwdrivers, flat and Phillips
hand tools	assembly	jeweler's screwdrivers
computer-controlled tools	cutting	laser cutter
computer-controlled tools	cutting	plasma utter
computer-controlled tools	cutting	water jet
electronics tools	cutting	wire stripper
hand or bench power tools	cutting	18V electric drill
hand or bench power tools	cutting	reciprocating saw
hand or bench power tools	cutting	plunge router
hand or bench power tools	cutting	Dremel

Table 7.2. Tools Sorted by Classification

Classification	*Category*	*Tool Name*
computer-controlled tools	cutting	laser cutter
computer-controlled tools	cutting	plasma cutter
computer-controlled tools	cutting	water jet
electronics tools	cutting	wire stripper
hand or bench power tools	cutting	18V electric drill
hand or bench power tools	cutting	reciprocating saw
hand or bench power tools	cutting	plunge router
hand or bench power tools	cutting	Dremel
hand or bench power tools	cutting	angle grinder
hand or bench power tools	cutting	bench grinder
hand or bench power tools	cutting	hot knife
hand or bench power tools	finishing	belt sander
hand tools	assembly	socket sets
hand tools	assembly	torque wrench

Tools themselves can be classified and categorized indifferent ways but generally fall in the following categories:

- Computer-controlled tools
- Electronics tools
- Hand tools
- Measurement tools
- Hand or bench power tools
- Large power tools
- Specialty tools

Eureka! Factory has developed an equipment budgeting tool that sorts tools by application and type that can help librarians see different ways to allocate tools and resources, and decide which combinations are the most cost effective for their needs. For our purposes, we'll take a look at some of the more common categories of library makerspace tools and their uses, starting with hand tools.

Hand Tools

Generally, if you'll be using hand tools in your library makerspace, these items are a solid bet:

- Combination wrench sets: SAE (Society of Automotive Engineers—also known as English or imperial measurements—inches, etc.) sizes ¼" to ¾" and metric sizes from 10mm to 24mm
- Socket sets SAE ⅜" drive, sockets from 5/16" to ¾"
- Wrenches, including adjustable "crescent" wrench 6" and/or 8" length, hex wrench sets SAE 5/64" to ¼" and metric 1.5mm to 8mm
- Bench vises 4" or larger jaws, at least two
- Claw hammer(s)
- Dial calipers
- Pliers, including slip joint, needle nose, square nose, and locking
- Utility knives with retractable blades
- Miter box, plastic or wood
- Hacksaw, open frame

- Center punch
- Scissors, including utility/EMT scissors, fabric shears, and embroidery scissors
- Tape measure 16' or longer
- Carpenter's square, steel 16" × 24"
- Clamps, bar clamp 24" or longer, C-clamps, 90-degree/framing clamps, 3" to 4" spring clamps
- Staple gun, heavy duty, manual
- Wire brush

Electrical Tools

- Pencil soldering iron 30w
- Basic temperature-controlled soldering station with replaceable/interchangeable tips
- Soldering stand with sponge (might be included with more advanced soldering irons)
- Helping hands, a device for holding materials being worked on
- Digital multimeter
- Oscilloscope, 2-channel or more, 500MS/s or better
- Wire stripper for 22- to 30-gauge wire
- Flush diagonal cutters
- Solder vacuum
- Solderless breadboard, "half size" 400 point
- Solderless breadboard, "full size" 800-plus point

Power Tools

- Drills, corded and cordless
- High-amp jigsaw
- Dremel tool sets
- Hot glue gun, full size, commercial, rather than "mini" or "craft" versions
- Heat gun, 300w or more

SPECIALTY EQUIPMENT

3D printers are probably the most familiar piece of "specialty" equipment for libraries with a makerspace program. When the earlier library makerspaces got underway, 3D printers were expensive, with a limited number of suppliers, Makerbot principal among them. Today, there are dozens, and prices range from a couple hundred dollars to tens of thousands of dollars. You can stick with the mainstream brands if your budget allows, but there are far less expensive and far more reliable new offerings. For the purposes of most libraries, with or without makerspaces, you don't need a makerspace to install a 3D printer in your facility. Some of the most cost effective and reliable machines are as follows:

- Prusa[5]
- XYZ Davinci and Davinci Jr.
- Anet A8 (This printer requires assembly but makes up for the investment of assembly time by the freedom from proprietary filament that many other printers necessitate.)
- Monoprice MP Mini Delta 3D (At the time of this writing, while not yet available, this printer was garnering a lot of attention as a low-cost, fully assembled, high-quality, open-filament printer [mpminidelta.monoprice.com].)

If your space will feature a textiles component for costuming and more, you'll want to include the following:

- Sewing machine(s), heavy-duty commercial brands like Janome
- Serger
- Seam ripper
- Cloth tape measure
- Steam iron, with an auto-off feature
- Ironing board, freestanding, collapsible
- Leather punch
- Snap setter with multiple sizes of bits/dies
- Sewing awl
- Embroidery hoops, 10" and 6"
- Knitting needle assortment, at least four pair of different sizes

Music and A/V equipment. ***Chuck Stephens***

If you'll have an A/V studio area, for video or audio recording, gaming, or animation, you'll want to make sure you have the following, with related editing software:

- DSLR camera
- Studio camcorder
- Photo/video studio light kit
- Studio camera tripod
- Music keyboard workstation
- Electronic drum station
- Blu-ray writer
- Webcam C920
- Lapel microphone
- Studio microphone
- Microphone preamp processor
- Premium 12-input 2/2 mixer
- Studio speaker system
- Over-ear headphones
- Soundproofing foam, acoustic tiles, and acoustic foam corner bass traps (if you're finishing out an enclosed recording area)

- 4-channel headphone amp
- Digital audio workstation and MIDI sequencer software

For an arts-related space—and we're talking more than basic arts and crafts here, wherever possible—you'll want:

- Easels, tabletop and floor
- LEGO wall materials
- High-end graphic editing computers and related software
- Silhouette digital cutter

Culinary arts is another increasingly popular offering in library makerspaces. While at the outset it seems like that might be a hard thing to pull off, if you've got easy access to water or even a library breakroom, it's not particularly complex to add cooking resources to your library makerspace. Some basic equipment that requires no additional library build-out to use include the following:

- Double-induction cooktop
- Single-induction cooktop
- Induction-compatible cookware
- Cooking utensil set

All of these items can be incorporated into a mobile cart for easy storage when not in use.

Kits

There are a number of resource and programming kits that have become staples in library makerspaces or libraries that offer Maker-style programming. These often include

- LittleBits[6]
- Bare Conductive (bareconductive.com), a great way to make interactive objects

- Boldport (boldport.club), a U.K. subscription-based electronics imitative
- Micro:bit (microbit.org), a BBC initiative to get British children to start coding (The micro:bit board will be introduced in the Netherlands and Iceland but will later expand to the United States and Asia.)
- MaKey MaKeys
- Snap Circuits
- Ozobots
- Cubelets

LARGE EQUIPMENT

While most library makerspaces won't have anything larger than a 3D printer or maybe a tabletop laser cutter, some may want to consider larger equipment—but if, and only if, there is clear and obvious demand for such equipment in your community. If you conducted sufficient stakeholder feedback and focus group sessions, you'll know whether your space can or should invest in large-scale equipment.

"With larger tool investments, there's a complex mental equation," said Chuck Stephens, "the usability versus the learning curve versus the price versus safety factors." He continued,

> A state of the art 3D printer is of little use if no one has an interest in learning CAD. A woodshop is awesome until the county lawyers shut it down as a liability. How many people would benefit from a laser cutter versus a new sewing center? All tool purchases have to fall within the ever-shifting "safe zone" of meeting multiple goals. It's a real challenge.

Large equipment can include the following:

- Floor drill press
- Table saw
- Band saw
- Lathe

This type of equipment requires supervised use, training, and regular monitoring and maintenance.

SOFTWARE AND HARDWARE

If your space will have any kind of programming and resources for things like music, filmmaking, animation, game design, graphic arts, or digital design, you'll want to have the following, at minimum:

- High-performance PC/laptop
- Video editing PC/laptop
- 3D Creation software
- 27" video monitor
- Color image scanner
- GarageBand (Mac)
- Acoustica Mixcraft (Windows)
- Gimp (free version of Photoshop)
- Corel Painter
- Artweaver
- Autodesk SketchBook Express
- Manga Studio software

TOOL- AND RESOURCE-LENDING SYSTEMS

In some cases, libraries might be interested in lending out their tools and resources, much like lending books and videos. The Public Library Association has a great resource page for nontraditional circulating materials.[7] The guide includes things like Wi-Fi hotspots, seed libraries, hand tools, kitchen tools, and appliances.

Berkeley Public Library (berkeleypubliclibrary.org/borrowing-tools) in California has run a tool-lending library for a while now, as does California's Oakland Public Library,[8] which has more than 5,000 tools available for checkout. In each case, local residents with library cards can check out any of a vast number and variety of tools, from garden tools to concrete and masonry tools and more, from anywhere from three to seven days. Obviously, there's a lot to consider if you decide to lend out tools. Sharestarter has a great page dedicated to starting a tool-lending library (sharestarter.org/tools/), and LocalTools.org features management software to help track and maintain your inventory.

Another lending system is mobile kits, or as they're called in the Blue Valley School District in Overland Park, Kansas, "Tinker Tubs"[9]: district-wide mobile makerspace kits made available through the school-district libraries. These mobile tubs may be checked out by school librarians for two weeks at a time, with the goal of testing the tools for future purchase and supplementing existing makerspace collections. Each wheeled tub contains the technology tool(s)—things like Sphero robots kits, virtual reality headsets and related equipment, and coding tools and resources—manuals, inventory sheets, and necessary supplies, including batteries.

"With limited budgets, the librarians wanted to get the best deal on many tech tools—many tried out the tubs and then were able to make purchases based on usability, comfort level, and integration possibilities. We also provided tools that would work for a variety of grade levels, so librarians could determine the best tool for their grade levels," explains Becca Munson in an article about the kits for *Knowledge Quest* magazine.[10]

This idea can also be rolled out effectively among branch libraries in a public library system. The biggest challenge with the loaner kits is consistently stocking and maintaining them, which leads us to our next section, where we discuss tracking and inventory of these great items.

TRACKING AND INVENTORY

So, if you've got all this stuff, you need to track it and maintain your inventory, not only of the tools and equipment itself, but also of related consumables. Consumables are things that are used up: 3D printer filament, fasteners, thread, and so forth. That also includes things that tend to be easily lost or carried out, like sewing needles or colored pencils.

"Blades, bits, belts, sandpaper, mineral spirits, solder, thread, and on and on—it all costs money and it all adds up," said Chuck Stephens. He added,

> That 3D printer is awesome, but if you didn't budget for the filament, it's just a conversation piece. If you have woodworking, you'll need sandpaper, nails, screws, varnish, glue, paint, bits, and blades—all of which wears out or gets used up. Do you limit tool time or charge patrons a nominal fee per gram of 3D printer filament used? Who organizes the donated hardware and paints? (There *will* be donated hardware and paints—the trick is knowing what to

recycle or dispose of and what's actually usable.) How will the periodic purchase of consumables fit into your current budgeting scheme?

Stephens advises having a policy in place regarding the use of unaccompanied and abandoned tools, as well as for public versus privately owned tools and tools owned by groups that use the space. "When something's missing, it's not the time to determine just whose drill it was to begin with," he noted.

The issue of donated items is a common one for makerspaces, both public and private.[11] A Tampa-area makerspace routinely finds donations of tools and equipment at their doorstep, like they're a tool shelter. While in one respect this is touching, in another it can be problematic, since donated tools may or may not be in the best of shape or have any value to the space. With a library, it's especially important that equipment is in good working order, for both safety and reliability.

To that end, it's especially important to have a preestablished donations policy. Appleton Makerspace in Wisconsin (appletonmakerspace.org/donations/), for instance, handles the issue online, with a clear list of needed items and a process for making donations. Decide early on what you're willing to accept and have a policy both for accepting makerspace donations and rejecting and disposing of unwanted contributions.

The Johnson County Public Library System (jocolibrary.org/makerspace) has a nice inventory and space reservation tracking and management system that allows users to reserve makerspace tools easily online and track use. They use an off-the-shelf solution sold by Springshare (springshare.com) for reservations and inventory their equipment via their IT department. Makerspace manager Meredith Nelson said they've also developed a custom replacement schedule for their equipment, as it is always a good idea to keep everything in good, safe working order.

Demco recently merged with Evanced (evancedsolutions.com), the system used by a large number of libraries for event, program, and space management, and, as of this writing, is working on developing new library makerspace management tools as well.

However you decide to do it, do it: Inventory your equipment on paper, or with barcodes or some other system, and track its use and maintenance regularly so you have a clear understanding of degrees of use and can maintain your equipment accordingly.

MAINTENANCE

Once you're stocked up with your tools and equipment, you're going to need to maintain them and the spaces in which they're located. Make sure your makerspace is well stocked with the following maintenance supplies:

- Shop vacuum
- Regular floor vacuum
- Broom and dustpan
- Ventilation equipment, portable or built in

Then for the best equipment longevity, safety, and user value, set up a regular maintenance schedule that staff and users adhere to. This can be as simple a weekly check of tools to make sure everything is in good working order—that cords aren't nicked or blades chipped or broken. Or you can turn to the pros, like the Occupational Safety and Health Administration (OSHA),[12] and employ industry best practices to evaluate equipment on a regular basis. The website Choose Hand Safety provides a helpful "Safety Walkaround Checklist" for hand tools.[13] Included on the checklist are the following common sense precautions:

- Ensure tools are used only for their intended purpose; make sure patrons use the right tools for the right jobs.
- Inspect tools daily or at least weekly to make sure they're in good repair and sharp when they need to be, with no chips, excessive wear, or metal fatigue.
- Clean and sharpen tools regularly, perhaps monthly or quarterly, depending on the extent of use.
- Make sure to remove or label damaged, defective, or worn tools and service or replace them in a timely fashion.
- Check workspace lighting regularly and make sure no lights are out or unevenly applied.

- Ensure that tools are stored in their proper places and in the right manner, with sharp edges and points sheathed, and not left lying around, especially in overhead workspaces where they could fall on people.

Proper Cleaning

Libraries should inspire patrons who use the makerspace tools to clean the tools and the space they used before leaving for the day. "Leave no trace," the mantra for outdoor ethics, is also a highly relevant mantra for makerspaces. If tools and workspaces are not given at least a basic cleanup after each use, their usability and usefulness will rapidly degrade into uselessness. Depending on the extent of use, tools and equipment should be given a thorough cleaning anywhere from once a week to once a month. Resources that get a lot of use should be disinfected as well. Cleaning is pretty straightforward with most things: wash or wipe down to remove residue or hand oils and treat with appropriate protectant. While tool users should be instructed to clean tools after they use them, it's a good idea to inspire a core group of volunteers to take ownership of the cleanliness and tidiness of the space as a whole.

Launder Those LEGOs

Library LEGOs—which are a tool as much as a toy—are an often-overlooked source of, well, grossness, and typically aren't cleaned as often as they should be—or more likely, in many libraries, at all. There are a few different ways to clean them. Some librarians have recommended washing LEGOs in a tub of hot water, with a half-cup of baking soda and a half-cup of vinegar, then rinsing them and laying them out on a towel to dry. Chuck Stephens however, has it down to a scheduled and less labor-intensive science. Said Stephens,

> I clean them every six to eight weeks. I make sure they are all separated, place them in a doubled-up mesh lingerie bag, and wash them in the washing machine with light detergent (about a quarter of what I'd use for a load of clothes). I use two sets of doubled bags so the load is balanced. Then I spread them on a sheet in the sun to dry, turning them over a few times throughout the process.

LEGOs. ***Chuck Stephens***

Hand Tools

With hand tools, a few times a year, depending on the extent of use, you can either clean them with a recommended commercial product (like Lestoil or Pine-Sol) or wipe them down with heavy-duty disinfecting wipes. Either way, dry the tools thoroughly, using a wire brush to remove any rust deposits, and spritz with a light coat of WD-40 and wipe with a clean rag. Wooden handles can be cleaned with a linseed-oiled cloth.

Power Tools

Check power towels regularly for nicks or breaks in cords or cracked cases or frames and clean them by wiping them down with disinfecting wipes and oiling as needed. Users should be instructed to at least wipe down power tools after each use, and the area around floor tools should always be swept and kept clean of debris.

Next up: How to help the people who make it all work, from your staff and volunteers to your community stakeholders, help your makerspace be as successful as possible.

NOTES

1. Kemp, Adam. *The Makerspace Workbench*. Sebastopol, CA: *Make:*, 2013. Accessed May 31, 2017. www.farnell.com/datasheets/1895152.pdf.

2. Cavalcanti, Gui, and Molly Rubenstein. "Make a Makerspace Worksheet." *Artisan's Asylum*. January 2015. Accessed May 31, 2017. http://artisansasylum.com/wp-content/uploads/2015/01/Make-a-Makerspace-Worksheet-2014-05-07.pdf.

3. Alper, Meryl. "Making Space in the Makerspace: Building a Mixed-Ability Maker Culture." *Annenberg School for Communication and Journalism*. March 2013. Accessed May 31, 2017. https://teethingontech.files.wordpress.com/2013/03/idc13-workshop_meryl-alper.pdf.

4. *High School Makerspace Tools and Materials*. *MakerEd*. April 2012. Accessed May 31, 2017. http://makered.org/wp-content/uploads/2014/09/Makerspace-High-School-Makerspace-Tools-And-Materials-April-2012.pdf.

5. "Original Prusa i3 MK2 Review: It Doesn't Get Any Better." *All3DP*. October 3, 2016. Accessed June 1, 2017. https://all3dp.com/original-prusa-i3-mk2-review-reprap-3d-printer-kit/.

6. Graves, Colleen. "The Librarians Guide to STEAM." *EDU Librarians Guide*. March 2015. Accessed May 31, 2017. https://d2q6sbo7w75ef4.cloudfront.net/EDU-LibrariansGuide-V1-7.pdf.

7. "Nontraditional Circulating Materials." *Public Library Association*. April 14, 2017. Accessed June 1, 2017. www.ala.org/pla/resources/tools/circulation-technical-services/nontraditional-circulating-materials.

8. "Tool List and Lending Guidelines." *Oakland Public Library*. Accessed June 1, 2017. www.oaklandlibrary.org/locations/tool-lending-library/tool-list-lending-guidelines.

9. Munson, Becca. "Tinker Tubs: District-Wide Mobile Makerspaces." *Knowledge Quest*. May 22, 2017. Accessed June 1, 2017. http://knowledgequest.aasl.org/tinker-tubs-district-wide-mobile-makerspaces.

10. Munson, "Tinker Tubs."

11. List, Jenny. "The Complex Issue of Hackspace Donations." *Hackaday*. April 14, 2017. Accessed June 1, 2017. http://hackaday.com/2017/04/14/the-complex-issue-of-hackspace-donations/.

12. *Hand and Power Tools*. *U.S. Department of Labor/Occupational Safety and Health Administration*. 2002. Accessed May 31, 2017. www.osha.gov/Publications/osha3080.pdf.

13. "Safety Walkaround Checklist: Hand Tools." *Choose Hand Safety*. 2001. Accessed June 1, 2017. www.choosehandsafety.org/sites/default/files/docs/walk_around_checklist_-_hand_tools.pdf.

8

MAKERS

The Human Element

You don't have to do everything! Do what you can do well, the rest will come. And use your community. I realized I don't need to be an expert at everything, someone else already is.

—Rasheil Stanger, Valley of the Tetons Library, Idaho

A makerspace isn't about the space, it's about the Makers, the people who use the space. It's also about the people who run the space, who teach and mentor there, who maintain it, who share what they create with one another, who inspire one another to new heights of creative and economic empowerment. Without the human element, a makerspace is worthless. It's just a space, like tools without hands to use them are just pieces of metal, plastic, and rubber. Of all the tools and resources in your library makerspace, none will be more important than the Makers—both your staff and volunteer Makers who make the space possible and the patron Makers who will use the space.

Your human capital is the heart of your makerspace and the most important part to nurture and develop. The more time, training, support, and personal engagement you invest in the people who will both make and use your space, the more effectively your library will build vital ownership and community pride in the space, and the more fiscal and moral support that can become available. In this chapter, we'll look at the different types of people who, with the right training, support, and empowerment, will make your space not only possible, but also effective and enjoyable. These include the following:

- Staff Makers
- Volunteer Makers
- Patron Makers
- Community Makers
- Funding Makers

We'll wrap up with a short overview of how to keep programing relevant and enjoyable. Let's start with staff and how to best engage them in Maker culture in ways they enjoy and that benefit your space.

STAFF MAKERS

In *Makerspaces in Libraries* we write,

> Before librarians can embrace Maker culture, they have to understand it. . . . For libraries, giving staff the opportunity to explore creative programming and to discover and build upon their own innate skills and interests can directly translate into empowered and impassioned librarians who can reinvigorate library programming and have a great time doing it.[1]

While "Maker culture" is a lot more familiar to most librarians today, if you're just embarking on the makerspace journey in your library, it's important to make sure everyone involved, first and foremost, staff, understand what's happening, why, and how integral they are to the process. While it's always important that employees are engaged in any programming, at a library or anywhere, with respect to the Maker experience, it's especially important that staff clearly understand what's going on and engage with infectious enjoyment wherever possible.

The very nature of the Maker experience is based on a community of joyful creation and a love of sharing the things created. In the same way people expect librarians to be authorities on books, or at the very least, to enjoy reading and book culture, patrons should see librarians in a makerspace as creative individuals interested in guiding them on the shared creative experience the space offers and excited to be using it with them.

Introduction to Maker Culture

A good way to introduce librarians to Maker culture is to show them that they're probably already Makers. This is a great opportunity to find out what staff members really like to do when they're not working or reading. Some may be avid board, card, or video game players, with a strong knowledge and appreciation for graphic arts, digital storytelling, animation, game theory, and game making itself. Others may have craft hobbies, like quilting, knitting, sculpting, or jewelry making. Some might belong to special interest clubs or organizations. Some may be movie buffs.

Having this conversation about what library staff does when not at work conceptually moves discussion from requirements-driven work to interest-driven living. The idea is to experience the opportunity to ask—and be asked—not only, "What do you like to read?" but also "What do you like to do?" Recognizing and honoring the creative abilities and interests of library staff is an integral part of building a Maker culture in the library and the first step toward changing public views of library culture. The two things are integrally connected: You can't build out an effective, sustainable makerspace in your library without first cultivating the Maker culture within it.

Staff Development

Holding a staff Maker program is a great form of staff development. Eureka! Factory has held a number of different staff development sessions on making, and they've been among the most popular staff development programs at the county library systems in which we've worked. In a an article on the benefits of holding a Maker program for staff, Holly Storck-Post, of Madison Public Library, identifies four main benefits to engaging staff in professional development making sessions:

- *Advocacy:* In the article, Storck-Post is referring to youth services advocacy, but Maker programming for staff serves as a form of advocacy for all departments, helping them see how their areas relate to Maker programming and ensuring that no librarian or library department is left out.

- *Marketing:* When library staff understands the maker culture, the goals, and the intent of library makerspace development, they can better explain its value and benefits to patrons.
- *Team building:* Maker programming naturally engages team-building skills. Many projects are collaborative, requiring many hands to make the light work or simply inspire mutual sharing of skills and talents.
- *Fun:* There's no way around it: Making stuff is usually fun. People get to work with craft materials, learn to solder, and make things light up, make sounds, or move. What's not to love?[2]

Of course, people being people, you'll find staff that doesn't enjoy the creative experience. That's okay. That gives you information, too. Don't assign those individuals to work in the makerspace area or in providing programming. It's okay for people to stay in their wheelhouse. That's an equally important reason to run staff development programming and give staff hands-on opportunities, to see how individuals respond and allocate them accordingly.

Staff Development Tools and Training

The best way to expose staff to Maker experiences is to hold staff Maker days. It's a good idea to hold individual branch or system-wide events, preferably in advance of any changes, to get staff thinking about what "making" is and comfortable with both the vocabulary of making and the hands-on nature of it all.

Some good staff development sessions include the following:

- *Squishy Circuits:*[3] Originally developed by the University of St. Thomas, in St. Paul, Minnesota, we include this project in *Makerspaces in Libraries*. Since the writing of that book in 2015, we've refined the project with the much less labor-intensive use of off-the-shelf play dough,[4] which cuts hours out of the preparation and yields equally fun, creative, and educational results.

- *Jitterbugs:*[5] Developed by Chuck Stephens of the Pasco County Library Cooperative, Jitterbugs offer a more interactive take on "brush bots."[6] Brush bots are typically made with a fingernail brush or toothbrush with a vibrating motor attached to it, powered by a small cell battery. Jitterbugs also employ a vibrating motor and battery but incorporate some simple soldering and adjustable wire "legs" and antennae that make the final product more fun and interactive.
- *Mindstorms robotics:* The LEGO Mindstorms education kit, which many libraries now stock, makes a great library staff development tool. Simple enough for a five-year-old to use, the drag-and-drop programming system makes it a fun intro to coding and robotics using the familiar format of LEGOs.
- *Music, instrument, or sound making:* Projects that make sounds are fun because of the immediate, often delightful feedback produced by the finished product. Simple handmade instruments can be anything from small or large cajon box drums and PVC pipe percussion instruments (ala the Blue Man Group) to kalimba or rhumba boxes. Sound projects like the Atari Punk Console[7] are less musical than noisy but just as much, if not more, fun, because it doesn't matter whether you can play an instrument or even if you have rhythm. These are opportunities to explore simple electronics and try out sound modulation. When we do the Atari Punk Console project with librarians, there's always this gentle wave of beeping and squealing that sweeps through the room, as one by one, the little sound devices come to life, followed by the delighted exclamations of librarians who just created an electronic device that makes sounds.
- *MaKey MaKeys or SnapCircuits:* Most libraries now stock these resources, but some librarians may not have had the opportunity to explore them. A staff tinkering session may be in order.

You can find many more professional development resources and ideas at the Making and Learning website.[8] The point here is that giving librarians the opportunity to experience the singular joy of creating something that didn't exist before is empowering and inspiring, and will, in turn, help them better connect with patrons trying out new tools, resources, and programs at their libraries.

Another thing to consider is what constitutes a "librarian" in the first place, especially in the 21st century, in a makerspace.

Rethinking Staff Requirements and Qualifications

In the thoughtful article "Re-Envisioning the MLS: The Future of Librarian Education," University of Maryland master in library science (MLS) professors and administrators propose that as we consider the future of public libraries, we also have to "consider the future of public librarians—and how we prepare them for a dynamic and evolving service context."[9]

In August 2014, the University of Maryland iSchool and Information Policy and Access Center (iPAC) launched the multiyear "Re-Envisioning the MLS" initiative to try to better understand, among other things, the following:

- What is the value of a MLS degree?
- What does the future MLS degree look like?
- What are the competencies, attitudes, and abilities that future library and information professionals need?

Among the key findings most relevant to our purposes here, with respect to makerspace programming, were the following:

- There has been a shift in focus to people and communities that de-emphasizes the physical collections (including digital content) and focuses more on individuals and the communities they serve, particularly through learning, making, content creation, and other forms of active and interactive engagement.
- The MLS degree may not be relevant or even necessary in all cases, with libraries increasingly reaching out to professionals in "instructional design/education; design; social work; public health; analytics; IT/IS; human resources management, and (those whose) skills might meet various needs better," recommending that "our information organizations should be open to those with a range of degrees other than the MLS."
- There is a need for information professionals who can understand and leverage their library community, people who are capable of identify-

ing the "different populations and needs of the communities that they serve, their challenges, and underlying opportunities. Additionally, our communities can serve as an extension of an information organization's services and resources. By leveraging the community's human resources, we can further enhance learning, education, expertise, and innovation."

- There is a need for library professionals who can effectively "foster learning by attending to an individual's particular interests, needs, and educational goals. An opportunity exists in focusing on youth learning, including Pre-K and 'readiness to read,' working with youth in schools, enhancing the understanding of primary data/information sources, including archival materials, facilitating learning in libraries through making, STEAM (science, technology, engineering, arts, and math), coding, and a range of other activities."[10]

It's increasingly up for debate whether the MLS is required at all or is even desirable for some new aspects of library work. In the same way the Fayetteville Free Library hired an educator to provide some of their programming (chapter 3), in 2014 the DC Public Library hired a social worker to be their "health and human services coordinator,"[11] to assist with the large homeless population that uses the library.

The practice of hiring outside the MLS degree is not without controversy, at least in the recent past. In 2010, the McMaster University Library in Hamilton, Ontario, Canada, was criticized for trying to hire PhD subject specialists and information technology professionals to run the library, and in 2011, there were raised voices in the library when the Alachua County Library District in Florida posted a job announcement for a non-MLS degreed director.

However, in the 2011 Evaluation and Measurement of Library Services survey, to which 500 academic library deans and directors representing more than 1,500 colleges and universities, and 370 public library directors representing more than 8,000 library systems, responded, more than 40 percent of the academic library directors felt there was a need to expand applicant pools beyond the MLS, with the nature of the work being the driving force behind not requiring the degree. Almost 80 percent of the public library directors said budget was the biggest factor in hiring outside the MLS degree.[12] But that was then and this is now, and libraries may want to start considering those with nondegreed skill sets as a valuable asset and reward expertise accordingly.

"The future belongs to those who are able to apply critical thinking skills and creativity to better understanding the communities they serve today and will serve five to 10 years down the road," the iSchool study's authors conclude, "and those who are bold, fearless, willing to take risks, go 'big,' and go against convention."[13]

One way to go big and against convention is to consider that perhaps a degree of any type may be unnecessary when hiring makerspace and related programming staff. Pasco County Library Cooperative in Florida hired Chuck Stephens on the strength of his skills and considerable experience as a tradesman, artist, and musician, fields of professional expertise that are not part of the typical MLS fields of study but are crucial to an effective makerspace. Stephens's background also helps him better communicate makerspace design and program needs to facilities personnel, and he brings a passionate, creative mindset to the programs he does with patrons, making him less of a distanced library professional and more of a peer Maker who makes programs enjoyable, inspiring, and empowering for participants.

It can take some courage to reach out into the community like that, and maybe the best way to embrace this type of "bold and fearless" risk taking in the hiring process is to reconsider some of the current staff titles and practices that may be holding libraries back from being truly innovative and game changing.

Rethinking the LTA and other Library Roles

Many of the library makerspace support staff running spaces and programming often fall under the handle of library assistant (LA) or library technical assistant (LTA). Stephens is technically a library assistant I, which doesn't adequately describe or financially reward the depth of passion and wealth of expertise he brings to his work or the positive impact he's making on the library system. Perhaps it's time to rethink the LTA position and look at some more accurate job titles with more appropriate pay for the individuals who leverage their innate skills and interests to the benefit of our public libraries.

Perhaps instead of LTAs, what library makerspaces are really looking for are jobs and positions more akin those in machine shops, craft studios, and woodshops, for example,

- Makerspace foreman
- Makerspace shop tech
- Makerspace program specialist
- Makerspace master craftsman

Another consideration in the 21st-century library should be the reallocation of positions that may have had their day, for instance, the sacrosanct "reference librarian" role. This is not to say that reference isn't important, but for the most part, the reference desk is Google for technophobes. This is an informed opinion with growing research and evidence to support the idea of changing up the reference-desk model in the library. Reference transactions, especially in large communities, have been falling steadily since 2003, with the advent of easy access to information on personal computers and smartphones, even while general program attendance has steadily increased. In the past 10 years, there's been about a 14 percent decrease in reference transactions overall.[14]

Yale's academic library closed their reference desk in 2008. In a 2016 article, Todd Gilman, librarian for literature in English at Yale University, writes, "It was *long* overdue. But when I mention this [to other librarians] elsewhere I can feel the anxiety in the room. 'Oh no! Not the beloved reference desk! What will we do all day if we can't sit there looking ready to help?'"

In the same article, Barbara Rockenbach, director of the humanities and history libraries at Columbia University, states, "It's not part of our mission to have a desk. It is our mission to be available to help with research and to partner with students and faculty on their research."[15]

The desk may be a symbol and part of the legacy of librarianship, she said, but that doesn't change the fact that they experienced a sharp decline in reference desk interactions and an increase in research consultations. Thus, the library combined their reference desk with their Digital Humanities Center to provide for more personal engagement and less transactional service.

Said Rockenbach,

> It is a library-centric view to say it's important and to keep the desk for its symbolic value. There is a rich tradition of reference and we want to honor that, but at the same time research is evolving and librarians have an opportunity to engage in partnerships with faculty and students that go beyond the reference desk.

There are lots of ways to provide reference support, and many libraries have turned to e-mail, instant messaging, and other mobile technologies, including social media, offering timely responses instead of static desk support. Libraries can stay true to the mission of reference, contends David Nolen, humanities reference librarian at Mitchell Memorial Library at Mississippi State University, without getting bogged down in the delivery or methodology of that mission.[16]

In 2012, the Dallas Public Library adopted a point-of-service reference model they called "Roving Reference," which removed the "reference desk barrier" for patrons and freed staff to be available to provide support without being confined to a reference desk.[17] The library system employed a variety of methods for their mobile reference program, including computer workstations outside the reference desk, where the librarians could work side by side with customers, or a combination of workstations colocated with the stacks, which used mobile technology. Among the results, within the first year of the reference desk redesign,

- Reference staff were more versatile and productive because they weren't tied to a desk waiting for patrons to approach but could help patrons at their point of need.
- The increased visibility of librarians in the public service areas decreased security and behavioral issues.
- Using mobile reference technology helped younger customers see libraries as more relevant.

Loosening degree requirements, creating more accurate job titles with commensurately appropriate compensation for 21st-century library professionals, and freeing library staff from outdated modes of providing library services will yield the best return on such 21st-century library efforts as makerspaces.

Leveraging Staff Interests and Talents

Regardless of what you call your library staff, as you embark on your makerspace journey, understanding what staff most enjoy doing in their spare time—what hobbies, skills, or trades they enjoy or have expertise in—can help you leverage those skills in the service of your new space and programs. The question floated earlier—What do you like to do?—is an important and potentially game-changing one.

Frequently, in the course of running professional development programs for librarians, we've found some amazing skill sets, of which library administration was sometimes unaware. One librarian had taught herself to make copper jewelry. Others sewed, gardened, or cooked at levels that would translate well into makerspace programming. Giving librarians the opportunity to do what they love at work is a gift to not only them, but also patrons, because there's nothing better than learning from someone who loves what they're teaching or sharing. Take the time to uncover and nurture those innate interests by doing the following:

- Survey staff early in your makerspace development efforts, identifying quick studies and curious and interested staff members during related professional development programs.
- Offer staff the opportunity to share their skills and interests wherever possible in makerspace programming efforts.
- Be approachable and supportive, providing a variety of ways for staff to share ideas and interests, for example, through comment boxes, periodic feedback opportunities, ongoing surveys, and staff meetings.

Celebrating and Empowering Innovation

Agile and open-minded library administration is key to a successful library makerspace program. Among other things, that means trusting and supporting staff engagement in the creative space you're developing. Once you get feedback on interests, skills, and talents, empower staff wherever possible to act on those interests, skills, and talents. If someone has an idea for a workshop or program, or a design idea for your new makerspace, give them an opportunity to try it. Nothing ventured, nothing gained is nowhere more true than in a makerspace program.

Consider a "Staff Project of the Month" as a great way to throw new ideas against the wall and see what sticks. Celebrate successes and take time to evaluate the things that didn't succeed. Consider what might be learned from less successful ideas as well as what might spin off from them. Prepackaged programming is fine, but your makerspace will be more interesting and exciting, and have greater staff—and patron—buy-in, if people with ideas for makerspace projects and programs feel heard and supported. Disengaged and disenfranchised library staff make for a disengaged makerspace community. Ownership at the staff level is every bit as important as patron and community buy-in, and maximizes the chances of sustainable and enduring success for your space.

VOLUNTEER MAKERS

Until now we've been talking about the importance of supporting and nurturing staff interest and engagement. But as most libraries know, volunteers are an almost equally important part of the library success story, with or without a makerspace. With respect to makerspace programming, however, your volunteer outreach is even more important and potentially more inviting to volunteers.

Finding volunteers to shelve books is one thing. Engaging volunteers who are woodworkers, sculptors, metalsmiths, animators, musicians, coders, good mentors, and so forth, is something else entirely. These skilled volunteers not only bring the potential of higher-level programming and alleviate the burden on staff to offer it, but also have the added benefit of drawing new patrons to the library. They also save the library time and money, bringing much-needed expertise to the makerspace table.

Sue Considine, executive director of the oldest library makerspace in the United States, the Fayetteville Free Library FabLab in New York, cites the book *The Abundant Community* as a transformational read that made her look at her community as much as an asset as a demographic to be served.

The Abundant Community, written by John McKnight and Peter Block (2012), maintains that, "Right in our neighborhood we have the capacity to address our human needs in ways that systems, which see us only as interchangeable units, as problems to be solved, never can. We all have gifts to offer, even the most seemingly marginal among us."[18] Each neighborhood, say McKnight and Block, is home to people with the gifts and talents we need to address challenges and fill needs. Considine would add that neighborhoods are also filled with people who will share their gifts and talents in our library makerspaces.

Volunteer expertise and interest is identified in much the same way as staff interests, through surveys and focus groups, regular feedback opportunities, and comment boxes. In addition, you can improve volunteer engagement for Maker programs through promotional materials, special events, and invitations for guest Makers, teachers, and presenters. A Maker-in-residence program is a great way to bring high-level volunteers on board.

Maker-in-Residence

Johnson County Library in Kansas (jocolibrary.org/makerspace) offers a four-month rotating Maker-in-residence opportunity, made possible by a grant from Black & Veatch,[19] to a local Maker of note. It asks interested participants about the type of Maker they consider themselves to be, why they want to be a Maker-in-residence at the library makerspace, how they envision engaging the public with their work, and if they're available to spend 10 hours a week at the library makerspace. The application sets the stage for the Maker experience for applicants and the broader implications of the Maker-in-residence program:

"We're looking for people who want to hang out, geek out, and share their love for making," it says, and then asks, "What are your thoughts about helping others with their projects? Teaching kids basic techniques?" It also asks, "What do you hope to get out of being a Maker-in-residence? How will it help you take your work to the next level?"

Both of these questions impart a sense of the higher value of the library's makerspace program, both to the patrons the resident Maker will be helping and the Maker-in-residence herself or himself.

Volunteer makers are crucial to the success of your library makerspace. Engage them early and often, and recognize and celebrate their contributions to your makerspace. Active and interested volunteers are a good sign of community engagement and the best way to grow your Maker programming.

PATRON MAKERS

Ideally, your patron Makers inform the programming and activities ultimately made possible by your staff and volunteers. For the most effective makerspace programming, you need to have buy-in from your patrons. Top-down, administrative-driven, and staff-driven programming may fill some gaps and bring some bodies in the door, but unless engagement is community driven, energy will flag and your space will most likely sit idle. If your space is only populated during library-organized programs, that's not a good sign.

As with your staff and volunteers, take the time to get patron feedback through focus groups and surveys, and take into consideration the feedback you receive. Even if volunteers and staff are totally into sewing but the patron feedback indicates an overwhelming preference for gardening-related activities, listen to your patrons and start that garden. You can always introduce sewing in relation to gardening—making garden hats, gloves, fabric awnings, planter bags, and so forth. But design for the interests patrons express, not necessarily, or only, the ones you want.

Once you've identified patron interests, float some initial programs that seem to fit what they've requested. There will always be a gap between what people ask for and what they actually participate in, so start small and go from there. To stay with the garden theme, for example, don't till up an acre of library ground for a giant community garden right away. Look at some small-scale hydroponics projects, do some greenhouse projects, or start a seed-lending library. Make butterfly houses or bat houses. If patron interest is consistent or grows, expand your related offerings accordingly. And keep listening to your patrons, with regular feedback opportunities before and after programs.

Be ready to pivot to new programming preferences at any time. Often, as makerspace users become more comfortable with the resources at hand

and learn new skills, their interests will expand beyond what was initially identified. Gardening may give way to woodworking or working with plant fibers. Regular communications is key to maintaining relevant programming and Maker opportunities.

It's also important to establish a makerspace culture not just of ownership, but also responsibility. Tools and equipment are expensive and need to be cared for properly so they last as long as possible. Patrons should be encouraged to be responsible makerspace users from the beginning, starting with required orientation and training programs before they can use equipment and clear messaging that sets ground rules for space and equipment use. It should become a matter of pride for users to clean up and restore the spaces they use. Setting the tone early on for that culture of ownership and responsibility will make responsible use an institutional given that everyone will work together to support and enforce.

Another way to instill that culture of shared responsibility is by encouraging patrons to share what they make, to teach and mentor one another within the space that's become their own. Create opportunities for Makers to showcase their creations in display cases or at special library Maker events, where the general public can see and be inspired by the things being made at the library. Consider featuring some of your patron Makers in special news features for the local news or your library media. Your makerspace is a big deal. Make a big deal out of it.

COMMUNITY MAKERS

Community Makers are your collaborative partners: larger formal groups like special interest clubs, companies, stores, artist collaboratives, musical groups, cultural associations, professional networks and meet-ups, retiree groups, entrepreneurial associations, chambers of commerce, other government agencies, and so on. Engaging these larger groups leverages a higher level of community involvement and buy-in, and can be helpful in engaging new patrons and bringing in different Maker components.

If yours is a culturally diverse community, for instance, engaging with local cultural associations can bridge the gap between community members who may not be sufficiently served by adding culturally relevant programming that they and others may enjoy. This type of programming can consist of everything from classes in ethnic cooking to traditional handcraft or related art or music programs.

Engaging with special interest clubs can also be a big boon for your library makerspace, as well as a potential bane. As with patron Makers, it's especially important to establish makerspace protocols and clear boundaries with special interest groups like art clubs and woodworking groups. It's easy for groups to become a little too comfortable in a welcoming space and maybe assume too much ownership. When programming becomes overly one-sided, it's important to carefully assess things to make sure the group is providing programming the community wants and not just enjoying free use of equipment and space without serving the library's mission and goals. It's also important to engrain that mantra of cleaning up and restoring the spaces they use before they leave.

It's great for groups to enjoy and use a space, but not to the exclusion of other patron or group interests. Again, consistently enforcing clear library makerspace protocols will go a long way toward equitable use of the space for as many people and community groups as possible. It's counterproductive to have a dominant group that excludes others through overuse or misuse of a makerspace, so set those guidelines early and post them clearly so everyone is on the same page.

That said, it's also important to highlight your community Maker groups, both in the space itself, perhaps with signage recognizing the different groups that meet at your makerspace, and through public displays and media opportunities. Your makerspace is a conversation piece, and the more often you display the work being done there, the bigger and more far-reaching the conversation will be.

FUNDING MAKERS

Adding a makerspace to a library can add some funding challenges, but the very nature of the space also opens up new opportunities for funding that may not have been previously available. The Hazel L. Incantalupo Makerspace,[20] a children's makerspace located at Palm Harbor Library, a municipal library in Florida, is funded through the purchase of naming rights and private donations, with no tax dollars allocated for the space.

Naming rights can also be leveraged for everything from tool collections to individual makerspace rooms or areas, for instance, a recording studio or large piece of equipment like a drill press. If your library already has a naming rights policy, you may want to update it to include makerspace opportunities or create a new one just for your makerspace. If you don't have a naming rights policy in place, you can find some good examples among other libraries.

The Highland Park Public Library in Illinois has a very clear policy on their website, along with a list of other ways to contribute to the library.[21] Like most libraries, Highland Park's Board of Trustees must approve naming rights for new or existing assets and sets the length of naming rights recognition according to the amount donated: Items costing less than $10,000 carry naming rights for 10 years, while those costing as much as $100,000 earn naming rights for 20 years. Naming rights donors should be recognized with generously sized and well-placed signage in the appropriate locations. Place clear signage in other areas where naming rights can also be employed to invite future donors.

In-kind donations are also valuable in a library makerspace, but it's important to be specific about the types of in-kind donations that are useful and the condition or quality of the equipment or resources that will be accepted. In-kind donations should have a significant dollar value, rather than just being old garage castoffs that people are trying to unload. Especially with tools and related equipment, safety and efficacy need to take precedence. Donations that are broken or unsafe are not assets. It's a good idea to recognize in-kind donors either on plaques in the makerspace or on the tools or equipment whenever possible.

Makerspaces allow for some unique and nontraditional partnerships with area businesses that can result in everything from the provision of equipment and build-out services to support for programs. The Highland Park Public Library, on their donor page, puts dollar amounts next to each of their major programs, inviting contributors to sponsor the individual programs. The same idea scales to makerspace programming, where you can leverage the support of area automotive companies, if you have a mechanical program, for example, or a frame shop for your art program. Business partnerships can be monetary in nature or physical, in terms of program mentors or contributions of physical labor or materials. Don't overlook local big-box stores like Lowes or Home Depot, either. They may have friendly managers interested in being part of any creative or constructive programming that may bring new customers to their stores as they learn to pursue new skills on their own.

Nontraditional grant opportunities also open up with the addition of a library makerspace. The Knight Foundation funds a variety of relevant projects in the United States and, in 2016, put out a call for library innovation projects in need of funding.[22] In Europe, libraries have been successful getting funding through the Erasmus+Programme,[23] which is focused on educational and youth projects. The Awesome Foundation, a microgrant agency, has a community-funded Innovation in Libraries initiative,[24] which grants $1,000 to one new library project per month. Other grant or funding opportunities that can be explored with the advent of a library makerspace include the following:

- Lowe's Toolbox for Education Grant (toolboxforeducation.com)
- Demco Grants Search Tool[25]
- Harbor Freight Donations (harborfreightdonations.com)
- DonorsChoose (donorschoose.org)
- TechSoup for Libraries[26]
- 3Mgives[27]

Be sure to check for local giving resources in your county or state as well, including such diverse sources as your local economic development office, humanities or arts grants, construction grants, and more. Think outside the usual library box and even more opportunities will become obvious.

KEEPING YOUR MAKER VILLAGE RELEVANT

If you've gotten this far, with library staff who understand and enjoy Maker culture, and feel empowered and supported by being an integral part of programming and the creative community you're building in your space, with an active and engaged volunteer community and a creative community of supporters and funders, congratulations! But don't rest on your laurels—you're not done. As a matter of fact, any library makerspace worth its salt is never done. Makerspaces, by their very nature, should be dynamic and agile, able and willing to change up programming and resources as user needs evolve—and they will.

The best way to remain relevant to your patrons and Maker community at large is by regularly assessing your offerings through periodic surveys, focus groups, or town hall meetings. The makerspace town hall is a great way to engage your users and help them continue to feel a sense of ownership of and responsibility for the space they use. Town halls, or something like a makerspace advisory group, where users can gather together to discuss everything from projects to makerspace needs or issues, can be held monthly or quarterly.

Empower users to bring concerns or ideas to library staff and provide ways to accept and act on feedback, and recognize individuals and groups that give back to your makerspace with dedicated energy and enthusiasm in their service. The best way to keep your makerspace active and serving your library mission is to respect, honor, and celebrate the Makers who make it possible.

NOTES

1. Willingham, Theresa, and Jeroen De Boer. *Makerspaces in Libraries*. Lanham, MD: Rowman & Littlefield, 2015, 69.
2. Storck-Post, Holly. "Four Benefits of a Library Makerspace Staff Day." *Demco*. August 30, 2016. Accessed June 1, 2017. http://ideas.demco.com/blog/4-benefits-holding-maker-program-library-staff/.
3. "Squishy Circuits: How To." *University of St. Thomas*. Accessed June 1, 2017. http://courseweb.stthomas.edu/apthomas/SquishyCircuits/howTo.htm.
4. Eureka! Factory. "Making Squishy Circuits from COTS Playdough." *Instructables.com*. June 2016. Accessed June 1, 2017. www.instructables.com/id/Making-Squishy-Circuits-from-COTS-Playdough/.
5. Stephens, Chuck. "Jitterbugs! Vibrating Robotic Bugs." *Instructables.com*. May 12, 2016. Accessed June 1, 2017. www.instructables.com/id/Jitterbugs-Vibrating-Robotic-Bugs/.
6. "DevineDIY." *YouTube*. August 7, 2013. Accessed June 1, 2017. www.youtube.com/watch?v=X4LEPZKVd7M.

7. Stephens, Chuck. "Eureka!Factory Atari Punk Console V2." *Instructables.com*. Summer 2015. Accessed June 1, 2017. www.instructables.com/id/EurekaFactory-Atari-Punk-Console-v2/.

8. "Introduction to Tools." *Making and Learning*. Accessed June 1, 2017. https://makingandlearning.squarespace.com/tools.

9. Bertot, John, Lindsay Sarin, and Paul Jaeger. "Re-Envisioning the MLS: The Future of Librarian Education." *Public Libraries Online*. January 6, 2016. Accessed June 1, 2017. http://publiclibrariesonline.org/2016/01/re-envisioning-the-mls-the-future-of-librarian-education/.

10. Bertot, John Carlo, Lindsay C. Sarin, and Johnna Percell. "Re-Envisioning the MLS: Findings, Issues, and Considerations." *College of Information Studies, University of Maryland College Park*. August 1, 2015. Accessed May 31, 2017. http://mls.umd.edu/wp-content/uploads/2015/08/ReEnvisioningFinalReport.pdf.

11. Jenkins, Mark. "D.C. Adds a Social Worker to Library System to Work with Homeless Patrons." *Washington Post*. August 27, 2014. Accessed June 1, 2017. www.washingtonpost.com/local/dc-adds-a-social-worker-to-library-system-to-work-with-homeless-patrons/2014/08/26/2d80200c-2c96-11e4-be9e-60cc44c01e7f_story.html.

12. Simpson, Betsy. "Hiring Non-MLS Librarians: Trends and Training Implications." *Library Leadership and Management* 28, no. 1 (November 2013): 1–15. Accessed June 1, 2017. https://journals.tdl.org/llm/index.php/llm/article/viewFile/7019/6260.

13. Bertot, Sarin, and Percell. "Re-Envisioning the MLS."

14. *Public Libraries in the United States Survey: Fiscal Year 2012. Institute of Museum and Library Services*. December 2012. Accessed June 1, 2017. www.imls.gov/sites/default/files/legacy/assets/1/AssetManager/PLS_FY2012.pdf.

15. "Are Library Reference Desks Obsolete?" *McGraw-Hill Education*. July 21, 2016. Accessed June 1, 2017. http://mcgrawhillprofessionalblog.com/reference-desks-obsolete-1acs/.

16. Nolen, David S. "Reforming or Rejecting the Reference Desk: Conflict and Continuity in the Concept of Reference." *Library Philosophy and Practice*. 2010. Accessed June 1, 2017. www.webpages.uidaho.edu/~mbolin/nolen.htm.

17. "Retooling Reference for Relevant Service @ Dallas Public Library." *Urban Libraries Council*. Accessed June 1, 2017. www.urbanlibraries.org/retooling-reference-for-relevant-service-dallas-public-library-innovation-151.php?page_id=38.

18. McKnight, John, and Peter Block. *The Abundant Community*. Oakland, CA: Berrett-Koehler, 2012.

19. "Application: Maker-in-Residence." *Google*. Accessed June 1, 2017. https://docs.google.com/forms/d/1nNaTs3h-qw_wWYfu2sblJkkTk7TiWd8bGAAk4hmWnHY/viewform.

20. Palm Harbor Library Children's Page. Accessed June 4, 2017. http://phlibkids.wixsite.com/phlchildren/makerspace.

21. "Gifts and Donations." *Highland Park Public Library*. Accessed June 4, 2017. www.hplibrary.org/volunteer-gifts-donations.

22. "Knight Foundation News Challenge on Libraries." *Electronic Librarian*. Accessed June 4, 2017. www.electroniclibrarian.org/2016-knight/.

23. "Erasmus+Programme - Call for Proposals 2017." *European Commission*. Fall 2016. Accessed June 4, 2017. https://ec.europa.eu/programmes/erasmus-plus/calls-for-proposals-tenders/2016-eac-a03_en.

24. "Innovation in Libraries." *Awesome Foundation*. Accessed June 4, 2017. www.awesomefoundation.org/en/chapters/libraries.

25. "Free Library and Education Grant Search." *Demco.com*. Accessed June 4, 2017. www.demco.com/goto?grants&intcmp=RC1_sep14_grants.

26. Gilbert-Knight, Ariel. "What TechSoup Offers Libraries." *TechSoup.org*. January 16, 2012. Accessed June 4, 2017. www.techsoup.org/support/articles-and-how-tos/what-techsoup-offers-libraries.

27. "Nonprofit Guidelines." *3Mgives*. Accessed June 4, 2017. http://solutions.3m.com/wps/portal/3M/en_US/Community-Giving/US-Home/nonprofits/eligibility-guidelines/.

9

RISK MANAGEMENT 101

At every level of the hierarchy, people need to be empowered to have big ideas and to take risks. This can only happen if both staff and management are not only tolerant of risk, but also able to effectively manage the risks. The culture of innovation needs to exist and be supported internally before being taken to the community at large.

—Lauren Britton Smedley, "A Fabulous Laboratory: The Makerspace at Fayetteville Free Library"[1]

We've said it before, and we'll say it again: If you want to be on the cutting edge, you can't be afraid of getting cut. You can, however, reasonably mitigate and manage risk without overly limiting creative freedom and innovation, and have a good first-aid kit handy. We'll start things off by borrowing a line from a presentation on legal issues in makerspaces: "Anything said here is not to be taken as legal advice. If you have a legal issue, please consult appropriate counsel."[2] What follows are basic recommendations based on best practices used by other libraries and organizations, along with references for getting more information. Always refer to your library system or county legal department for protocols and procedure best suited to your library.

Generally speaking, risk falls into three broad categories in library makerspaces:

1. Patent and copyright issues
2. Risks of defects or harm
3. Free speech and privacy

The main ways to address these risk categories are through

- Waivers and agreements
- Equipment safety
- Personal safety
- Appropriate training for staff and patrons
- Signage

The recommendations here are equally broad but hopefully can help you think about some of the issues of relevance in your makerspace and give you the start of a road map for working with the risk management professionals in your library system.

WAIVERS AND AGREEMENTS

Risk management is a challenging topic, at best. Lock everything down for safety and nothing creative, enjoyable, or transformative happens. Your makerspace is useless, and your programs are uninspiring and ineffective. Make your rules too open-ended and you endanger people and property, and can ruin the fun for everyone. But there's a sweet spot in the middle that most libraries with makerspaces have found and execute effectively. Of the almost 20 library makerspaces that have been in existence for more than two years and completed the survey for this book, only a couple reported injuries, and they were minor.

Most of the libraries surveyed handled risk management in three basic ways:

1. Waivers and hold harmless agreements
2. On-site supervision
3. Lockout devices on equipment

Others placed age limits on equipment use or simply didn't use any equipment that posed user hazards. By far the most common safety precautions, however, involved the use of waivers and agreements and on-site supervision.

Having clear, reasonable, and easily accessible makerspace policies and agreements is important. The Powers Memorial Public Library Makerspace has a good example online.[3] It describes the makerspace, what can be found in it, and clear conditions, rules, and requirements for use of equipment. Like many library makerspaces, Powers Memorial requires orientation classes before anyone can use equipment.

Cleveland Public Library's TechCentral Makerspace also has an online user agreement for patrons to complete and return.[4] Upon completion of the user agreement, patrons receive a "Makerspace ID" that signifies the agreement has been completed and filed by the library. Certain materials, equipment, and tools require either a MakerspaceID or library card to use or check out.

Fayetteville Free Library (FFL) FabLab in New York requires certification for the use of some of their equipment, including their 3D printers,

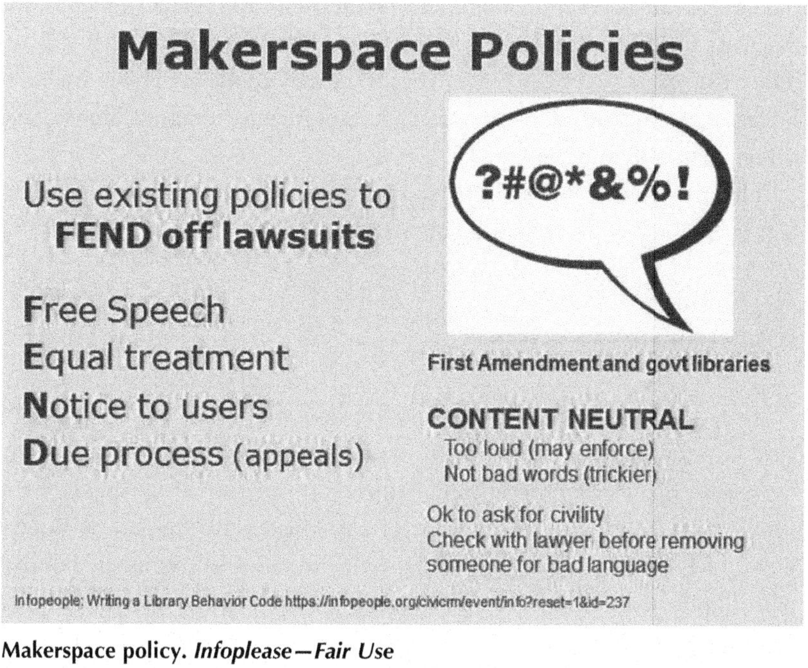

Makerspace Policies

Use existing policies to
FEND off lawsuits

Free Speech
Equal treatment
Notice to users
Due process (appeals)

?#@*&%!

First Amendment and govt libraries

CONTENT NEUTRAL
Too loud (may enforce)
Not bad words (trickier)

Ok to ask for civility
Check with lawyer before removing
someone for bad language

Infopeople: Writing a Library Behavior Code https://infopeople.org/civicrm/event/info?reset=1&id=237

Makerspace policy. ***Infoplease—Fair Use***

sewing machines, laser and vinyl cutters, and CNC mill. The certification training can be completed online or in person. The online version can be accessed from their website (www.fflib.org/make) and consists of watching a training video and taking a quiz. Upon satisfactory completion of the training, patrons get an identifying note on their library cards, which lets staff know they're cleared to use the relevant equipment. The library also has a "FFL FabLab Maker Agreement," which includes makerspace rules and policies, as well as a hold harmless agreement.[5]

Most library makerspace user agreements briefly touch on copyright issues, usually with respect to A/V products produced in a makerspace. But there are also issues related to 3D printing. In an excellent article for the Association for Information Science and Technology (www.asist.org), Barbara Jones, director of the American Library Association's (ALA) Office for Intellectual Freedom, lays out the case for simple policies that take advantage of already existing laws. Simply stating on a library makerspace agreement that "illegal activity is prohibited" covers a range of illegal content, including intellectual property infringement and safe use of 3D printers. The article also covers important principles to include in 3D printing policies, including ethical, intellectual freedom, and privacy considerations.[6] Much of the language for this and related policies can be found on the ALA's Privacy Tool Kit page (www.ala.org/advocacy/privacy/toolkit), which includes boilerplate templates and other useful resources for crafting library user agreements and policies.

The main point here is to get your policy and procedure ducks in a row before you open your space, not after.

ON-SITE SUPERVISION

Waivers and agreements are necessary, and well-crafted ones will take care of most areas of concern. But there is no substitute for trained and experienced on-site supervision. Before you open up your space to the public, make sure staff and volunteer supervisors are trained on equipment that requires some level of expertise to use and intimately familiar with library makerspace use protocols. On-site supervisors should also be people who

- Enjoy making things
- Are warm, friendly, and encouraging to patrons using the space
- Can teach and share easily and articulately
- Have first-aid training

There are few things less inspiring than entering a makerspace with a disinterested supervisor waving patrons in. Library makerspaces should be interesting and inspiring from the moment a patron enters the space to the moment they leave, and on-site supervisors can help set the creative and empowering tone of the space just by the way they greet and support users. Engaged site supervisors are also vital for safe and productive use of the space. Thus, it is important to be sure to make "customer service" a key part of staff and volunteer training for those who will be supervising the space.

The on-site supervisor should also be someone who is proactive in managing the space, as opposed to just reading behind a desk. The library makerspace supervisor should actively engage in helping patrons use the space, be knowledgeable about equipment and general tool and resource use, and help guide patrons in the proper use of equipment. The supervisor should also have the authority to enforce policies and procedures, remove patrons for unsafe or inappropriate conduct, and act as a site foreman within the guidelines for education and creative use set forth by the library.

On-site supervision and oversight is also important when there are community groups using your space. While it's important to encourage ownership by creative groups that use the space, and especially those that provide creative services in the way of programs or active clubs that meet there, it's also crucial that groups use the space respectfully and safely. It's easy to get too comfortable with regular groups, but it's important to keep the mission and goals of the library front and center, and maintain professional working relationships with the organizations and individuals that use the space, either for themselves or to provide programs or workshops.

A CULTURE OF SAFETY

In addition to waivers and well-trained on-site supervision, you can make safety first a key cultural ingredient of your makerspace by designing, organizing, and enforcing safe space use at all levels. Some of the easiest and most effective safety measures you can implement include the following:

- Use clear, specific, and abundant signage.
- Provide easy access to safety equipment.
- Use lockout devices on more hazardous or delicate equipment.
- Implement regular maintenance procedures.
- Establish and enforce cleanup procedures.

Signage is often underutilized in makerspaces of all types, but it provides an easy and effective way to keep safety and other policies and protocols a top-of-the-mind issue. Put big, clean, clear, and bold signs everywhere that indicate the following:

- Makerspace sign-in areas
- Tool storage and instructions for returning tools to their proper places
- User instructions or policies on equipment that requires it (bulleted, not text heavy)
- Cleanup policies
- Safety reminders for safety glasses, gloves, hearing protection, or other relevant protective needs
- Location of first-aid kits, fire extinguishers, and other emergency resources
- Instructions for emergencies, with relevant phone numbers and contact information

The more eye-catching the signs the better. Use icons whenever possible to bridge potential language barriers and improve adherence. The ALA online store sells a "Makerspace Safety Poster" (www.alastore.ala.org/detail.aspx?ID=11244) that covers most of the basics and other related signage.

Other basic safety features include the following:

- Lockout devices on specialty equipment (Seton[7] is one option)
- Nonslip flooring material (e.g., rubber workshop mats in front of workbenches or freestanding equipment)
- Easily available wipes and cleaning resources like vacuums

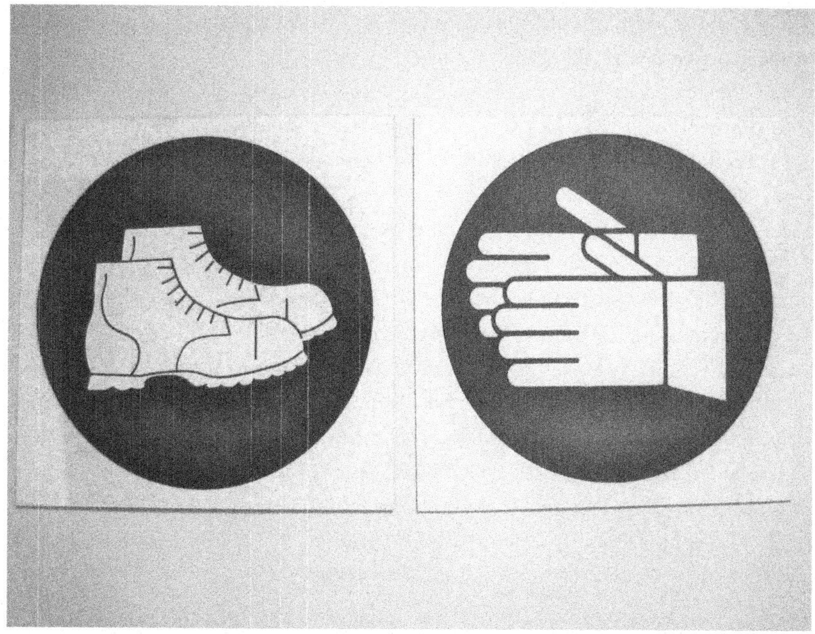

Signage. ***Copyright Free CC***

- Readily available equipment manuals
- Well-maintained safety equipment (check, clean, and refill consumable safety gear like ear plugs and disinfect safety glasses regularly)
- Well-maintained equipment and a feedback process for users to report damaged, worn, or poorly operating equipment

With common sense and advance planning, libraries can manage risk reasonably and effectively in ways that protect patrons from harm and libraries from lawsuits, while maintaining an inviting and productive space and preserving the intellectual and creative freedom library makerspaces make possible.

NOTES

1. Smedley, Lauren Britton. "A Fabulous Laboratory: The Makerspace at Fayetteville Free Library." *Public Libraries Online.* October 26, 2012. Accessed

June 1, 2017. http://publiclibrariesonline.org/2012/10/a-fabulous-labaratory-the-makerspace-at-fayetteville-free-library/.

2. "Makerspaces: Library's Legal Answers Workshop Slide Deck." *LinkedIn SlideShare*. June 18, 2015. Accessed June 1, 2017. https://www.slideshare.net/ALATechSource/makerspaces-librarys-legal-answers-workshop.

3. "Powers Memorial Library Makerspace Policy." *Powers Memorial Library*. Accessed June 1, 2017. http://www.palmyra.lib.wi.us/makerspace-policy/.

4. "Cleveland Public Library TechCentral Makerspace User Agreement." *Cleveland Public Library*. October 13, 2013. Accessed June 1, 2017. https://cpl.org/wp-content/uploads/MakerSpace-Agreement-Final-Plus-FORM-12.27.16.pdf.

5. "FFL FabLab Maker Agreement." *Fayetteville Free Library*. Accessed June 1, 2017. https://www.fflib.org/sites/default/files/fflfablabmakeragreement2015.pdf.

6. Jones, Barbara M. "3D Printing in Libraries." *Association for Information Science and Technology*. October 5, 2015. Accessed June 1, 2017. https://www.asist.org/publications/bulletin/oct-15/3d-printing-in-libraries.

7. "Lockout Devices." *Seton*. Accessed June 1, 2017. http://www.seton.com/safety-security/lockout-tagout/lockout-devices.html.

10

FINISHING TOUCHES

Putting It All Together

Here we are. You've made it to the end, but it's only the beginning. By now you should have a better understanding of the following:

- The history, progress, and goals of the library makerspace movement
- Best practices for developing a community-driven space that reflects the interests of community stakeholders
- Resources for stocking, staffing, and managing makerspaces and running related programs
- Best practices for staff development, volunteer recruitment, and community engagement
- Ideas for funding resources
- Creating and maintaining a culture of safety and managing risk in a way that preserves intellectual and creative freedom in your makerspace

There's a lot of information to sort through. In this chapter, we provide a few checklists to help you get to the information you need quickly.

KICKING OFF YOUR MAKERSPACE PLANNING

Your makerspace program development can be a multiphase rollout, as outlined in chapter 2.

- *Milestone 1:* Ensure Administrative Support
  - Organize administration and library staff meetings to ensure everyone is on the same page with mission and goals of the space, and expectations of outcomes.
  - For most effective makerspace operation, administrative oversight needs to be reasonable, and the library has to have creative freedom and operational agility with respect to programming, budgeting, and management.
- *Milestone 2:* Assess Community Needs and Interests
  - Organize focus groups.
  - Launch surveys.
  - Evaluate results of focus groups and surveys to determine stakeholder preferences at all levels.
- *Milestone 3:* Develop Community Asset Maps
  - Formulate community asset maps to identify potential community partners and resources to support identified needs and interests.
- *Milestone 4:* Develop a Makerspace Budget and Plan
  - Make a budget and plan for your makerspace based on results of surveys and community assets and support.
- *Milestone 5:* Create Organizational Documents
  - Use organizational documents to codify your library makerspace mission, goals, safety, and code of conduct.

CONSIDER BEST PRACTICES

Chapter 3 provides an extensive overview of best practices from a variety of libraries with established makerspaces. These successful spaces, ranging from FabLabs to K-12 school library makerspaces and public library pop-up makerspaces, have the following main features:

- Community-based focus
- Intentionality in design and programming
- Adaptability and flexibility to change with user interests
- Empowerment and the ability to be empowering, freeing those who run the spaces, from volunteers to staff, to exercise creativity and originality in the work of managing their spaces

- Ability to fail forward by not being overly risk averse and being able to learn from projects, programs, and efforts that may not work as intended or hoped
- Comfortability with the noise and mess active makerspaces generate
- Ability to actively leverage community expertise

DESIGN FOR EVERYONE

In chapter 4, we look at makerspace architecture, specifically issues related to:

- *Accessibility and usability:* Workshop areas should allow 75 to 100 square feet of independent work space per person and be ADA (Americans with Disabilities Act) compliant.
- *Lighting:* There should be an appropriate amount of light for working with machinery and tools.
- *Power distribution:* Outlets should be easily accessible, with dedicated circuits for power-hungry electrical equipment.
- *Storage:* Having enough storage for everything from consumables to tools to patron projects should be part of your makerspace build-out plan from the beginning.
- *Safety and security:* Ensuring safety and security should be first and foremost in planning out a makerspace, allowing for the 25 to 35 percent of open floor space required by most fire codes, with easy access to first-aid stations and exits, and good signage, throughout.
- *Adaptability:* Your space should be easy to adapt to changing needs and interests.

PROGRAMMING UNLIMITED

Chapter 5 looks at the different types of programming possible in a library makerspace. Programs typically fall into a few basic categories:

- Hobby programming (the different things people like to do that aren't work related)

- Professional programming (including skills development and entrepreneurial programming)
- Educational programming for adults and youth (including skills development)
- Youth-specific programming
- Civic programming (e.g., community gardens or community improvement projects)

For all types of programming, there are some basic best practices to help create the most successful outcomes and community engagement. They are as follows:

- Respect user feedback to ensure your programming reflects what patrons are interested in and have requested.
- Promote early and often, leveraging social media and abundant signage.
- Engage local experts to teach and share their crafts and skills.
- Create library displays as a form of show-and-tell for the things made in programming sessions.
- Tie in related books and other media from your collection in special displays leading up to sessions.
- Take photos and share the activity as it happens and afterward via social media, articles, and blog posts.
- Try the same idea a couple of different ways to see which one engages people best.
- Ask for participant feedback and listen to it.

In running your programs, keep these things in mind:

- Have more supplies and materials than you think you need.
- Set up workstations in advance with the materials and tools participants will need for the program.
- Know how to do the activity or program being offered. Don't host a program you don't understand or can't source to an experienced teacher.

- Put safety first. Make sure to have the needed safety equipment (e.g., safety glasses or hearing protection) on hand.
- Start and end on time.
- Factor in time for questions and show-and-tell afterward so everyone can enjoy seeing everyone else's work.

CELEBRATE AND INSPIRE WITH EVENTS

Chapter 6 explores the different Maker-style events you can host at your library to raise awareness of your programs and show off the great things being made in your space. The different types of possible events include:

- Maker festivals
- Coding events
- "Open make" events (including build contests)
- Pop-culture events (e.g., cosplay, gaming, comic and anime festivals)
- Entrepreneurial events (e.g., 1 Million Cups, Alligator Zone, hosting your own pitch events)
- Other special events (e.g., youth robotics events, deconstruction, fix-it clinics, TEDxLibraries, webinars, community service projects)

Regardless of the type of event you're putting together, you'll need these essentials:

- Form a planning team made up of people who really like the things you'll be doing at the event.
- Set a good date and allow sufficient planning time. Give yourself at least six or more months to put together an event, especially the first time out.
- Ensure you have sufficient space for your event, indoors or out.
- Identify collaborative partners who can help produce different aspects of the event.
- Plan for entertainment and presentations to make it fun and educational.
- Promote, promote, promote.

BUILDING OUT YOUR MAKERSPACE INVENTORY

In chapter 7, we take a close look at makerspace inventory, including a detailed overview of the different types of tools and categories of tools and their uses. As you build your inventory of equipment, tools, and resources, keep the following crucial considerations in mind:

- *Facility focus:* What's the intent of your makerspace?
- *Power availability and allocation:* Do you have sufficient power access and can your library handle the load for things like large-scale power tools, 3D printers, laser cutters, sewing machines, or other equipment that requires electricity?
- *Physical work space:* Allow 50 square feet of space per person and take into consideration accessibility for differently abled users.
- *Noise issues:* Plan accordingly for noisy equipment and programming.
- *Ventilation:* Plan ahead to install appropriate filtration and ventilation systems while you're building out your space, and don't colocate sensitive equipment like computers for computer-aided design (CAD) or digital editing, or A/V visual equipment, with debris-producing equipment.
- *Storage:* For every piece of equipment and its related materials or supplies, plan on appropriate storage.
- *Safety:* Make safety an integral part of your makerspace planning and an unnegotiable part of your makerspace culture.

NURTURING THE HUMAN ELEMENT

Chapter 8 looks at the most crucial part of any makerspace: the people who make it possible, viable, and enjoyable. In the case of library makerspaces, that means

- Staff Makers
- Volunteer Makers
- Patron Makers

- Community Makers
- Funding Makers

This section looks at everything from professional development for staff to engaging volunteers and community groups who can bring different types of "Maker"-style expertise to your library to help with programming and community engagement, as well as Maker-in-residence programs. It also does the following:

- Explores updated research and changing attitudes about the value of the master in library science (MLS) degree, especially with respect to makerspace hiring
- Rethinks such current library staff titles as the library assistant (LA) and library technical assistant (LTA)
- Invites reconsideration of the static reference desk model

MANAGING RISK

Chapter 9 touches on balancing risk management with supporting the intellectual and creative enjoyment inherent in a library makerspace. Risk falls into three basic categories:

1. Patent and copyright issues
2. Risks of defects or harm
3. Free speech and privacy

And the main ways these risks are mitigated in library makerspaces are through

- Waivers and agreements
- Equipment safety, with lockout devices and on-site supervision
- Personal safety
- Appropriate training for staff and patrons
- Signage

The most important consideration with respect to risk management in a library makerspace is establishing a culture of safety at the start of your makerspace planning and maintaining that culture at all levels, from expectations of staff and volunteers to patron use of the space.

So, there you have it. We started this book with the goal of helping libraries begin the intentional journey of developing makerspaces that matter and serve the needs and interests of their communities in new and exciting ways. We hope *Library Makerspaces* has given you a solid road map for that journey and inspired you to move beyond the ideas presented here to take the future of library makerspaces into your own creative hands and Make it amazing, and Make on!

APPENDIX

Sample Documents

[LIBRARY LETTERHEAD]

Dear Innovative Thinker:

__________ Library is on the forefront of creating a landmark creative space for our community. Imagine using tools and equipment at your local library to realize your own creations. Designing, building, and creating things you've only imagined can be possible at the __________ makerspace being planned for the __________ Library.

In an effort to further advance and focus our vision, and to better serve not only our current library patrons, but also our entire community, on <date> at ____ p.m., the __________ Library is partnering with the Eureka! Factory to hold a focus group with <group name>, and we sincerely hope you will be able to join us. The focus group will last approximately 60 minutes and be led by a nonbiased moderator, who will facilitate and engage conversations based on discussion topics that may include, but are not limited to, the following:

- Currently use of the library
- Thoughts on new services, events, programs, or partnerships that might improve the library experience
- The role of the library in the community now and in the future
- Types of resources that might be helpful for business development, academic and skills development, and personal fulfillment

The purpose of this focus group is to gather thoughts, recommendations, insights, and possibilities related to the new library makerspace and related services we may provide to you and your friends, colleagues, family, or team. Your valuable insights and suggestions will be an integral part of the development of makerspace and creative programming offered at the library. Data collected during our session is for internal use and will not be publicized without your permission.

We encourage you to join us to share your thoughts and opinions, and help us gain a clearer understanding of your vision and needs, and how we can work to best accommodate them. Please RSVP no later than <date>, by <state how they are to RSVP>. If you have any questions or concerns, please feel free to contact __________.

Add a short description of the library and proposed makerspace/creative programming.

[LIBRARY LETTERHEAD]

Library Makerspace Survey

A "makerspace" is a physical place set aside for creative, hands-on endeavors ranging from arts and handcrafts to mechanics, electronics, Web and app development, and more. They are becoming increasingly common in libraries and schools, providing a new level of library services and public resource availability. Your library is exploring the development of a makerspace, along with creative programming, and would appreciate your feedback regarding the resources, tools, and activities you might value in such a space. Thank you for taking the time to complete this survey.

1. Are you a regular library user?
   - ☐ yes
   - ☐ no
2. If yes, how often do you use the library now?
   - ☐ daily
   - ☐ weekly
   - ☐ monthly
   - ☐ a few times a year
3. Do you think you would use a makerspace in this library?
   - ☐ yes
   - ☐ no
   - ☐ maybe
4. What elements/activities/ideas would make a makerspace most interesting to you or your family?
   - ☐ game design
   - ☐ hobby electronics
   - ☐ computer programming
   - ☐ 3-D printing
   - ☐ app development
   - ☐ A/V creation
   - ☐ graphic design
   - ☐ music making
   - ☐ traditional craft (woodworking, metalsmithing, textiles, etc.)
   - ☐ general tinkering (inventions, prototyping, etc.)
   - ☐ small household repairs (small appliances, mending broken items, etc.)
   - ☐ robotics
   - ☐ other: ___________________

5. What kind of tools and resources would you most value in a library makerspace?
   - ☐ hand tools
   - ☐ power tools
   - ☐ multimedia equipment (cameras, A/V equipment, etc.)
   - ☐ 3D printer
   - ☐ sewing machines
   - ☐ electronics equipment (multimeters, oscilloscopes, etc.)
   - ☐ laser cutter
   - ☐ Web and app developer resources
   - ☐ other: ________________
6. What types of workshops and classes would you value?
   - ☐ electronics
   - ☐ woodworking
   - ☐ mechanical design
   - ☐ CAD (computer-aided design)
   - ☐ 3D printing
   - ☐ sewing
   - ☐ animation
   - ☐ moviemaking
   - ☐ household repair
   - ☐ Web development
   - ☐ product development (patents, marketing, etc.)
   - ☐ robotics
   - ☐ other ________________
7. Do you think a makerspace would increase your use of the library?
   - ☐ yes
   - ☐ no
   - ☐ maybe
8. What are some of your current skills, hobbies, or trades, and would you be interested in sharing your skills or interests at a library makerspace with others? ___ Yes ___ No

   ____

   ____

   ____
9. Questions, comments, ideas?

   ____

   ____

   ____
10. If you wish to remain updated on makerspace progress at this library, please share your name and contact information.

    ____

    ____

    ____

[LIBRARY LETTERHEAD]

Makerspace and Creative Programming Focus Group Proposal/Outline

Focus Group Purpose

The purpose of these makerspace/creative programing focus groups is to learn the preferences, recommendations, and insights of current and potential library patrons, and how to develop the most relevant and useful spaces for the immediate patron and service area community of the library.

Focus groups consisting of a select 10 to 12 people may be conducted for each of the following stakeholder categories:

- current library patrons
- current user groups (clubs/organizations)
- teen advisory board/youth group
- library staff and volunteers
- nonlibrary users from the community
- immediate business community

Focus groups will last approximately 60 to 90 minutes and be led by a nonbiased moderator, who will facilitate and engage conversations based on various discussion topics. Data collected during our session is for internal use only and will not be publicized without the participants' permission. A full report, with recommendations, will be provided to the library, along with a makerspace programming plan.

Goals include, but are not limited to, the following:

- Introducing potential new uses for library spaces and new types of programming
- Learning about stakeholder perceptions and expectations of the library as it currently exists
- Learning how users feel about current services, events, and programming, including which are considered most helpful and which are not
- Gauging awareness and interest in new programming and space usage
- Learning about existing skill sets and interests among patrons, staff, and volunteers

- Discovering challenges to and opportunities for makerspace-style development by gaining a better understanding of the stakeholder community

Possible main discussion topics are as follows:

- How patrons currently use the library
- Thoughts on new services, events, programs, and partnerships
- The present-day role of the library in the community and the possible role in the future
- Types of resources that might be helpful for business development, academic and skills development, and personal fulfillment

BIBLIOGRAPHY

ARTICLES

"#HACKLIBSCHOOL." *In the Library with the Lead Pipe.* www.inthelibrarywiththeleadpipe.org/2010/hacklibschool/.

"Hiring Non-MLS Librarians: Trends and Training Implications." *Texas Digital Library.* https://journals.tdl.org/llm/index.php/llm/article/viewFile/7019/6260.

"How Libraries Are Becoming Modern Makerspaces." *Atlantic.* \www.theatlantic.com/technology/archive/2016/03/everyone-is-a-maker/473286/.

"Launching a Makerspace: Lessons Learned from a Transformed School Library." *KQED News.* ww2.kqed.org/mindshift/2016/07/31/launching-a-makerspace-lessons-learned-from-a-transformed-school-library/.

"Libraries for All: Expanding Services to People with Disabilities." *Illinois Library Association.* www.ila.org/publications/ila-reporter/article/55/libraries-for-all-expanding-services-to-people-with-disabilities.

"Makerspace: Towards a New Civic Infrastructure." *Places Journal.* https://placesjournal.org/article/makerspace-towards-a-new-civic-infrastructure/.

"Making a Makerspace? Guidelines for Accessibility and Universal Design." *DO-IT.* www.washington.edu/doit/making-makerspace-guidelines-accessibility-and-universal-design.

"Power, Access, Status: The Discourse of Race, Gender, and Class in the Maker Movement." *Technology and Social Change Group, University of Washington.* http://tascha.uw.edu/2015/03/power-access-status-the-discourse-of-race-gender-and-class-in-the-maker-movement/.

"The State of the European Sharing Movement." *Resilience.org*. www.resilience.org/stories/2014-04-21/the-state-of-the-european-sharing-movement.

"Wikipedia: The 'Intellectual Makerspace' of Libraries." *Programming Librarian*. http://programminglibrarian.org/articles/wikipedia-intellectual-makerspace-libraries.

"Young Digital Makers." *Nesta*. www.nesta.org.uk/publications/young-digital-makers.

Asset Mapping

"Assessing Community Needs and Resources." *Community Tool Box*. http://ctb.ku.edu/en/table-of-contents/assessment/assessing-community-needs-and-resources/identify-community-assets/main.

Asset Mapping Toolkits

"Asset Mapping." *National Endowment for the Arts*. www.arts.gov/exploring-our-town/project-type/asset-mapping.

Participatory Asset Mapping. Community Science. www.communityscience.com/knowledge4equity/AssetMappingToolkit.pdf

BOOKS

Batykefer, Erinn, and Laura Damon-Moore. *The Artist's Library: A Field Guide from the Library as Incubator Project*. Minneapolis, MN: Coffee House Press, 2014.

Hamelink, Mariska, Ista Boszhard, and Karien Vermeulen. *Teacher Maker Camp Cookbook*. http://waag.org/sites/waag/files/public/media/publicaties/teacher-maker-camp-cookbook_0.pdf

Kemp, Adam. *The Makerspace Workbench*. Sebastopol, CA: *Make:*, 2013. www.farnell.com/datasheets/1895152.pdf.

Maddigan, Beth Christina, and Susan C. Bloos. *Community Library Programs That Work: Building Youth and Family Literacy*. Santa Barbara. CA: Libraries Unlimited, 2013.

Weber, Mary Beth, ed. *Rethinking Library Technical Services: Redefining Our Profession for the Future*. Lanham, MD: Rowman & Littlefield, 2015.

WEBSITES

Abundant Community, www.abundantcommunity.com
ALA Privacy Toolkit, www.ala.org/advocacy/privacy/toolkit
Black Girls Code, www.blackgirlscode.com
Blockly, https://blockly-games.appspot.com
Business Reference and Services Section (BRASS) www.ala.org/rusa/sections/brass
Code Academy, www.codecademy.com
Cosplay, Comics, and Geek Culture in the Library, http://ccgclibraries.com
Definitive Maker Map Mapping, http://district.life/2015/04/21/definitive-maker-map-mapping/
Dialog on Public Libraries, http://csreports.aspeninstitute.org/Dialogue-on-Public-Libraries
Digital Commons Network, http://network.bepress.com
Directory of Tool Lending Libraries, http://localtools.org/find
DIYability, http://diyability.org
EIFL (Electronic Information for Libraries), www.eifl.net/page/about
Essential Elements of Digital Literacies, www.digitalliteraci.es
Evolve Project, https://evolveproject.org
Find 3D, www.ifind3d.com
Fixit Clinics, http://fixitclinic.blogspot.com
Future of Libraries, http://tascha.uw.edu/research/libraries
Girls Who Code, https://girlswhocode.com
Grants for Makerspace Schools, http://makergrants.blogspot.com
Great Science for Girls, www.fhi360.org/projects/great-science-girls
Hack Library School, https://hacklibraryschool.com
Idaho Libraries Programs and Activities, http://libraries.idaho.gov/page/program-ideas-activities-and-events
In the Library with a Lead Pipe, www.inthelibrarywiththeleadpipe.org
Let's Make Guide, www.letsmakeguide.com
Libraries and Makerspace Culture, http://library-maker-culture.weebly.com/makerspaces-in-libraries.html
Library as Incubator Project, www.libraryasincubatorproject.org
Library of the Future, www.ala.org/transforminglibraries/future
Library Programming Catalog, www.ctlibrarians.org/?page=programming
Library Publishing Toolkit, https://rusapubtools.wordpress.com
Maker and DIY Programs Wiki, http://wikis.ala.org/yalsa/index.php/Maker_%26_DIY_Programs

Maker Bridge, http://makerbridge.si.umich.edu/makerspaces-in-libraries-museums-map

Maker Library, http://design.britishcouncil.org/projects/makerlibraries

Makerspaces and Programming, https://colleengraves.org/makerspace-resources-and-programming-ideas

Makerspaces in Libraries, www.urbanlibraries.org/-makerspaces-in-libraries-pages-338.php

Makerspaces in Libraries, Museums, and Schools, www.google.com/maps/d/viewer?mid=1wKXDd1rOs4ls1EiZswQr-upFq7o&hl=en_US

Mobile Lab Coalition, www.mobilelabcoalition.com/wp

Model Programme for Public Libraries: Spaces and Zones, http://modelprogrammer.slks.dk/en/challenges/zones-and-spaces

New Mexico Makerstate Initiative, www.newmexicoculture.org/libraries/new-mexico-makerstate

Open Dataset of U.K. Makerspaces: A User's Guide, www.nesta.org.uk/publications/open-dataset-uk-makerspaces-users-guide

People First Language, www.disabilityisnatural.com/people-first-language.html

Program Ideas, Activities, and Events, http://libraries.idaho.gov/page/program-ideas-activities-and-events

Programming Librarian, www.programminglibrarian.org/programs

Public Libraries 2020, http://publiclibraries2020.eu

Shapeways, www.shapeways.com

Tech Soup for Libraries, www.techsoupforlibraries.org

TinkerCad, www.tinkercad.com

Tool Lending Library Directory, http://localtools.org/find

Tool Library, http://torontotoollibrary.com/about-2/ourlocationandhour/

Urban Libraries Council, www.urbanlibraries.org/workforce-and-economic-development-pages-533.php

Virtual Makerspace Canada, http://library.georgiancollege.ca/c.php?g=192109&p=1565637

Young Adult Services Wiki, http://wikis.ala.org/yalsa/index.php/Maker_%26_DIY_ProgramsResource Directories

PAPERS, GUIDES, AND WEBINARS

"Final Recommendations Europeana Association Network Task Force on Public Libraries." *Europeana Pro.* http://pro.europeana.eu/files/Europeana_Professional/Europeana_Network/europeana-task-force-on-public-libraries-final-report-dec2015.pdf.

Gaming in Libraries: Building Relationships between Communities and Libraries. Colorado Department of Education. www.cde.state.co.us/cdelib/teengaming-pack.

"Makerspaces in Libraries: Legal Issues." *Infopeple.* https://infopeople.org/sites/default/files/webinar/2014/07-22-2014/Makerspace_Libraries.pdf.

Mobile Makerspace Guide. San Jose Public Library www.sjpl.org/sites/default/files/documents/MobileMakerspaceGuideBook.pdf.

INDEX

Note: Page references for figures are italicized.

ABOUT THE AUTHOR AND CONTRIBUTORS

Theresa Willingham is director and chief operations officer of Eureka! Factory, where she works to help libraries and other organizations develop public creative spaces and programming. She was the regional director for *FIRST* youth robotics in central Florida from 2011 to 2017. More importantly, she loves making things. She is a writer, photographer, and artist; author of two books on health; and coauthor of *Makerspaces in Libraries* (Rowman & Littlefield, 2015). Willingham believes in the value of collaboration and the strength of mentor-based learning, and has more than 30 years of social entrepreneurship experience across a diverse spectrum of fields and interests, focused on doing work she's passionate about in a way she hopes will make her corner of the world a better place.

. . .

Chuck Stephens makes things, from crafts to boats to synthesizers, and otherwise keeps himself occupied with a never-ending series of artistic, musical, and technological projects. He works as a makerspace coordinator for the Pasco County, Florida, library system, where he develops STEM programs and coaches multiple *FIRST* teams.

Steve Willingham, president of Eureka! Factory, has 30 years of experience in systems engineering and has been a key team leader on a variety of government projects for manned space flight, satellite communications, civil aviation, and commercial venues, including insurance, financial services, medical technology, and accounting. He designed the original space plan for the HIVE, a 10,000-square-foot public community innovation center at the John F. Germany Library in downtown Tampa, Florida, which opened in the fall of 2014, and with his wife Theresa, has facilitated the development of library makerspaces throughout three counties in Florida. Willingham is also a longtime *FIRST* robotics volunteer and producer and organizing partner of the offseason event Tampa Bay ROBOTICON, which has been attended by teams from throughout the world.

Jeroen De Boer, coauthor of *Makerspaces in Libraries* (Rowman & Littlefield, 2015), has years of experience in the cultural sector, education, government, and arts education. He currently works in the public library sector, focusing primarily on innovation and the digital domain. He led the development of Frysklab, Europe's first mobile makerspace, in the Netherlands.